CONTENTS

 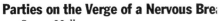
4 vols
£15

GW00750562

EDITORS
Stuart Hall
Doreen Massey
Michael Rustin

POETRY EDITOR
Carole Satyamurti

ART EDITOR
Jan Brown

EDITORIAL OFFICE
Sally Davison
Lawrence & Wishart
144a Old South Lambeth Road
London SW8 1XX

MARKETING CONSULTANT
Mark Perryman

Soundings is published three
times a year, in autumn,
spring and summer by:
Soundings Ltd
c/o Lawrence & Wishart
144a Old South Lambeth Road
London SW8 1XX

ADVERTISEMENTS
Write for information to Soundings,
c/o Lawrence & Wishart

SUBSCRIPTIONS
1995-96 subscription rates are (for three issues):
UK: Institutions £70, Individuals £35
Rest of the world: Institutions £80, Individuals £45

BOOKS FOR REVIEW
Contact Soundings Books Editor,
c/o Lawrence & Wishart.

ISBN 0 85315 817 7

Text setting Jan Brown Designs, London
Cover photograph: © Simon Norfolk

Printed in Great Britain by Cambridge University Press,
Cambridge

NOTES ON CONTRIBUTORS

Stuart Hall is Professor of Sociology at the Open University.

Barbara Castle, now Baroness Castle of Blackburn, was a member of four Labour cabinets between 1964 and 1976, with responsibilities during this period which included transport, health and social services, and employment.

Beatrix Campbell is a print and television journalist. Her most recent book is *Goliath: Britain's Dangerous Places* (Methuen).

Lynne Murray is Senior Research Fellow at the Winnicott Research Unit at Cambridge University, where she is investigating the effects of maternal depression on infants and young children.

Mae-Wan Ho is a bio-physicist and Reader in Biology at the Open University. She is author of *The Rainbow and the Worm* (World Scientific).

Lola Young is Senior Lecturer in Media and Cultural Studies at Middlesex University. She is author of *Fear of the Dark, Race, Gender and Sexuality in the Cinema* (forthcoming 1995, Routledge).

Ingrid Pollard is a photographer and lecturer. Her two most recent exhibitions, *Boxer* and *Self-Evident*, are currently on tour in the UK.

Maggie Mort is a journalist, currently researching issues in the sociology of technology and the politics of healthcare.

Kerry Hamilton is Director of Environmental and Transport Studies at the London Research Centre. She has written widely on social aspects of transport policy, especially women and transport, and is co-editor of *Travel Sickness* (Lawrence & Wishart).

Max Dixon is a researcher in Environment and Transport at the London Research Centre.

Graham Smith is Principal Lecturer in the School of Architecture at Oxford Brookes University.

Heather Hunt is a consultant community psychologist. She is a longstanding campaigner on women and peace issues, and more recently was involved in the campaign against the M11 in East London.

Michael Rustin is Dean of Social Sciences at East London University.

Carole Satyamurti has had three volumes of poetry published by Oxford University Press – *Broken Moon, Striking Distance*, and *Changing the Subject*.

Carol Rumens currently lives and works in Belfast. A new volume of her poetry, *Best China Sky*, is due to be published this year.

Judith Kazantzis' *Selected Poems 1977-1992* was published by Sinclair-Stevenson earlier this year.

John Burnside was born in Fife in 1955. A new collection of his poems, *Swimming in the Flood*, is due to be published this year.

Susanne Ehrhardt was brought up in Germany and lives in England. A selection of her poems was published in *New Chatto Poets II*.

Sylvia Kantaris' most recent collection is *Lad's Love*, published by Bloodaxe in 1993.

James Berry was born in Jamaica. A new collection of his poems, *Hot Earth Cold Earth*, was published by Bloodaxe in 1995.

Simon Edge is a journalist and a former editor of *Capital Gay*.

Andrew Blake teaches in the Department of Cultural Studies at the University of East London, and writes on music in popular culture.

Doreen Massey is Professor of Geography at the Open University. Her recent books include *Space, Place and Gender* (Polity).

Fred Halliday is Professor of International Relations at the London School of Economics. He is the author of *The Second Cold War* and many other books and articles.

SUPPORTING SUBSCRIBERS

We are grateful to our
pre-launch subscribers for
their supporting subscriptions.
They are:

Alex Afaxenidis
David Albury
K.J.W. Alexander
Sharon Alperovitz
Geoff Andrews
Leighton Andrews
Derek Antrobus
James Avis
G. Barr
Nick Bentley
Irene Breugel
Alan Bullion
Robert Chase
Cynthia Cockburn
Hilary Cottam
Tim Dawson
Jill Ebrey
Adam Edwards
Dave Ely
Alan Finlayson

Joan Fletcher
Rosalind Gill
Angel J. Gordo-Lopez
Bharat Goswami
John Grahl
David Grugeon
Carole Hanmer
Alex Hughes
Richard Kuper
Kathy Jones
Prof & Mrs D. Judd
Michael Keating
Maria Lauret
Matthew Lockwood
Kathy Loundon
Steven Lukes
David Macey
Peter Mandler
Graham Martin
Carolyn Miller

Henry Miller
Richard Minns
John Morgan
Andrew Morgan
Mica Nava
Mark Perryman
Andy Pratt
Ali Rattansi
Dan Rubenstein
Jonathan Rutherford
Andrew Samuels
James Scarth
Anne Showstack Sassoon
Jenny Shaw
Kate Steele
Nigel Thrift
Michael Tiller
Andrew Trigg
Michael Waite
Sue Way

iv

Uncomfortable times

Stuart Hall, Doreen Massey, Michael Rustin

T hese are uncomfortable times. Capitalist forms of society are enjoying an almost unchallenged triumph throughout the world. Global markets in capital, labour and commodities are transforming the economies of virtually all states, even those, like China, which remain under ostensibly Communist government. Socialism, as an alternative economic system based on democratic decision by government, party or working class, seems to have little remaining intellectual or political credibility. We need look no further than the New Labour Party of Tony Blair to see the profound effects on our political culture of this ideological victory of the right.

Yet the shift to the right of the political culture of the West gives rise to deep anxiety and concern. Many of the compromise structures set up in the post-war period to balance the benefits of capital accumulation with security for working and dependent populations have been attacked and dismantled. National governments have generally lost their power to determine levels of taxation, welfare expenditure and employment. 'Flexibility' in forms of production and distribution, and financial assets which can be traded worldwide, have dematerialised formerly solid structures and

5

exposed individuals and communities to remorselessly competitive pressures.

The Communist economies of the former USSR and Eastern Europe collapsed in part because of the inferiority of their performance to those of the West. At the same time, those social-democratic 'mixed economies' have encountered fiscal crises as they have faced international competition based on lower levels of wages and social benefits; even the former social-democratic strongholds have unravelled in the face of these pressures. But the 'free market' which was propounded in the 1980s as the only alternative to these regulated systems has failed to generate general economic benefit even in its ideological heartlands. The economic insecurity which seems inseparable from global competition has not been confined in its disciplinary effects to unionised workers (as was originally intended), but threatens to engulf the growing middle class too. Substantial levels of unemployment are now taken for granted as an unalterable condition in the advanced economies – this despite the fact that unemployment brings social exclusion, polarisation, and racial stigmatisation, and precludes the development of integrated democratic societies.

One political reaction to this insecurity has been a politics of enragement. Racism, right-wing fundamentalism, punitive treatment of the poor and a generalised resentment against others follow the experiences of downward mobility and loss of hope, among threatened population groups. Isolationism, indifference to injustice and hostility to 'immigrants' are widespread reactions to the insecurities produced by market forces among those who wish to defend their existing advantages. Governments find themselves caught between demands to do something to repair this damage and restore some measure of stability to living standards, and the need to adjust to a competitive environment in order that their economic problems do not grow still worse. No solutions to these dilemmas are presently in sight. J.K. Galbraith, who described an earlier period as one of 'private affluence and public squalor', has characterised the new predicament as a 'culture of contentment', by which he really means the indifference of the 'two-thirds society' to the plight of the marginalised third.

A historical perspective: two cheers for Fordism

The post-war period, across Western Europe and North America, saw an attempt to create a kind of social democracy, following the example of the 1930s New Deal in the United States. The political right had been discredited, in part because of its compromises with Fascism and Nazism before the war and during the various occupations, and in part because of the catastrophe which befell *laissez-faire* economies in the inter-war period. Working people anticipated *and obtained* some benefit from their role in securing victory for the democracies. Governments expected to take an active part in economic and social reconstruction, and did so according to their various national political traditions. These circumstances led to an unprecedented era of full employment and rapid economic growth, from about 1950 to 1975, in which social expenditure rose to take a much greater share of gross national product.

'Access and adequacy, rather than choice and diversity, were the priorities'

T he main engine of growth of this social order was manufacturing industry. Together with mining and transport, manufacturing came to employ a majority of the workforce and to generate a huge range of mass consumer products, creating a moving equilibrium of supply and demand. Corresponding to the mass organisation of production in the factories and the standardised lines of consumer products was a pattern of social welfare provision, in housing, education and health. Organised or supported by government, this welfare provision involved major social investment in house-building, school-building and in the development of universal access to benefits such as pensions. Except for the upper segments of the population able to make their own private provision, access and adequacy, rather than choice and diversity, were the priorities. This compromise struck between market and state led to extended rights and powers for trade unions, whose members also enjoyed greater bargaining power thanks to the conditions of full employment.

This 'Fordist' system eventually came to generate its own tensions, expressed in rising inflation, growing trade union militancy and falling profit levels. The long post-war boom created heightened levels of aspiration which it could not ultimately satisfy. So long as citizens looked backwards to the pre-war and war-time periods, there was a sense of relative satisfaction. ('You've never had it so good,' as Harold Macmillan put it.) But once they began to examine their present situation and the differences in opportunities between themselves and fellow-citizens, the limitations of the system were more apparent. At the same time, the structures of familial, class and bureaucratic authority which had remained intact for the older generation became matters of contention for the young. The relative affluence of the 1960s was greeted with a widening of politics beyond its previous bounds. Many new voices – speaking for class, gender, race, nation and region, and alternative life-styles – insisted on being heard. New arenas of cultural and social contestation opened up.

These tensions might have been accommodated, both in Europe and the United States, but for the Vietnam War, which destroyed the Democrats as a ruling party and the optimism of Lyndon Johnson's 'Great Society' programme of social and racial inclusion. It also provoked world-wide inflation and set the stage for the huge rise in oil prices of the 1970s. The great inflation which followed brought the Fordist era to its time of crisis.

The left lost the battle to resolve this crisis, with the consequences of the defeat felt most severely in the United States and Britain. In other parts of Western Europe, though, much of the former social compromise remained intact. Right-wing governments, allied with the financial and corporate sectors, initiated programmes whose object was to discipline the labour force by raising unemployment, to expose national economies to greater competition, to reduce the 'safety net' of welfare programmes, and to attack the legal rights and powers of trade unions. Changes in the dominant forms of economic activity, from large-scale mining and manufacturing, to tertiary sector activities (such as finance, tourism, distribution and producer services) which were much less favourable to established forms of collective organisation, altered the balance of industrial power. For many working people, the economic situation grew sharply worse.

'The left lost the battle to resolve the crisis of Fordism'

The economic restructuring also meant that a greater diversity of consumer products, and the diffusion of rapidly evolving kinds of communications technology, brought a change in patterns of consumption; the new middle class became the style-leaders. Citizens accustomed to a greater degree of choice in the consumer marketplace came to value this freedom in other spheres of life. Just as Fordist production and consumption provided the dominant model for the boom of the 1950s and 1960s, so 'post-Fordist' ideas of 'flexible specialisation' were extended from car models to portable pensions, to right-to-buy council houses and modular degree courses. The fact that opt-out pension schemes were sometimes a fraud, that house purchases may have left their owners with negative equity, and that class sizes in universities may have doubled, has not altogether discredited this vision of enhanced freedom.

Beyond the frame of the merely economic, both right-wing and social-democratic governments found themselves virtually mute in the face of a whole range of new social movements organised around gender and sexuality, ethnicity, and the environment. The old political establishments attempted to cast these as 'local', special issue causes, not to be integrated into, and certainly not to affect, the 'real business of politics', but they have proved far more durable and universal concerns since.

This cumulative destruction of the post-war settlement has created acute problems for the established political left in Britain. Local authorities, although almost entirely in Labour and Liberal Democratic hands, now have only shadows of their former powers. Trade union membership has declined significantly as a proportion of the workforce. The public sector of industry, which had provided significant guarantees of job security and trade union recognition to its workforce, has been decimated. The directors of the former public utilities are becoming millionaires on the strength of the profits, which in part they make by dismissing 'surplus' workers. The building societies, formerly co-operative institutions

'Governments found themselves mute in the face of new social movements'

designed to extend house-ownership and to provide secure forms of savings, are becoming just another arm of the financial sector; a potential resource for social responsibility in the housing sector is thus disappearing. The public on whose loyalty Labour had primarily relied and whose lives had been shaped by relative job security and by the welfare state, was being rapidly fragmented and transformed. While Labour was still preaching collectivism, they began to sing to the tunes of enhanced choice, freedom and material gain played so confidently, if deceitfully, by the Thatcherites. While some guilty concern for the worst-off and an apparent regard for public services remained evident in attitude surveys, these residues of egalitarianism did not carry much political weight. To take one glaring example, the very modestly redistributive tax increases announced by John Smith seem to have scared away a decisive tranche of voters at the 1992 general election.

There is, nevertheless, a bright side to these transformations. New voices, new diversity and greater choice have broadened the spectrum of politics in these 'New Times', as they have been called. Assumptions which before had been barely noticed, conventions and forms of authority which previously had not been exposed to view, were now refreshingly challenged. Some radicals have sought to ride the waves of anti-statism and anti-corporatism, saying that the institutions of the old left have deserved their fate, and that it is time to make a completely fresh start. Some of these activists *have* identified real needs and opportunities in the more individualised and differentiated world of post-Fordism, and these have to be taken seriously.

Yet perhaps the old values, institutions and beliefs have been given up a little too easily – certainly by those in party politics. The Mephistopheles of market economics has said to the new radicals, 'if you follow me, and denounce these relics of the past as loudly as I do, you can have electoral success too and escape from perpetual defeat.' But every repudiation seems to call forth the need for a fresh one, every position abandoned seems to expose another principle which was not even thought suspect before. Worse, in most cases, this denunciation of 'the old' has not in fact been accompanied by any acknowledgement of the potential new agendas.

Tony Blair's New Labour is in the middle of this journey, in which old political garments are being removed in a succession of encounters with different power brokers – the latest at the time of writing being the Media Mephistopheles himself, Rupert Murdoch. Abolishing Clause IV, as the totem of Old Labourism, placing an emphatic distance between Labour and the trade union movement, declining to make any commitments whatsoever to restore any industry to public control, refusing to grant local authorities their former powers to manage education, and looking to a new electoral base in 'Middle England' – all these strategies separate New Labour from the collective institutions and loyalties which sustained it in the past. The apparently imminent self-destruction of the Conservative Party, now hijacked by its own sectarians and ideologues, has left a gaping electoral space which New Labour now looks likely to seize. But whether this amounts to anything more than a promise to provide a new political management for a now fully-marketised system remains to be seen. Of course, this new management will be more sensitive to social needs than its predecessor, more committed to social compromise, and more far-sighted about the needs of economic development where this requires an active role for government. We

'Every repudiation seems to call forth the need for a fresh one'

hardly need reminding how desperately such a political spring-cleaning is required.

But for this new start to mean more than a fully-marketised society 'under new management', a different vision of social progress is needed. Part of *Soundings*' aim is to help develop this, from a position of critical independence from New Labour – welcome though its advent to power would certainly be.

The democratic state, for a start

Much was wrong with the governmental forms through which earlier collectivist liberals and democratic socialists sought to redress the harm done by private property and the market. The agencies of mass democracy, new to the world in this century, were only to a limited degree properly democratic. The emerging leaderships of working-class movements and their middle-class allies had to make use of the political machinery to hand to redress inequality, impose some measure of planning and defend living standards. These systems were often bureaucratic or authoritarian, and they remained in the hands of too narrow a spectrum (male and white, typically) of the population.

'The democratic state has been, in broad terms, an effective vehicle for the empowerment of citizens'

It is these contradictions in the forms and uses of power by social democrats which have been exploited so effectively to attack the achievements of full employment and welfare states in the past twenty years. In a more extreme form, the monopolisation of power by political parties and central government has also been the downfall of the state socialist regimes of the East.

We shall have plenty to say about the limitations of statist politics, and even of formal politics, as means of social improvement and transformation. But here at the outset of *Soundings* something different needs to be asserted, against the grain of the market and the compromises with its ideology which are now to be found virtually everywhere. This is that the democratic state has been, in broad terms, an effective vehicle for the economic and social empowerment of citizens, and not an incubus laid upon them. Democratic governments have brought guarantees of living standards, health and education, where none previously existed. They have acted to limit the powers of monopolistic property owners to extort profits from both producers and consumers, especially in the field of basic goods and services (such as energy, water and communications). They have ensured that social goods, and long-term interests are taken into account, for example in the provision of transport networks and social services. They have acted to establish public spaces, for recreation and assembly, and, equally, they have provided the infrastructure necessary for a public culture, in broadcasting, education, and the arts. (It is important to recognise this, even though we might now question that received definition of 'the public'.) And democratic governments have acted to ensure that all citizens gained some sense of economic, social and legal membership in society, something that does not happen once disparities of circumstances become too gross and too general.

Social democracy, in its various secular and religious traditions, has to this degree been a signal success in this century; and local, regional and national levels of government have been its principal instrument of betterment and emancipation. Why then are New Labour, the Democratic Party in the United States and social democrats more generally now so reluctant to defend these achievements or to promise to advance them further? Why is a market of some kind now deemed to be the best means of allocating every good and service, when it is clear that markets generate inequalities as their intrinsic driving force? And why is the role of the democratic state, with its formal promise of political equality among citizens, no longer proclaimed as a basic good of a civilised society, when – without its strong agency – inequality and injustice will undoubtedly grow?

'Why is a market of some kind now deemed to be the best means of allocating every good and service?'

Internationally, too, the role of states and associations of states should be to redress inequality and protect the public good. The European Union now has a limited social agenda of this kind, which *Soundings* will strongly support. This commitment to a measure of international social justice should be, but is not, the function of agencies such as the International Monetary Fund, the World Bank and the United Nations.

Those who support democracy should also support democratic states acting to defend the well-being of majorities against powerful and propertied minorities. Instead, formerly socialist parties rush to deny that they have any special intimacy with active government, and prefer to protest that no-one is now closer to the market or the sacredness of private property than they. This is the way of political disaster. Socialists must defend the role and value of the democratic state, or they become nothing.

Beyond the (conventionally) political

If our first argument is that the achievements of the democratic state deserve defending, and where necessary restoration, our second is that there must be more to radical politics than what is accomplished by governments, or even by politics as it is conventionally understood. Indeed over-estimation of what can be achieved by 'political' means has been a major source of failure in the socialist project, just as excessive belief in what can be achieved by economic agency has been the principal cause of disaster in market-driven societies. The gains in social citizenship which were achieved through government are not in doubt, but they also contained their own contradictions and limitations. Some of the institutions of actual existing social democracy were in part an alienation of democracy, or its sequestration in limited and self-interested hands. It is these inherent contradictions and limitations which the right has been able to exploit in its attacks on the state, and on the kinds of tacit elitism, paternalism and vanguardism with which these agencies have colluded.

'There must be more to radical politics that what is accomplished by governments'

What, then, could be the shape of such a 'politics-beyond-politics'? What spheres of action and agencies of change lie beyond the antagonistic categories of market and state? Even though we would most often side, within democratic capitalist societies, with the latter in its struggles against the former, we have no illusions that such a choice is any longer a sufficient basis for a left politics. It is the identification of this third sphere which is essential both to the project of *Soundings* and to the revival of a new left. This sphere is often described as 'civil society', although unlike some we wish to distinguish it from the market as well as from the state.

The distinctive analytic strength of the 'regulation school' (and other theories of Fordism and post-Fordism) was that it sought to *relate* technological, economic, social and political changes as elements of a whole system. 'Fordism' was an equilibrium, a point of balance between contending social forces operating in a particular context of technological development and social

13

aspirations. The transformation of this Fordist compromise has involved several linked changes, although these are not equivalent in their power: we would hold, for example, that the driving force of capital accumulation has counted for more in these changes than the resistance of particular local communities or social classes, where in earlier phases the balance of power was sometimes different. But there are, nevertheless, many different spheres within which these changes have been effective; these include new aspirations for greater choice in goods and public services; emergent public voices of women and ethnically more diverse communities; technologies of communication which may enable the circulation of new ideas and images of the world as well as of commodity prices and mass-produced information; and scientific discoveries and technologies – socially contested and debated as never before because of their environmental and social consequences.

'Mass populations are being awakened and enfranchised worldwide'

Capitalism may now dominate this post-Fordist social order, having resolved largely in its favour the moment of crisis of the previous regime. But it does not exhaust the possibilities of this social order. Besides powerful agencies of capital, embodied in huge flows of mobile assets as well as in corporations, mass populations are being awakened and enfranchised worldwide. Claims to fundamental rights continue to be made. The great moment of democratisation in South Africa and the overthrow of the tyrannies of Eastern Europe mark not an end of politics, but its revival and renewal.

While consumption grows, so do demands to regulate it in relation to ecological and aesthetic concerns, such as the preservation of landscapes or town centres. Mass communications seek to standardise and homogenise outputs of information, to realise economies of scale and consequent profits, as much as to influence beliefs. But mass communications also mean *more* information and greater access to it for more people. Who can now say whether the net effect of these changes will be to concentrate or to diffuse power and opportunity? Our contention is that this remains to be determined in many spheres of public debate and action. Some of this engagement will be of a conventionally political kind, some will not. For example, the greater independence and equality of women, the decline of marriage, and the emergence of vigorous gay and lesbian cultures in the large cities of the West, are examples of major changes in society which are more the causes of legislation than its consequences.

Our object in *Soundings* will be to register changes taking place in many domains of life, both in the major thematic section we will carry in all subsequent issues and in our editorial. We see the narrow definition of politics as a mis-appropriation of the democratic process by both left and right. We shall argue that change can be achieved in many social spaces besides that which is normally designated as political. We will report specific interventions in what is often described as 'civil society', and support them in the cause of a fuller process of cultural and social democratisation. There is a need to interpret these changes – for example, in the changing patterns of family life, in scientific understanding, or in the uses of space or buildings – and to link them where appropriate to more conventional political practice.

The fact that we think that society is much broader than formal politics implies does not mean than we are indifferent to what happens in the narrower political sphere. We believe, though, that political actors, narrowly defined, are normally carried along by these larger currents. Our primary interest is to try to understand these shaping events, trends and spheres of social action, and by interpreting them to inflect them in more democratic and egalitarian directions.

We do not agree that the ideals of democracy and equality have been permanently defeated by the success of the right, and by the pressure to reach an accommodation with the claims of the market as the price of political survival, either in Britain or elsewhere. The defining political achievement of Thatcherism was to represent its real project of re-empowering the propertied and of reimposing a coercive social hierarchy in a language of popular rights, social citizenship and enhanced choice and freedom. The new right has paid unconscious tribute to its actual democratic enemy in its adoption of a radical populist rhetoric. But now that this politics has been largely discredited, and market ideology can again be seen as one-dimensional and partial, it becomes possible to return to a larger agenda of democratisation, with the aim of distributing power and opportunity among all citizens.

'The ideals of democracy and equality have not been permanently defeated by the success of the right'

Soundings

Soundings will be a political journal, but its overriding interest will be in the relation between political thought and action, conventionally conceived, and the larger social processes which shape and limit their possibilities. The narrow conception of politics is itself a legacy of pre-democratic times, a hangover from a monopolisation and centralisation of power in society. The institutions of modern democracies – mass parties, universal franchise and general elections – were devised as means of extending and legitimising powers whose origin lay in monarchies and aristocracies. The assumption that power is exercised inevitably by minorities, usually seeing themselves as a ruling class or coalition of ruling classes, deeply shapes modern political processes. Even radicals who are educated in elite institutions – the Grandes Ecoles, Ivy League Colleges or Oxbridge – to share habits of natural authority with those whose substantive politics they oppose may tacitly accept this minoritarian conception of who, in reality, should rule. Parties, whether in government or opposition, usually seek to concentrate, not distribute power. New Labour's backtracking on constitutional and electoral reform is a worrying sign. A new agenda of pluralism requires a more open political process, not a reversion to the hegemonic ambitions of the Labour Party of old.

'The assumption that power is exercised inevitably by minorities deeply shapes modern political processes'

We are not, however, utopians who imagine that governments are dispensable or redundant, and that all power can be dispersed in some magical way 'to the people'. But we do hold that governments, even progressive governments, are and should be only one locus of power among many. It is the construction of these alternative locations of power that most interests us, and which we intend to map in this magazine. We do not believe that a progressive political project can any longer be formulated in the narrow terms of politics alone – to adapt C.L.R. James's memorable remark about cricket, 'who knows politics who only politics knows?' The real problem now is to reformulate the radical democratic project in its full cultural and social scope.

There are continuities between *Soundings* and the earliest projects of the New Left, which from its beginnings in the 1950s insisted on a redefinition of politics to include much that the mainstream political system left out. In seeking to create a space outside social-democratic or communist parties, the New Left argued that the reduction of politics to the 'line' of the vanguard party, or even to the programme of the parliamentary socialist party, was never going to be enough. The democratic revolution is a broad river, never containable within the confining channels constructed by politicians and their specific operations. What the New Left has recognised in its various populist, euro-communist, feminist, and now green versions is that formal political action is merely one expression of this transformative process, often as much its enemy as its agent or interpreter. It is vital not to equate the definitions laid down and enforced by political parties with the democratic revolution itself.

This was why the New Left found itself everywhere a critical presence – an opposition or revisionist voice within communist parties, part of extra-parliamentary movements in Western democracies protesting in the streets against colonial wars, the arms race or racism. The New Left defined its function as above all one of critique. This position could at times risk a 'false innocence', where the compromises unavoidable in all political practice were defined as betrayal, or where marxism as a programme was too easily exempted from the failures of 'actually existing socialism'. But, generally, the role of this New Left – more outside the formal political system than within it – has been a principled and productive one. It has contributed much to the widening of the democratic agenda, and we will try to sustain this tradition.

These assumptions explain the format and the name of *Soundings*. The coherence of the worldview of political journals and magazines has often functioned as a generative structure, which at worst allows every happening to be encoded, as by some ideological translating machine, into a predictable 'position' or 'line'. Usually such coherence derives from the primacy of a particular agency (that of class or party, for example, or in the case of some right-wing organs, the all-pervasive and absolute sovereignty of markets over everything).

'Our generative structure is a commitment to a continuing democratic revolution in a multitude of forms'

Our own generative structure is more minimal than this and amounts to a commitment to a continuing democratic revolution in a multitude of forms. *Soundings* will carry in each issue a wide range of articles whose purpose will be to keep open debates that others (including the New Labour Party) might now prefer to see closed, as well as to focus attention on new points of growth and

17

conflict in our society and culture. To say that politics now has to be seen as a space of interaction between competing voices is not to say that it naturally presents itself in that way: we will defend a conception of radical political pluralism and publish voices from its different locations with the aim of sustaining the most open democratic discussion possible. We aim, too, to keep the field wide in terms both of topics and of modes of expression. We would, for instance, like to broaden the usual social science view of politics and to link up actively with cultural concerns and especially with developments and debates in the natural sciences.

Our 'minimalist generative structure' will not produce a position for this journal on every topic that might occur to us: there needs to be a more exploratory debate. A continuing radical programme today needs to be built on a 'decentred' basis, sphere by sphere. Relations to systematic, unifying ideas (for example, to the force of capital accumulation and to the countervailing principles of popular democracy and individual freedom) need to be worked out for each sphere as a new agenda evolves.

For this reason, *Soundings* will offer in each issue an exploration in depth of a particular theme relevant to the radical agenda in this broad sense. Our overall programme can only be constructed through these explorations, drawing on the capabilities and experiences of contributors who write from their understanding and knowledge of a specific field. Early issues will explore the themes of 'Law and Justice' and 'the Public Good'. 'Law and Justice' will be concerned with the rights of citizens, both as individuals and as participating members of a political community, and it will be written for the most part by radical lawyers and others at the sharp end of legal practices. 'The Public Good' will explore the interaction between public and private spheres, questioning the relations between state and market, and the meaning of markets for all of us. We are also planning issues on 'Heroes and Heroines', on 'Living in a Global Economy', on 'Risk, Science and the Environment', and on 'African Political Writing'. These 'theme' features will usually take up about half of each issue.

We should like *Soundings* to be able to relate to the world, not only through contributions by individual authors, but also through the varied but interconnected voices of people active in specific communities and spheres of society. We hope to make *Soundings*, if only in a small way, a participatory project which over the years will involve a wide network of people. Welcome

Parties on the verge of a nervous breakdown

Stuart Hall

Both right and left of British politics are in need of a 'grand idea'. Stuart Hall examines the dangers on both sides of the political spectrum: the possibility of a new grand idea from the far right, and the lack of one – so far – on the left.

The Tory Party: devices and desires

The more one sees of political parties, and the ways they are driven hither and thither, often at the whim of deeply irrational and unconscious forces, the more one is tempted to anthropomorphise them. They behave like partially crazed adolescents, tossed about by powerful undercurrents of emotion and uncontrollable spasms which are not amenable to a purely rational or empirical analysis. The Tory party is undergoing this kind of 'crisis', and nothing will 'resolve' it until some catharsis, the shape of which we cannot fully foresee, intervenes. Mr Major's leadership election 'gamble' has only postponed this. It is not enough to have saved the Conservative Party from the collective nervous breakdown which is afflicting it.

At a tactical level, however, the move was rather effective. It has temporarily silenced his Euro-sceptic critics and enemies, that party of *enragés* now glowering in silence behind him on the back benches. It has temporarily seen off the rivalrous knights, jostling around his back to deliver the final *coup de grâce*. Portillo is temporarily stymied, and safely tucked away in an armoured vehicle temporarily on its way – figuratively – to Bosnia. Lamont made a fatal hesitation at the final hour and is lost. And Heseltine played the loyalty game so long and so deviously that he seems to have become trapped by his own web. This is bad news for the Heselteenies, but worse for Labour. The latter still seem to believe there is mileage to be made out of speculating on what the enhanced job of the Deputy Prime Minister could be. It is no mystery. His task is to clobber

'A large proportion of the Conservative Party is bewitched by the dream of an extremist, Thatcherite, revivalism'

the Opposition, mercilessly and relentlessly, for the next eighteen months, a task for which he is superbly well fitted. He will also take some prisoners from John Humphreys on the *Today* programme – particularly bad news for Labour, since he is manifestly the only politician of any party currently capable of doing so.

Will all this save John Major? Can it save the Tory Party from electoral defeat? I doubt it. But, in my view, it will be a closer-run thing, when we come to the election, than the Labour leadership, the press, Rupert Murdoch and Paul Johnson seem to think. Tactical moves won't save John Major because, given the mood to be found at the centre of gravity of the Tory Party, and the delicate balance of factions clustering there, his brand of low-flying pragmatism is not enough. Too large a proportion of the Conservative Party, inside and outside Parliament, are bewitched by the dream of an extremist, Thatcherite, revivalism to settle for 'wait and see'. I don't mean that they want Lady Thatcher back – one look at her performances on TV makes it abundantly clear that, though she no doubt harbours illusions, her moment has passed. What the Tory faithful, of whatever faction, simply cannot exorcise is that deep hunger, that un-nameable desire, that gnaws at their political guts, for the return of the 'feel good factor' which Mrs T at the height of her powers gave them – which has very little to do with economic performance, consumer confidence and growth rates, and everything to do with being part of a revivalist crusade, of marching in the ranks of the latter-day free market 'Saints'. It is a conversion experience, not just an electoral victory, they are after: the 'two intellectual leaps' which Enoch Powell made first and 'which Keith Joseph and I would only make some years later' (*The*

Path to Power); what Peter Clarke has recently identified, in his review of Lady Thatcher's book, as the Joan of Arc moment, summoned by voices – 'I heard myself saying, "Look Keith if you're not going to stand, I will because someone who represents our viewpoint *has* to stand"' ('Maggiefication', Peter Clarke, in *London Review of Books*, 6 July 1995).

If the Tories are ever to recover from their collective derangement, then only such a spirit of revivalism will do, and in that respect, Mr Major is not for burning. Where then is it to be found? How long would it take to get it into place to carry a 'popular majority' in the country (i.e. a tactically composed, geographically dispersed minority, which is what has actually 'won' elections in our system since the 1970s)? And who could 'personify' it (for, like all charismatic sectarianisms, it requires its 'personification')?

There is only one such political configuration on offer, only one place for the Tory Party, constituted as it currently is politically, to go: that is, towards some reconstituted or reconfigured combination of virulent, sectarian, free marketism, coupled (paradoxically) with a massive dose of social ravanchism masquerading under the umbrella of 'family values', secured below by a revivalist 'Little Englandism'. The same basic ingredients as 'Thatcherism', but revamped and reshaped to the new conjuncture. The recipe, when concocted, will appear to have been sutured together with, I suspect, a very strong infusion of 'Gingrich-ism', borrowed from the highly successful example of the American Republican revival – dissolution of the welfare state and 'contract with the British people' and all. Even now, late at night,

'Even now, late into the night, Mr Portillo is studying the Gingrich blueprint'

the lights in his private sanctuary high in the Ministry of Defence blazing into the darkness, Mr Portillo is studying the Gingrich blueprint. Every time one hears on late night radio the voices of the pentecostalists of the Adam Smith Institute as they tremble with a deep irrationalism, one knows that the free market extremists, with their crack-pot Benthamite schemes and their loony remedies, are on the loose again, waiting in the wings for their conduit to power.

As for 'Little Englandism', for a deep, deeply irrational, largely unconscious, defensive and ab-reactive chauvinism, this is the most powerful and the most popular vein in the whole ensemble; and the name which summons it is not, as it was in Mrs Thatcher's more optimistic time, 'Great Britain Limited', but

'Europe'. Europe has become the fetish, the displaced signifier, the repository into which all those dark and unrequited elements of the collective British psyche have been decanted: the hatred of all foreigners, not just black or brown ones; the deep resentment at the transformation of what used to be 'Great Britain' into some ill-defined and ignominious third-rate, off-continental, junior partner in the affairs that now shape and drive the world; a profound sense of 'loss' of the old values, the old ways of life, the old customs, the old verities – the sort of dissolution of past glories in which a people are profoundly invested, which drives nations crazy. This is what 'being against Europe' has come to stand for. And though no-one can suppose that Mrs Gorman will be able to personify this mood on the highest political stage, everyone in the Tory Party knows that this heady ensemble, this mix, is the only popular current of feeling in the country into which a disaggregated party of the right can tap. So all the jockeyings represent a collective, instinctive search for someone who can do what Mrs Thatcher in her time did: embody, represent, personify – effect the linkage between this inchoate surge of feeling in the country and the main thrust of policy in government and the state.

> **'Europe has become the fetish, the displaced signifier, of the dark and unrequited elements of the collective British psyche'**

'Personally, I was conscious that in some strange way I was instinctively speaking and feeling in harmony with the great majority of the population. Such moments are as unforgettable as they are rare. They must be seized to change history' (*The Path to Power*). It is the dream – the illusion – that such a moment, though extremely rare, must and will come again, which keeps the uncertain heartbeat of the Tory Party going. My guess is that, now Mr Major's position has been temporarily secured, the party cannot nurture, cultivate and crystallise such a popular mood in the country into an active electoral constituency before the election; and that, without it, it will do considerably better than anyone seems to expect at the election, but cannot, or may not, recover sufficiently to win.

Everything, then, cannot be resolved until *after* the 'catharsis' of the general election. It is in the wake of electoral defeat that the final reckoning with Mr Major will probably come; and, as they see it, it is in a brief but necessary period in opposition that the internal reconstruction will be undertaken to prepare the renovated party and the revitalised constituencies in the country for another long, hegemonic period in office – a second Calvinist dispensation. In short, the resolution for the Tories lies in a 'knight's move' – finessing through Mr Major to …? I think this particular future belongs to Mr Portillo, who, despite his *gaffes* and hesitations during the leadership crisis, is the only figure of Cabinet rank and seniority, apart from Peter Lilley, with that demoniacal light of exaltation in his eye, and a certain passionate, romantic nationalist wildness to carry it off. But here the crystal-ball begins to darken over …

The Labour Party and the Blair resolution

What, then, of the alternative – the camp of the modernising saints and the Blair revolution? With a remarkable show of political courage and a flair for presentation, Mr Blair has set out to conquer Labour and to colonise political opinion in what by any reckoning has been a remarkable year, if not exactly an *annus mirabilis*. It is safe to say that Mr Blair has done what no Labour politician – including Mr Kinnock and Mr Smith, significant though their contributions were – has been able to accomplish, or what indeed has seemed impossible in the dark night of the Thatcher years: reconstruct an electable Labour Party and put it in a possible winning position. It has been a considerable achievement – so unlikely, indeed, that it sometimes appears that those who have participated most in bringing it about can hardly breathe, in case they bring the whole edifice tumbling down like dominoes. For the realists know it is not as sure-fire and foolproof as it appears to be. Despite the distance travelled, given the electoral arithmetic, it may not be quite enough. And there are many signs, of which Mr Blair is perfectly aware, that a lot of the support is as 'soft' as new-fallen snow. A puff of wind, or the announcement of the date of the election, will sweep a good 20 per cent of it away, for a start.

We know what the Tory 'revolution' would be, if only they could bring it off. But what is the 'Blair' revolution? What shift or current of feeling among the great majority of the population is he 'instinctively speaking and feeling in harmony with'?

Reshaping the Party

The first question is much easier to answer than the second. The 'Blair revolution' has been pre-eminently focused on transforming and reshaping the Labour Party, making it electable and, at the same time, the effective engine of his political

Soundings

ambitions and aspirations. No-one should underestimate the achievement here. There were always two aspects to any Labour revival: the first had to do, broadly speaking, with *modernisation*, the second with a political strategy and programme for the country which *both* addressed the major social and economic problems confronting the society in a novel and distinctive way, clearly contrasting its approach with that which had governed the previous regime, *and* at the same time captured the popular imagination, crystallising the disparate and sometimes contradictory elements of dissatisfaction into a new configuration, a new kind of politics. It is clear that, for Mr Blair, the test-bed of the first aspect – modernisation – has been the Labour Party itself, and there quite remarkable things have been accomplished. It is also no secret that this has been a far more successful venture than the second strand, where the 'seizing of moments' is less in evidence.

The refashioning of Labour – the apotheosis of the dreadful sloganised 'New Labour' – was necessary, but always promised to be a painful task. Political traditions are absolutely necessary for any political party, but there is all the difference in the world between confronting the radical novelty and contingency of the future from within a deeply grounded 'sense of history', as a resource, and being imprisoned – frozen – by the past.

The Labour Party has, for long, been immured in the second of those positions and it is, largely if not entirely, to Mr Blair's credit that he has courageously grasped the necessity of blasting the party free of some of these encrustations. The idea that the Labour Party ought to be more open and democratic in its procedures, less governed by caucus and clique, was instinctively right. The need to make it more of a recruiting party with a mass membership that meant something, less of a party whose *raison d'être* rested on bureaucratic forms of representation, seemed both right and inevitable.

Being old enough to remember when the trade union barons were regularly wheeled out by the right to clobber any radical or democratic initiative, I could never persuade myself that this was a good way of conducting democratic business for a political party that needed to be constantly in touch with the actual movement of political opinion. So that when the same bureaucracies were persuaded to use their muscle in defence of left-wing causes, it seemed to me that it was the principle and the method not simply the expedient result, which was the problem. It is certainly the case that certain sectors of workers in the labour market have never needed the protection of the unions as much as they do now. But, with certain key exceptions, these are not the union leaderships that have had most influence in reshaping Labour thinking or culture. Few of them have been in the vanguard of rethinking the relations of representation between unions and their members in ways which make the critical move from being an interest-group to becoming a 'national' form of political representation (i.e. one which could see that the struggle between miners and the Coal Board, or between train drivers and British Rail is, and is likely to be in the future, 'settled' by the weight of feeling amongst the great majority of 'consumers' who are neither). Without that shift, Mr Blair was right to think that the old way of giving the unions a voice inside the Labour Party was one which would only operate on the side of conserving and preserving the old bureaucratic culture of Labour, rather than on the side of modernisation, democratisation and change. This is not to support every move he has made in the area of rethinking the relations between the party and the unions, but it is to commend the instinct of modernisation that took him to this difficult front.

> 'The Labour Party has never been within a million light years of taking all of industry into common ownership'

Clause IV and public ownership

I am even less in sympathy with conventional left thinking on these issues where Clause IV is concerned. It is not as if the revision of Clause IV represented a major decommitment from a policy of principle to which Labour was formerly committed and which was a centrepiece of Labour's strategic thinking. As far as I am aware, the Labour Party has never been during my lifetime, and certainly is not now, within a million light-years of taking all of productive industry, of the full fruits of workers' labour by hand and brain, into common ownership. Such a commitment *may* just have made sense when it was first stitched up, in one of those clever, backstairs, conference redrafting 'deals' in which the Webbs so often had a hand. But it has absolutely no bearing, in its old form, on the world of the later twentieth century; nor does it represent an adequate response of a party to the whole, disastrous experience of 'state socialism' which came to so abrupt and dramatic an end in 1989, in the light of which the entire historical basis and trajectory of 'the left' in serious politics has *had* to be rethought. The opinion which was expressed at the time of its revision, that Labour needed Clause IV, not because anyone believed in it or intended to implement it, but because, like Everest, 'it was *there*', is the remnant of a totemistic form of thought, and has nothing to do with a modern political party attempting to develop a serious alternative political position for the twenty-first century. The opinion, which some serious figures on the left expressed at the time, that Labour could no more send its troops into electoral battle without Clause IV than Britain could send its troops into battle without the Union Jack, was so unnerving, so revealing in its unconscious implications, so eloquent of a political culture rivetted to empty symbols and a vacuous rhetoric, as to be seriously embarrassing to contemplate.

Of course, there is a place for forms of public ownership, social intervention and regulation in a variety of forms in the so-called market economy, as the public response to, say, the privatisation of water, the unscrupulous greed of the managements of the new public utilities, the scandal of rail privatisation and the effective derailing of Heseltine's attempt to privatise the Post Office clearly demonstrates. Of course, this real, substantive, issue of economic regulation and the harnessing of market forces within a social framework has been hopelessly fudged by the Blair reforms. The new wording for Clause IV is grammatically – not to mention politically – incomprehensible. It reveals, in the nervous incoherence of its syntax, its failure to think through serious issues in depth. But it was not wrong to try to reword it so as to bring it a millimetre closer to something that might and could actually come to pass in our lifetimes. Here, Mr Blair's instinct – that no party could survive so enormous a gap between words and deeds, rhetoric and intention – was correct; and the result is not to be dismissed as yet another inevitable example of a 'sell-out', as the absolutely predictable and automatic 'hard left' response would have it.

By these and other measures, equally courageously undertaken, Mr Blair has not only been consistent to the political 'project' which brought him to power, but courageous in the way he has pushed it through. In terms of the parliamentary battle, he has proven himself an excellent and articulate performer. The leadership 'machine' is also in much better shape – though it is being run as a 'tight battle ship', on the inner-circle basis, by a smart but over-confident kitchen cabinet-in-waiting, with an extremely limited range of intellectual and policy-sensitive views available to it, a few chosen academic and journalistic voices managed into place when the young tyros run out of fresh ideas themselves, and is powerfully 'Presidential' in style. It may be that successful modern political parties have to be run along these lines. But the one crucial ingredient which is conspicuously lacking, and for which the inner Praetorian guard are themselves serving as the inadequate substitute, is an open, and public *dialogue* with a very broad section of what may be called organic intellectual opinion (in which, of course, I include those critical *cadres* who run the voluntary organisations, or those with bright ideas to reform public administration, the NHS and local government, just as much as free-floating academics). Yet this is exactly the sort of construction of a public forum, of an intellectual ferment of ideas (not from a few, tame, party intellectuals only) which one would *expect* from a radical party facing office in profoundly changed social, economic and global conditions after sixteen years in the political wilderness. Here, the technical successes of the Blair style of New Labour leadership begin to reveal their limits.

> 'The one crucial ingredient which is conspiciously lacking is an open and public dialogue'

New ideas for new times?

What of the other prong of the 'project'? ... the opening up of a new political alternative; the sketching out of a viable new politics of Labour for 'new times'; clearly addressed to what is novel and dislocating in the global circumstances in which Labour might return to office; realistic in its recognition of the limits in speed and scope imposed both by the decline in manoeuvrability of the nation-state in the new global environment *and* by the fact that Britain remains fundamentally one of the least successful, declining members of the new economic club; and yet *selectively* directed at sketching out, by way of a sort of demonstration effect, some radically bold and novel ways of tackling *some* of the key issues; enough at least to show that Thatcherism, which appeared inevitably to command the first stage of these 'new times', was only one, possible, deeply flawed, way of addressing the dilemma; and thus capable of constructing a political constituency for change out of the varied and dispersed or disaggregated movements. Any signs of this in the 'Blair agenda'? I am afraid there are not. For some months, many of us who were fundamentally well-disposed to trying to make the Blair reform movement work persuaded ourselves that the reason none of this was in evidence was *tactical*. They had lots of plans, lots of ideas bubbling around, had drawn very widely on the thinking that had been going on during the Thatcher era. It was simply that they weren't going to just spill them out and get caught, like last time, on the hook of 'how does Labour propose to cost these?' They were biding their time. The ideas would be 'unveiled' at the strategically correct moment, each accompanied by a well-directed popular mobilisation building one key constituency after another – disgruntled NHS patients here, disillusioned parents and teachers next, traffic jammed commuters there – leading up to the crowning issue: how to remodel the welfare state while sustaining the basic public philosophy out of which it sprang. But this hasn't happened.

'There must be a better way of doing things than this lot'

I used the term 'demonstration effect' because I recognise that the discipline of popular opinion, which has moved significantly against the Thatcher tide, but certainly not as far as a massive redistributive programme, would place considerable constraints on what Labour could promise to do – *and* get elected. That made it doubly important that each part of the reform policy programme, though limited seriously in scope and effect, would clearly and publicly exemplify the radically new and distinctive thinking it embodied, clearly demonstrating precisely that here *is* an alternative (to the Thatcherite, free market forces, little England chauvinist way of thinking) and that Labour has some conception of what this other kind of politics might be – and of how it would make the country feel, look and be a different place to live in. If there is a post-Thatcherist mood in the country, this surely is what it is. There must be a better way of doing things than this lot. We've tried their way and it's failing. What other reason would there be for voting Labour for the vast majority of non genetically-programmed potential Labour voters?

It was always a possibility that the Labour modernisation programme would read the lessons of Thatcherism incorrectly. The lesson was – the times they are a-changing, and Thatcherism is the most effective way of trying to colonise these changes within a radical programme from the right. The left, however defined, must respect and address the changes – but from its own distinctive analysis and programme, with its own historic alternative. Instead 'New Labour' seems to have interpreted the lesson of Thatcherism as – the times are changing and

Thatcherism managed for a while to hegemonise them for the right. The left should therefore model itself as closely as possible on what the right did. This strategy of accommodation wins certain friends and influences certain people – especially detached voters and the press. As to whether it constitutes a powerful and persuasive enough reason for ordinary folk to vote Labour remains open to considerable doubt.

There is a simple test. Ask any potentially sympathetic but non-politically committed person, who has some grievance with any aspect of current policy, to describe how they imagine things will or could be done differently under Labour. I am willing to bet good money that they will be unable to do so. They know that under the Tory health service reforms one of the most precious, efficient, cost-effective and socially-supportive measures ever put forward to win public support in a modern democracy was put in jeopardy. They know that all was not well with the old NHS, but they know that what has happened to it under the Tories is of a different order of obscenity. The notion that *only* by faithfully 'mimicking the market' can an organisation be made efficient is basically unsound. People know that the pall of hypocritical double talk, the concealing cloak which Mrs Bottomley dispensed over the whole scene, was absolutely paradigmatic of the mode of institutionalised deceit which characterises the current Tory form

> 'How will this complex of issues be addressed under a Labour government? We do not know'

of government. How will this complex of issues be addressed in the NHS under a Labour government? We do not know. The public has no clear conception. It sort of knows that some bits of the reforms are to be kept, and some are not. People have a vague feeling, since Britain has the most cost-effective public health system and spends a lower proportion of its GDP on health than most advanced industrial societies, that, though 'we can't just throw money at it', the proportion of national wealth 'transferred' by public means through the NHS ought to rise. Under Labour, will it? It will not.

Well, why not? Because this is actually the right proportion to spend on health? Not at all. It is because Labour is so committed to out-doing the Tory government in public financial probity that no further funds can be raised by public taxation for *anything*. Now it is perfectly true that public spending and borrowing levels will have to be rigorously controlled by a Labour government.

On the other hand, a Labour government which cannot spend an extra penny from any source on health, the education system, public housing, community, family and caring services, transport and a strategic element of security in the labour market, is not worth voting for. Money isn't everything. But nothing fundamental will happen in *any* of these social areas which is cost-free. It follows that two or three of these areas should have been prioritised, the limited tax targets to fund them clearly and firmly established, the immediate 'ratepayer reaction' weathered at least two years *before* the election, and then the slow reconstruction of an element of public funding and targeted redistributive taxation begun as a long term project to turn the tide of the 80s 'ratepayer revolution' as part of a wider Labour strategy. One law of the Medes and Persians is that Labour is *always* more cautious, more conservative, in office than before it. What it does not campaign about beforehand, it will be mastered and driven by afterwards. The 1970s immigration legislation was the paradigm case where, having failed to campaign to educate its own and other constituencies while out of office, it found itself driven in office hurriedly to legislate in a basically anti-immigrant and racist way. This writing on the wall is now staring us in the face again, over the whole critical range of social policies which is precisely where the Thatcherite consensus fractured. Not to address this agenda in an accent and voice significantly clear, unambiguous and distinctive from that of your rivals, is a fundamental, strategic political miscalculation.

> 'What Labour does not campaign about before office, it will be mastered and driven by afterwards'

Labour's conservative modernity

When Bill Clinton took office, there was a feeling among many younger Americans that at least here was a figure who had had the kind of political experience they had, who somehow belonged to the same political generation as they did. It didn't last. There was a similar phenomenon with Tony Blair. Here was someone who seemed to be born and to have grown up in the same political generation, through the same historical experiences as younger voters. He actually knew the Sixties, had participated in the social movements, was married and bringing up young kids in Thatcher's Britain, may even know an unmarried mother or even have a friend who was HIV positive. He was, in generation at least, a post-feminist man. We could expect him, not to become the mouthpiece for these 'new times', but to know on his political pulses what it was all about. Out of office, he seemed to be a personable young politician, who had the great virtue of being able to listen to people, who might be looking for ways of enabling these novel sociological currents of feeling to break back into, and wreak a subtle transformation of, the traditional culture and programme of Labour.

But, in leadership, the impression he creates is almost the diametrical opposite. Mr Blair is a sort of 'new' or modern man, but a deeply conservative version of the species. On crime, on family values, on one-parent families, on questions of sexuality, on the particular variant of communitarianism which he espouses, one can find no echo at all of the underlying sociological analysis that one would expect of a so-called 'moderniser'. The idea that, at the end of the twentieth century, after the revolution in the position of women and in sexual attitudes we have passed through, it would be possible to advance the 'modernisation' of British society by an ideological commitment to the monogamous nuclear family as the only credible and stable family form, gives 'modernity' such a deeply conservative inflection that it hardly deserves the name.

Of course there are serious questions to be asked about parenting, about a sense of responsibility and mutual reciprocity and commitment in relationships, as there are about standards in education and the dissolution of the social fabric under the assault of 'there is no society' Thatcherite familial individualism. But a species of communitarianism which depends on sending women back to the hearth to 'conserve social values', which stigmatises the possibility of creating caring and loving places for children to grow up in who don't conform to the traditional nuclear norm, where the sense of community is most effectively embodied in the local

'It's back to tough on the causes of women's oppression, tough on women'

noise patrol, is fundamentally regressive socially. It derives from that spurious new-Democrat, neo-Republican Etzionian model – one of the very few ideas which seems to have penetrated the core of Blair thinking – whose main function is somehow to promise to square the circle between a new deal for 'women' *and* an old deal for 'mothers'. To adapt another too frequently quoted Blair slogan, it's back to 'tough on the causes of women's oppression, tough on women'!

On education, where if anywhere there is a popular agitation waiting to be developed, Mr Blair seems profoundly, one might even think wilfully, blind to the way a so-called modernisation programme, which takes 'standards' seriously but neglects the demands of the great mass of the children's education, aids the creeping advance of 'selectivity'. His stance – including I'm afraid the lack of touch with respect to the education of his own children – reproduces the most ancient and reactionary of the old class structures of educational privilege, totally at variance with any serious 'modernising' project, and in terms of the new global competitive environment, sociologically naive. And so on down the list.

> 'Mr Blair's stance reproduces the most ancient and reactionary of the old class structures of educational privilege'

'Modernisation' depends on raising the general level of educational achievement, but there is hardly a sound to emerge from the Blair camp about the 'costs' of the Tory expansion of higher education without investment, the crisis of student grants, or the chaos of technical education. Instead Labour is toying with selectivity, with schemes for combining the education and training of young adults with work experience which would take us back to the days before the 1944 Education Act, and a 'university of industry'.

The search for the grand idea

Mr Blair seized his chance in the Labour Party in the period when, on all sides, the search was on to substitute for the exhausted Thatcher project, some alternative 'grand idea'. It never appeared – 'grand ideas', looked for in this way, almost never emerge. However, though it was not of such stunning originality, there was always a very strong and distinctive 'idea' awaiting its Labour personifier.

Fundamentally, what seemed to have 'won' in the long night of Thatcherism was the gut sentiment that, essentially, there was no alternative to a way of life founded on the principles of the unregulated free market. Of course, not many people bought in to this idea wholesale. Still, even those who did not like what it delivered seemed for a time to settle reluctantly for the view that a 'society of the market' works and there was no alternative. What is manifestly clear now, in retrospect, is that this idea, though it provided the spear-head of a massive project of social reconstruction – what elsewhere I called 'regressive modernisation' – has not worked and cannot work.

For a long time, the distinction between the right and the left was stabilised by the polarisation of attitudes towards markets. The left was characterised by the belief that, since 'the market' *always* creates winners and losers, always creates deep inequalities, and social fragmentation, its remedy was the opposite, the abolition of markets and the absorption of state and economy into the so-called 'planned society' – state socialism. Now we know this doesn't 'work' either. Its costs are writ large in the collapse of the so-called Soviet model and its many variants and the catastrophes which its inauguration in that form brought in its train.

It does not take a genius to work out what, in such circumstances, constitutes 'the grand idea' of democratic politics. Is it possible, and in what form, to harness the significant advantages of the market (supposing for the moment that there is any *one* such thing – which there isn't – and that it is 'free', which it certainly is not), within a logic of social calculation which transcends a market forces conception of society and social need, and an 'economic man' or 'entrepreneurial subject' conception of human nature? Can one show, in thinking, in forms of organisation, in policy and strategy, that there *is* such a thing as 'society', though it is not the closed totality, the sutured closure conceived of by state socialism and all its derivatives (including much of Labourism), but remains fundamentally open to the contingency of historical movement and change – a place of calculation and strategic operations, not an ultimately predictable social essence. This may sound broad and vague – but then all 'grand ideas' usually do. The trick lies in giving this vague and open-ended idea a concrete, late twentieth century 'content' and form.

Somehow, in the back of his head, Mr Blair knew that 'seizing the historical moment' depended on being able to constitute political forms which would enable a society, mesmerised for a time by the chimera of 'market forces', once again *to imagine the social* in the context of the twenty-first century. But the effort to think through in depth what this would mean seems to have been a task too difficult to accomplish, a 'grand idea' too far. In its place, we stand a chance of getting a Labour Government in power again. But I have my doubts that it is driven by an idea, strategy or perspective large enough to capture the popular imagination. Of course, 'such moments are as unforgettable as they are rare', as Mrs Thatcher reminded us. They can also be rather short lived and can end in disaster. One hopes, but without much confidence, that Labour is headed for something a little less ignominious than that dismal scenario.

Lawrence & Wishart
New Books 1995

THE FIRST NEW LEFT
British Intellectuals After Stalin
Michael Kenny

In the late 1950s Stuart Hall, Edward Thompson and Raymond Williams, among others, came together as part of a promising new political formations, the New Left. The six years of the group's formal existence represents one of the richest and most exciting periods in the intellectual history of the left in Britain.

Michael Kenny documents and analyses the debates of the New Left, showing how their preoccupations prefigure many contemporary concerns such as the broadening of the previously narrow definition of politics and the development of an interest in popular culture.

Paperback £14.99   ISBN 0 85315 797 9   216pp

AYES TO THE LEFT
A Future for Socialism
Peter Hain MP

Is there only one vision for New Labour? Here, Peter Hain, a leading figure in current debates about the future of the Labour Party, presents his case for a modern and participatory socialism. He makes an intelligent and coherent case for a radical, popular and decentred socialism – an alternative to both the social democratic and communist traditions. This offers attractive policies for regenerating the economy, democratising the British state and creating a people's Europe.

Paperback £9.99   ISBN 0 85315 832 0   224pp

CULTURAL REMIX
Theories of Politics and the Popular
Edited by Erica Carter, James Donald, Judith Squires

'Culled from the pioneering journal of cultural studies, *New Formations*, this presents muscular theoretical writings on topics ranging from black hairstyles and satellite dishes to democracy and parliamentary debates on Section 28 ... A challenging read, it reflects the complex paradigmatic crisis that has bedevilled the discipline in recent years.' *Sight and Sound*, August 1995

Paperback £14.99   ISBN 0 85315 794 4   332pp

Lessons for Labour

Barbara Castle

Barbara Castle recounts from her experience how much 'old Labour' achieved in its periods of office. She warns New Labour against the accommodations to financial orthodoxy which wrecked previous Labour governments, and declares that unemployment is the blight that most needs to be challenged.

I think it is common knowledge that I am 'Old Labour'. At 84 some people would describe that as 'Very Old'.

As a schoolgirl in Bradford in the 1920s I rubbed shoulders with party veterans like Fred Jowett who was to become a Cabinet Minister in the first ever Labour Government in 1924. He had been brought up in the infamous back-to-back slum terraces whose sanitation consisted of a row of 'privy middens' – a chain of earth closets between the terraced houses, serving all of them. No water flushing, of course. Just the nightly clearance of the accumulated excrement by mysterious 'night soil' men. Fresh air never blew through the back-to-backs and bathrooms were unknown.

So am I just an old sentimentalist living in the past? I only wish this degradation of so many of our fellow citizens *was* past history. Of course, we all have water closets today – if we have a home. At least Fred Jowett had a roof over his head which is more than we can say of everyone in our 'prosperous' society 70 years on from my Bradford days.

In fact, the technological revolution has left as many human scars as the industrial one did. The privy middens may have gone, thanks to the tireless war waged on them by men and women like Fred Jowett and Margaret Macmillan, pioneer of the nursery school; between them, they literally cleansed the conditions under which thousands of Bradford people lived. But we have only got to look round so many of our inner cities with their down-at-heel housing estates, littered with discarded condoms and syringes, to realise that we have hardly begun to build the new Jerusalem.

The point I am trying to make is that there is a continuity in the Labour Party's history ever since Keir Hardie encouraged working men and women at the beginning of this century to break with the Liberals and form an Independent Labour Party of their own. It was not a narrow sectional movement. Middle-class reformers, writers and intellectuals flocked to it: Fabians like George Bernard Shaw and the Webbs; scientific visionaries like H.G. Wells; fighters for sex equality like Richard and Emmeline Pankhurst. They were attracted by the ILP's challenge to an economic system which treated human beings as units of production rather than as sentient individuals with a right to fulfil themselves.

I am not pretending for a moment that these ILP pioneers were an angelic host. I have lived too close to politics ever since I joined the ILP Guild of Youth at the age of 16 not to know how often we fell short of our ideals. But the important thing was that we always followed our guiding star, however often we stumbled on the way. As a result, the achievements have been prodigious. Most of them were very down-to-earth, such as the abolition of the slums, the end of sweated labour conditions, the opening-up of educational opportunities. The achievements of the first majority Labour Government of 1945 are now legendary: not only its great reforming programme, but also the way it changed the whole moral and intellectual climate of the country.

'We have hardly begun to build the new Jerusalem'

In fact we swung millions of people from a cowed acceptance of the social evils of *laissez-faire* into the belief that they could mould a better society. In his seminal Report Sir William Beveridge hammered on them that the five giant evils – ignorance, squalor, disease, idleness and want – were man-made, not acts of God.

We could cure them by organising our national resources more effectively. By the 1945 election it was already clear that Churchill, whose wartime coalition Government had commissioned the Report, was planning to jettison it. One of the first acts of the victorious Labour Government was to implement his concept of the welfare state in full. It was to survive unchallenged for 30 years.

The National Health Service which Aneurin Bevan as Minister of Health forced through the 1945 Parliament against Conservative opposition has proved an enduring monument. It is based on pure socialist principles: you pay through your taxes according to your ability when you are fit and working and when you fall ill you are entitled to draw free at the point of use on the best medical resources the country can provide.

> 'I approved of the direction of Harold Wilson's governments, though not of the deviations on the way'

Yet the vast majority of people of all parties jump to its defence when it is under threat. Even Margaret Thatcher dared not attack this piece of socialist legislation frontally and was forced to try to undermine it surreptitiously.

Ah, critics say, those were the halcyon days: circumstances have changed and so have Labour governments. The first fine idealism is dead and selfishness is king.

We certainly live in a different world. Thanks to technological advance austerity has given way to relative affluence. This has made Labour's reforming task more difficult, particularly since Margaret Thatcher set out ruthlessly to reverse that unifying philosophy which Labour launched in 1945 and substituted the doctrine that it is everyone for him- or herself – the devil and drugs take the hindmost. It has been an uphill task to fight the materialist values which increasingly dominate our lives. But it would be dangerous folly to dismiss the post-1945 Labour governments as proof that socialist principles have been discredited.

That is, of course, nonsense – as I know from firsthand experience as an MP for 34 years and as a member of Harold Wilson's four Cabinets between 1964 and 1976. Of course I had plenty of criticisms to make of those governments, but looking back I am struck by the continuity of purpose if not always of practice. I approved of the direction, though not of the deviations on the way.

Some of them were forced on us. It was always our lot to be elected when the Tories had got the economy into a mess. In 1964 for example Reginald

Maudling's ill-planned 'dash for growth' had left us to face a record balance of payments deficit. Nevertheless, Jim Callaghan's first budget fulfilled a number of our commitments, notably to the pensioners, and covered the cost by a sixpence increase on income tax; so it was not inflationary.

This did not satisfy the speculators. The City was outraged, not that we were being spendthrift, but re-distributive. Unfortunately the inner triumvirate of the Cabinet – Harold Wilson, Jim Callaghan and George Brown – had fallen victim to the City shibboleth that defence of the currency must always have overriding priority. Devaluation being ruled out, deflation became the only alternative. The cut-backs began.

But the general direction of our social policy towards a more equal society remained unchanged. Legal aid, which Labour had introduced in 1949, was strengthened and a tax-free redundancy payments scheme was introduced. Overseas aid was marginally increased despite a chorus of 'charity begins at home' in the tabloid press. Comprehensive education was launched too. And, as Minister of Transport, Harold encouraged me to draw up an integrated transport policy giving public transport a central role. I was even allowed to put the first ever all-embracing Equal Pay Act on the statute book. Harold himself doggedly pursued his two favourite aims: to promote women to jobs no woman had held before (such as Transport), and to open the doors of educational opportunity through his brainchild, the Open University.

> 'The city was outraged, not that we were being spendthrift, but re-distributive'

By 1970, we had balanced the nation's books, but at a political price which cost us the election and let in Edward Heath. Ironically, one of his first acts was to float the pound – for which some of us had been pressing since 1964. But he threw away the benefits in his disastrous struggle to put the unions in a legal straitjacket so complex that it was unworkable; he was forced to dump his Industrial Relations Bill. Even Margaret Thatcher did not attempt to resurrect it, preferring more subtle means of weakening the trade unions.

So Labour was back in office in 1974. It was the same grim inheritance. In his fight with the miners Ted Heath had left British industry throttled by a three-day working week. Prices were rising and so was the trade deficit. Once again, we had to put the economy to rights and, once again, the Treasury moved in with its only recipe for a strong economy – cut public expenditure.

So the battle over the cuts began again: it was long and bitter precisely because every member of the Cabinet was determined to safeguard his or her department's contribution to a better society. I was lucky because as Secretary of State in charge of the DHSS, I was the custodian of sweeping social reforms to bring the welfare state up-to-date. In this capacity I was able to introduce the most exciting advances in social policy since 1945: the State Earnings Related

'Wilson had been exhausted by the strain of keeping left and right together'

Pensions Scheme which gave manual workers and women a new security and dignity in retirement; child benefit which gave mothers their own wage for the first time; a charter for the disabled; new status for nurses and para-medics through the Halsbury Reports; and curbs on the encroachment of private medicine in the NHS. It was all part of the Social Contract which we had entered into with the trade unions, guaranteeing a 'social wage' in return for their sharing the responsibility of making the national economy work by voluntarily moderating their wage demands.

The policy was beginning to tell when a weary Harold Wilson resigned in 1976. As he had hinted to me more than once, he had been exhausted by the strain of keeping the left and right in the government together with cunning compromises and by the resulting denunciation of him in a hostile press as 'unprincipled'. In fact his eel-like qualities were employed in the service of his guiding principle – his duty to preserve party unity at whatever cost to his own reputation. A left-winger at heart he had to manoeuvre to get his way as much as possible without splitting the Cabinet.

His successor, Jim Callaghan, was of a different mould. He was more orthodox and less flexible. He sacrificed the party to another orthodox economic priority, to get inflation down at any social cost. In fact inflation had been falling steadily from its high peak of 1975, thanks to the co-operation of the trade unions which the social contract had won for us. But it was still running at 10 per cent when in 1978 Callaghan demanded his colleagues' support for a ruthless new 'norm' for wage increases. I was no longer in the Cabinet, Jim having sacked me when he took over in 1976, but Denis Healey describes the scene in his autobiography, *The Time of My Life*. 'Jim had preferred a zero norm and actually proposed 3 per cent at one meeting... Cabinet finally settled for a norm of 5 per cent.' Even this would have amounted to a cut in wages against which prospect the unions finally rebelled, plunging the country into the strikes of the winter of discontent which brought down the government.

H arold Wilson would never have been guilty of such rigidity. 'You know me', he used to say to me, 'I hate to be painted into a corner.' He would have manoeuvred himself out of this one. By asking less from the unions he would in fact have got smaller wage increases than Jim Callaghan's confrontational formula actually achieved – and he would have averted the disastrous wave of strikes. I believe that if Harold Wilson had not resigned Labour would not have lost the 1979 election.

In other words, Margaret Thatcher would never have had her opportunity to launch her counter-revolution, reversing all Labour's policies in a free-for-all in which government washed its hands of all responsibility for unemployment and poverty. The market was to decide everything. It was socialism, she claimed, which had brought us low and must be destroyed.

So what are the lessons of Labour's long struggles? The first is that we must regain our pride in our accomplishments and confidence in our analysis of what is wrong. For one thing Margaret Thatcher's counter-revolution has not worked economically. In the past 16 years the economy has been put through a disastrous cycle of boom and bust, plunging us into a recession

'It is absurd at this moment to boast of a break with our past'

of which any Labour government in which I have served would have been ashamed. As Will Hutton, economics editor of *The Guardian*, points out in his penetrating book *The State We're In*, her deliberate policy of widening the gap between rich and poor has been responsible for the low economic performance from which we are still suffering today. Poverty and inequality can never make for economic stability. No entrepreneur is going to invest in an economy which deliberately shrinks demand. As 'Old Labour' I used to tell my audience that the only way to expand wealth is to share it more equally. That is still relevant today, globally as well as nationally.

The second lesson is that it is absurd at this very moment to boast of a break with our past. Of course, we made mistakes, and we need to be quite clear what they were. But there was nothing wrong with our aims: I was fighting for new Labour's 'core values' before Tony Blair was born. Or perhaps they *are* being changed: 'Diversity and excellence' is a worrying title for an education policy, smacking of a return to selectivity rather than a genuine equality of opportunity and of esteem.

But what about wholesale nationalisation? Old Labour – apart from a few Stalinists and loony left – has believed in a mixed economy for years. There is nothing new in the idea of partnership between the public and private sectors. The SERPS which I introduced was a perfect example of the need for co-operation between the state scheme and private occupational pension schemes as the best way of bringing Beveridge up-to-date. SERPS also costs

'There is nothing new in the idea of partnership between the public and private sectors'

the taxpayer less than the Tories' fraudulent attempt to snare people into private personal pensions schemes which will reduce millions of people, particularly women, to abject poverty in old age. In a few years time the country will be faced with a mounting bill for income support just to keep them alive in penury. Yet our leaders have not yet committed themselves to restoring SERPS.

What about Labour's relations with the trade unions? New Labour tells us that old Labour (by inference the left) was too much in the pocket of the trade unions and that the modernisers will assert the party's independence. This version of history is the complete opposite of my experience. It was the old left which always asserted the rights of the individual members of the constituency parties against the trade unions' dominance of the party conference. There was no objection to the block vote by the 'modernisers' of the time, led by Hugh Gaitskell, so long as the unions were safely in the hands of right-wing bosses like Will Lawther of the miners who supported them.

I t was only when left-wing leaders like Frank Cousins took over the Transport and General Workers Union that the mood changed, though Frank as a good democrat was always ready to submit himself to the decisions of his union conference.

It was the same story when I became Secretary of State for Employment in 1968. I spent two turbulent years telling my trade union friends that the industrial anarchy caused by wild-cat strikes was no way to secure the fundamental political reforms their members were looking for. All it did was to strengthen our political enemies. The unions, I urged, must learn to accommodate their sectional demands to the wider economic aims of their Labour government as the only way to safeguard their members' long-term interests.

But when I embodied this thesis in my now notorious White Paper, 'In Place of Strife', it was 'moderates' like Jim Callaghan who led the attack on me and stirred up the trade union storm, arguing that we must not interfere with union rights. Even Social Democrats like Roy Jenkins, who secretly agreed with me, lost their nerve and let me down. I like Roy Jenkins personally and admired many of the 'permissive' reforms he carried through as Home Secretary, but the idea that the wooing of former SDP quitters back into the party will stiffen the party's backbone is spurious. I welcome them back, but I think they should show some humility.

I also welcome Tony Blair's determination to reduce the role of the block vote and to give a greater say to the individual membership. But I reject with alarm the suggestion now coming from certain quarters, including Roy Hattersley, that the next step should be to end the party's constitutional links with the trade unions. This is like saying that the Tory party should break all ideological and financial links with the powerful forces which dominate industry, and we are a long way from that.

'It was "moderates" like Jim Callaghan who led the attack on "In Place of Strife"'

The need for employees to have a strong organisation to protect them from exploitation has never been clearer than it is today. With the Major government constantly shedding its duties to protect the health and safety of workers from the risks of a profit driven society, the rate of accidents in agriculture and other industries is rising ominously. Strong trade unions must fill the gap. We should be proud of our links with them as part of our pluralist democracy.

Again, this should be the last moment for us to apologise for our record when widespread disillusionment with Thatcherite and Majorite policies is setting in. Even the Chancellor Kenneth Clark, in a remarkable recent interview in *The Guardian*, admitted that he was a 'One Nation' pre-Thatcherite Tory who was sickened by the public spending cuts which have robbed so many of the essentials for life in a civilised society.

It has been amusing, too, to watch Tory MPs from rural areas panic at the idea of privatising the Post Office. They realise what we have always known: that the only way to guarantee a universal system serving all parts of the country equally is through public ownership. Having failed in his attempt to break the Post

Office up into private lots, Michael Heseltine has been forced to give it the commercial freedom it has always been denied. The result has been a spectacular development of its activities, as we see from its television advertising. New Labour must demand that other publicly-owned services like the railways be given the same freedom so that they can remain in public ownership.

There are indeed lessons we can learn from our past mistakes. One of the most important is that previous Labour governments only failed to the extent that they were hypnotised by the monetarist dictums of the City and the Treasury. Examples abound, starting with Philip Snowden's destruction of the 1929 Labour government by his insistence that Britain must remain on the gold standard at all costs. Keynes' opposition was brushed aside. The savage spending cuts needed to sustain this policy only deepened the depression and brought in the National Government. When its first step was to take Britain off the gold standard Sidney Webb remarked wistfully, 'Nobody told us we could do that.'

'Labour governments failed to the extent that they were hypnotised by the monetarist dictums of the City and the Treasury'

Forty years later nobody told Denis Healey, then Chancellor, that the Treasury figures designed to prove that public spending and borrowing had gone through the roof were wrong. He was induced to negotiate a loan from the IMF on tough deflationary terms only to find that the Treasury estimates had been twice as gloomy as the facts warranted. He writes bitterly in his autobiography, 'If I had been given accurate forecasts in 1976 I would never have needed to go to the IMF at all.' But the political damage had been done.

Under Margaret Thatcher these mistakes were compounded by establishing monetary criteria as the sole arbiters of economic and social policy. Her two famous dictums – 'you can't buck the market' and 'there is no such thing as society' – were complementary. If the market is king no-one can object to its social consequences, whatever the ensuing loss of jobs and the resulting poverty.

The climax of the monetarist approach came with her government's decision to put sterling into the Exchange Rate Mechanism (ERM) at a value our economy could not sustain. In her autobiography Margaret Thatcher claims that on this and on other blunders she had not been told what was happening. In fact she had been a consistent party to the view that financial criteria should dominate economic policy. It has never worked. British industry, which had begun by welcoming the currency stability which membership of the ERM seemed to offer, was soon up in arms against the flood of bankruptcies, loss of export markets and rising unemployment which followed the attempt to put our economy in a financial straitjacket. It was not until the Tory government was forced by this outcry to withdraw sterling from the ERM that there was any chance of pulling us out of the recession which was swamping us.

How, then, does New Labour intend to learn these economic lessons from our history? Old Labour has always been broadly Keynesian in the sense that it believed – and still believes – that government must take responsibility for securing a high level of employment by demand management. Some of us are worried by the priority given to the supply side in New Labour's economic policy. It is not enough to stress the need for better training and education, important though both are. Their value soon vanishes if well-trained people find there is no demand for their services. I have too many highly-trained friends whose self-confidence is punctured by the endless rejection of their job applications and who are trying to live on £47.00 a week.

'Some of us are worried by the priority given to the supply side by New Labour'

Nor is it any good calling on industry to invest in long-term development unless it can see a market for its products. Demand must always lead supply. Margaret Thatcher's pet nostrum, zero inflation, would stultify demand and put an end to growth. We must remaster the art of demand management and revive the social contract as its focal point.

Our democracy cannot withstand the Tory policy of competitive deflation which tries to force our people to accept wage levels and working conditions which will enable them to undercut, among others, the Koreans. If the Western world does not work out policies to protect our own people's right to work on the basis of civilised standards, dictatorship, whether communist of fascist, will win the day.

With his usual competence Gordon Brown has produced two documents setting out New Labour's economic strategy. It includes some important institutional reforms, but it has one serious omission. We must, he argues, have a target for growth as well as inflation, but he does not mention jobs. Yet, as we all know, investment in new technology can actually put people out of work. It is only the public sector that can provide the labour-intensive services.

The battle for fuller employment will not be an easy one, but unless we win it we will never get rid of the dependent society and give our people dignity and hope.

The first step must be to compel economists of the Western world to accept this goal as the centre piece of economic policy. We must set ourselves a jobs target as one of the indices of economic health and the test of any government's claim to economic recovery.

In other words we must change the mental climate of this country once again as we did in 1945. If Tony Blair will emblazon this goal on his election banner, he will romp home.

Old fogeys and angry young men

Beatrix Campbell

Beatrix Campbell *argues that communitarianism represents the latest in a long line of attempts by men to reassert their power over women. Its focus on the family as a major source of community problems is a thinly disguised attack on women. And its refusal to investigate the parenting deficit between women and men is symptomatic of its wilful resistance to the insights of feminism.*

'He seemed paranoid', said someone referring to a speaker promoting communitarianism at a local government conference during the summer of 1995. It was a sign of something strange. Communitarianism is a barely-understood and little-read thesis in political circles, yet it has prospered handsomely in Britain under the patronage of the new boys in the Labour leadership and the think-tank Demos.

The wariness of its advocates at the local government conference was suggestive, however, of an unexpected challenge from something seething below the threshold of consciousness: their fugitive Furies perhaps.

Buoyed by the pundits' endorsement of communitarianism's resurrection of universal moral verities, nevertheless communitarianism's New Labour advocates seemed piqued in the spring of 1995 when their guru the American-Israeli sociologist Amitai Etzioni – hosted by Demos and *The Times* – was chided both by scholars and by activists drawing directly on experience.

Communitarianism is a rather biblical notion that emerged as a third way between liberal individualism and statist socialism in philosophical debates in the USA during the 1980s. Its attraction, no doubt, comes from what it connotes: community action. But its parameters and preoccupations come from neither the drift of popular culture nor the vigorous networks of active citizenship stirring in civil society. The theory comes from the dialogue between liberal individualism and classical philosophy and belongs to a political culture in the United States which – unlike the UK, despite the best efforts of Thatcherism – is potently anchored in individualism and anti-statism.

Amitai Etzioni notes in his book *The Spirit of Community* that although 'it is common to romanticise the Greek *polis* as a place in which all free people participated in public life, which is equated with political life ... an important way to build community is to ensure that there are numerous occasions for active participation of the members in its governance.'

The appeal to ancient civic values is not only an argument against the market rampant, it is (not only in Etzioni's influential text) also an attempt to restore the authority of values and structures already winded by a medley of new and previously marginalised interests and identities. For communitarianism in Britain provides the theory for a political practice that has already been bested by Thatcherism, an audacious 'regressive modernisation' deployed with surgical elan by Britain's first woman premier. Unlike Thatcherism, though, communitarianism is a *contingent* politics; it is associated with a political project that is both *abject* and *authoritarian*; it is dependent not on radicalism, on a culture of challenge fertilised by the conflicts and solidarities of popular culture, but on the traditionalism reinstated by the very same Thatcherism it purports to oppose.

But the British feminist critics of the liberal-communitarian debate, Elizabeth Frazer and Nicola Lacey, have cautioned against the communitarians' conservative potential. Their critique alerts us to the attempts within radical liberalism to advance progressive discourses – the one 'more resonant with the more social-democratic version of liberalism espoused in the early twentieth century', the other more inclined to jettison order and certainty as an authoritarian attempt to impose universal values on a heterogeneous universe. In the context of the rush rightwards in governance in Britain and the USA in the 1980s, this 'has helped to emphasise both the progressiveness of liberalism and the dangers of the potential conservatism of communitarianism.'[1]

1. Elizabeth Frazer and Nicola Lacey, *The Politics of Community, A Feminist Critique of the Liberal-Communitarian Debate*, Harvester Wheatsheaf, Hemel Hempstead 1993.

The challenge to the traditional verities, explains the feminist philosopher Susan Bordo, 'first occurred not in the course of philosophical conversation, but in political practice. Its agents were the liberation movements of the sixties and seventies, emerging not only to make a claim to the legitimacy of marginalised cultures, unheard voices, suppressed narratives, but also to expose the perspectivity and partiality of the official accounts. Now those accounts could no longer

'What communitarianism gives to the new boys is traditionalism'

claim to descend from the heavens of pure rationality or to reflect the inevitable and progressive logic of intellectual or scientific discovery.'[2]

Communitarianism is a response both to the potency of traditionalism and the New Right, and to the liberation movements. It speaks to anxiety about the seismic shifts in relations between genders and generations, an anxiety which is often expressed in more or less covert misogyny and old fogeyism. It is sustained by the effects of the asymmetry between the transformations of 'private' relations and the priorities of public institutions.

What communitarianism gives to the new boys in the White House and Walworth Road is traditionalism, or as Demos director Geoff Mulgan – communitarianism's centurion in Britain – puts it, a swing away from ideology and back to ethics.[3] This vacuity allows its advocates to pour their fears and fantasies into its shapeless form; it allows 'progressive' traditionalists to re-group and to solidify their evaporating political authority; above all, it enables 'respectable', white, mainstream masculinity to exempt itself from the critique – now well-rehearsed as common sense – of the masculinities that make life a misery in hard-pressed places. It allows angry white men to compose themselves and close the conversations with the insurgents – primarily women – that they never wanted to have.

Communitarianism's relevance to *fin de siècle* Britain derives not from its connection with community concerns but from its rhetorical resonance for a *party* political culture whose centre of gravity has tilted dramatically to the right, and is grievously detached from the drift of popular discourses. The argument here is that communitarianism, so far as it has been popularised in this country,

---

2. Susan Bordo, 'Feminism, Postmodernism and Gender-Scepticism', in
    Feminism/Postmodernism, Linda J. Nicholson (ed), Routledge, London 1990.
3. Geoff Mulgan, 'Beyond the Lure of Off-the-Shelf Ethics', *Independent*, 30 January 1995.

is precisely about *policing* popular cultures, identities and interests which have disturbed the ancient pillars of traditional power – both personal and public – and party politics.

Although focused on the social space of community, communitarianism looks at the micro-metamorphoses of the landscape of locality from a distance: and after that, of course, the detail dies. It takes the side of white men in the twentieth century's second great effort to effect a new historic settlement between men and women; it takes the side of affronted white men in the wake of new settlements between regions and races; it recoils from the redistribution not only of resources but respect.

> 'Communitarianism takes the side of white men in the effort to effect a new historic settlement between men and women'

It is the rhetorical resonance, the primitive moral polarisations, of communitarianism, that have brought it to the British political table. This is what has given it the frisson of a *new idea* and put it to the service of the New Labourism's quest for a new political project.

Since both liberalism and communitarianism lack a theory of power and a sensitivity to the dominant political solidarities that derive from exclusive, masculinised modes of assembly, neither have a theory of oppression.[4] It is difficult to imagine, therefore, how this debate can yield personal and global redistribution and solidarity.

Within communitarianism there is a palpably masculinist moralism. The communitarians have been stung by the feminist critique – Geoff Mulgan petulantly notes 'an extraordinary range of attacks from all sorts of *guardians of orthodoxy*, whether liberals or feminists...'[5] However, communitarianism occupies some of the same terrain as feminism. Its appeal to ethics could echo the feminist mantra: the personal is political; but there is a determined, indeed sometimes desperate, disengagement from the insights of feminism. Since communitarians appear to be interested in the boundary between public and private, which is nothing if not the terrain of feminism, the erasure of feminist scholarship and politics reveals something about the interests that are defended by communitarianism.

---

4. Frazer and Lacey, *op. cit.*
5. Mulgan, *op. cit.*

Community – the Holy Ghost

Communitarianism celebrates a holy trinity of family, community and nation, as if community represented a halcyon pasture, small but perfectly formed, an immaculately conceived domain of homogeneous kinships, shared interests and common histories. This notion of community enlarges the fantasy of family as 'personal' and 'natural' that was shaken by feminism's scrutiny of its secret life; the discovery that families are not only the locus of passionate care, but also that 'thoroughly permeated with power, they are the site of egocentric, strategic and instrumental calculation as well as sites of literally exploitative exchanges of services, labour, cash and sex, not to mention coercion and violence.'[6]

The imaginary unity of community or family has been exposed not only by the very movements that are again under threat of being marginalised by communitarianism, but also by the fallout in the 'distressed areas' where community and family are no less fissured by power and subordination than class, nation and empire are.

Sex and self-interest

Etzioni's book *The Spirit of Community* was the text which Demos selected to initiate British readers to communitarianism: their orientation is revealed in the book's core chapter: 'The Parenting Deficit'.

'Nobody likes to admit it, but between 1960 and 1990 American society allowed children to be devalued, while the golden call of "making it" was put high on the pedestal,' remarks Etzioni. 'Some blame this development on the women's movement, others on the elevation of materialism and greed to new historical heights. These and other factors may all have combined to devalue children.' Women, he insists, share the same entitlement as men to pursue self-interest, but a society in which sexual equality means women behave as men do (as if they do!) is unacceptable. This does not take Etzioni or Demos into a critique of the political and cultural histories of masculinity, however.

On the contrary, 'Over the past 20 years millions of American mothers have sharply curtailed their work in the "parenting industry" by moving to work outside the home.' If this had happened in any other industry, 'we would be

---

6. Nancy Fraser, 'What's Critical About Critical Theory? The Case of Habermas and Gender', *Feminist Interpretations and Political Theory*, Mary Lyndon Shanley and Carole Pateman (eds), Polity Press, Cambridge 1991.

considered crazy. But this is what happened to parenting.' And, 'whatever the cause, the result is an empty nest.' Children, Etzioni told a meeting in London, have been abandoned to the drinks cabinet and the television.

Frequently slipping from one argument to another – now it's a defence of two parent families, then a defence of parents staying home to be with children – the confusion is instructive. The history of the modern era is littered with men's crusades to control women's freedom of movement, to constrain their participation in the paid labour market and to secure the care of men and children safely at the centre of women's attention. Etzioni's lament echoes the familiar refrain of 'latch-key children' which characterised an earlier era in the post-war reconstruction of Britain and America when women's confinement to homemaking was subject to renewed cultural pressure, when public child-care was privatised, and yet women were re-entering the paid labour market. The lament was always a reproach to women. The rehabilitation of the notion by Etzioni is indicative: despite caveats, his critique of contemporary parenting is directed *against* mothers. He marks the beginning of the end for children as the point in the 1960s when women rejoined the paid labour market *en masse*. His caveat that his case is against delinquent fathers as well as mothers cannot be taken seriously. His work reveals a fury, not with fathers, but with mothers.

'The modern era is littered with men's crusades to control women's freedom of movement'

Feminist scholars have criticised liberalism, classical philosophy and communitarianism for their failure to reckon with the structural polarisation of private and public which is founded on the regulation of women. 'Sexual difference is central to the distinction between public and private,' argues the feminist philosopher Nancy Fraser. There is a substantial feminist and socialist literature which has mapped the historical separation of these spheres and its consequences for both individuals and institutions; its impact on subjectivity, citizenship and political systems.

But this is not on Demos' or Etzioni's agenda. Their project is not the reform of the institutions so that adult time and space synchronise with children's. Etzioni's case leads inexorably to an impasse. He argues that 'all women did was demand for themselves what men had long possessed...', but this is not true. In Britain, women's waged work did not abandon children *en masse* to a Home

Alone syndrome. Nor have women consigned the work of care to the Other – men. Motherhood is not fading, it is changing and challenging men, and the institutions they made in their own image, to deliver the thing women long for – co-operation.

T he politics of time has long been a feminist pre-occupation, not least because of the temporal polarisations between men and women produced by the regulation of 'separate spheres'. Indeed, it was the women's movement that invented the politics of time.[7] None of this has been assimilated by Etzioni or Demos.

Etzioni's crude claims about mothers are not supported by empirical research. Studies of time-use in the UK and the USA show different patterns of parental employment and parenting. (British conditions cannot be extrapolated from US data as if British culture were merely a colony of its American Big Brother.) According to the most authoritative comparisons by Gershuny and Robinson, 'time spent in child-care seems to be increasing in the UK but decreasing in the USA.'[8] They qualify this conclusion, however, by noting that once structural changes and scale are factored in, then 'child-care time actually increases in both countries', and there is an 'underlying trend upward'.

In earlier time-use studies child-care could have been hidden as a secondary activity happening at the same time as housework. What Gershuny and Robinson chart from daily diaries recorded by parents, however, is the dedicated time parents give to their children. Gershuny's research on British domestic labour and child-care not only shows that time spent with children is increasing among both fathers and mothers, but among those mothers working full-time the time spent with children is actually greater than the time given to children by full-time homemakers three decades ago. But Etzioni's complaint against mothers averts his attention from the disappearing father: when children are young and

---

7. See Anne Phillips, *Hidden Hands: Women and Economic Policies*, Pluto, London 1983; Jenny Hurstfield, *The Part Time Trap*, Low Pay Unit, London 1978; Hilary Land, 'The Family Wage', *Feminist Review*, No.6, 1980; Beatrix Campbell and Valerie Charlton, 'Work to Rule', *Red Rag*, 1978; Beatrix Campbell, 'United We Fall', *Red Rag*, 1980; Michael Anderson, Frank Bechhof and Jonathan Gershuny, *The Social and Political Economy of the Household*, Oxford University Press, Oxford 1994. For a model of indifference to gendered time differentials see Geoff Mulgan and Helen Wilkinson, 'Well-being and Time', in *Demos Quarterly*, No.5, London, 1995.
8. Jonathan Gershuny and John P. Robinson, 'Changes in Household Division of Labour', in *Demography*, Vol.25, No.4, November 1988.

most sequestered at home, fathers are most absent.

In her 1989 presidential address to the Population Association of America, Harriet Presser clarified the familiar pressures that have centrifugal effects on men's and women's time. She concluded that American mothers with children under 14 are working fewer hours and days than other women, while fathers living with children under 14 are out working longer than other men. The gender gap in working time between men and women is thus at its greatest when children are most needy. Contrary to expectation, Presser found that temporal flexibility in the workplace, far from increasing parents' time with children and reducing the stress of finding appropriate, affordable child-care, has a minimal effect on parental time with children. 'Greater job flexibility seems to reinforce rather than mitigate gender differences among dual-earner couples.'

> 'The gender gap in working time between men and women is at its greatest when children are most needy'

This echoes the trend in Britain. Here, too, the greatest time differential is between parents and non-parents, and between mothers and fathers. Women's earlier and more substantial return to the labour market in Britain (beginning in the 1960s rather than the 1970s as in the USA) has been primarily part-time. It has always been contingent on women continuing to care, almost exclusively, for their men, their children and their homes. The *British Social Attitudes* surveys of the 1980s showed that about 90 per cent of women working part-time did *all* the washing, ironing, cooking and cleaning (like full-time homemakers). More than two-thirds of women with *full-time* paid jobs also did all of the domestic work at home. Jonathan Gershuny's research on time spent caring for children shows that the full-time mother in 1961 spent 95 minutes a day with her pre-school children, compared with 107 minutes a day by the full-time working mother in 1985.

Etzioni's fire has been directed at mothers and not at the democratic deficit in domestic love and labour. His parenting deficit does not describe the reality of lived life so much as men's reluctance to share the work that they consigned to women, in an era in which the culture of childhood itself has been transformed by the expectation that parenting is not only about care but also companionship.

The travails of parenting have also been compounded by the failure of institutions to plan with parents and children in mind. It is salutary that the great movement of fathers in the 1990s has not been to reduce working time, nor to desegregate men's and women's incomes and social security benefits (which would mitigate the pressure on poor men to become itinerants, moving between giro drops, their own mothers and the mothers of their children), but to protest against the Child Support Agency's attempts to make them pay for their children.

The model of the working week has not been reorganised to synchronise with children's time. And the transformation of the locale of community by public planning and the dominance of the car has merely intensified the pressure on parents to protect children from the hazards of community space – the street space children share with their peers – from the uncontrolled conquest of the car.

No party endorses the exhausted efforts of mothers to reform fathers. Politicians' failure to confront the 'parenting deficit' between men and women is a strategic silence. 'The Etzioni argument helps men *not* to think about that problem,' comments Jonathan Gershuny.

There is also a strong sense in the debate about community and crime that the failure to extend empathy to women, particularly single parents, represents another kind of complaint. What to women may feel like equality may to men feel like a loss of control over their own freedom of movement, a loss of control over women and their own loss of mothering.

Converging concepts

Communitarianism's influence in Britain synchronises with the race and class contempt that infuses the ideology of the 'underclass', popularised in Britain by the *Sunday Times* and the Institute of Economic Affairs, which have assiduously promoted another American sociologist, Charles Murray. His case is that a criminalised 'underclass' is spreading in British and American cities not as an effect of pauperisation caused by global economic restructuring, but of the moral failing of mothers. Indeed an anxiety about mothers and mothering is where these two distinct, antagonistic discourses meet.

Etzioni's hypothesis, the notion of the 'parental deficit', converges with the misogynist tirade against poor mothers as the incubators of an 'underclass' in Murray's incredibly influential tracts.[9] Murray's portrait of a spectre haunting Europe has become almost hegemonic in Britain. He correlates the rise of crime

---

9. Charles Murray, *The Emerging British Underclass*, IEA, London 1990.

and the purported collapse of community with the alleged purge of the father from the family: it is thus the morals of mothers that are to blame for the bad behaviour of the boys.

U p to fifteen years ago every poor neighbourhood had 'plentiful examples of good fathers around them'. These days, however, a 'generational catastrophe' has been induced by inflammatory, independent mothers. Norman Dennis and George Erdos, who claim to be 'ethical socialists', also invoke the 1950s as a golden age of fatherhood in the respectable working class before the descent into depravity inaugurated by the supposedly sexy 1960s. Indeed Dennis exemplifies the way these two approaches bleed into each other.[10]

'There was no golden age of fatherhood, there was a regime of respectability'

But Gershuny's time-use research shows that the average father in 1961 spent an average of just eleven minutes a day with his pre-school children. There was no golden age of fatherhood. What there was, however, was a regime of respectability that regulated the roles of men and women, that disciplined mothers as carers in a relation of economic dependence upon fathers, that privileged fathering within the public and private economy not as a *parent* but as the *provider*.

Norman Dennis has clearly forgotten his own account of the family life of an archetypical proletarian homestead in his book, *Coal is Our Life*, written in the golden age of fathered families, the 1950s. Fathers were visitors to their families, wrote Dennis, preferring to both work and play with other men rather than the women and children of their kin and community.

Women's long march into public space, into the wage economy and the political domain, has not been matched by an equivalent revolution in domestic democracy. If there is a parenting deficit then it is between men and women. Fathers still give much *less* time to their children than mothers; and fathers spend *more* time at work than other men. 'Parenthood seems to reduce the extent of maternal employment and increase the extent of paternal employment.'[11]

Although the revolution in sexual manners and marriage has taken place across all classes, Dennis locates the cultural revolution in the poor. It is not their

10.Norman Dennis and George Erdos, *Families Without Fatherhood*, IEA, London 1992.
11.Harriet Presser, 'Can We Make Time for Children? The Economy, Work Schedules and Child Care', *Demography*, Vol.26 No.3, August 1989.

economy but their morals that are creating community crisis. This approach is adopted by Dennis and Erdos in their IEA tract. They argue that it is not poverty that is sustaining crime, nor the problem of marauding masculinities; it is mothers. Driven by marxism and feminism they are purging families of fathers. This eccentric text has enjoyed widespread endorsement from such disaffected Fabians and liberals as Professor A.H. Halsey and the columnist Melanie Philips, in what can only be described as a realignment in British politics – the detachment of reformers from the progressive portion of society. These are protagonists whose politics have placed them as agents rather than subjects of reform. Suddenly challenged by their children, by women, by black people, by crusties and ravers, they seek solace in the defensive fortress of the *traditional family*.

> 'A re-alignment in politics, the detachment of reformers from the progressive portion of society'

Grandpa power

Communities need fathers, insists Murray, and without marriage there is not only no father, but 'grandfathers and uncles, too, become scarce.'[12] Research has confirmed what common sense already knows, that it is *grandmothers* who are typically the most important relative in children's care beyond their parents. She is the most significant *relative* in the provision of child-care support, although we also know that many grandfathers discover the pleasures of child-care for the first time in their old age. Stephen Sedley's seering inquiry into the murder of Tyra Henry – a disaster that illuminated the state's partnership with parents – provides a poignant caution against the tendency to render the dependable grandmother invisible. The child's father, her killer, was treated by the statutory services 'not as an aggressor but as a parent.' But the child's grandmother, who was designated 'her front-line protector', was left to manage a man who aroused fear all around him, while caring for a dying husband, grieving for a dead son, and bringing up five other children on social security. There is a danger, warned Sedley, in believing that 'the poor are so accustomed to poverty that they can be expected to get by in conditions which no middle-class family would be expected to tolerate. There is also a 'positive', but nevertheless false, stereotype in white

---

12.Murray, *op. cit.*

British society of the Afro-Caribbean mother figure as endlessly resourceful, able to cope in great adversity, essentially unsinkable.'[13] While this unsinkable woman was reduced to a type, rather than an individual, she was left to police a man who could not be controlled by either the statutory services or the criminal justice system.

The grandmother disappears in Murray's lexicon of family, while Dennis and Erdos recite the lament of the grandfather deprived of access to his grandchildren and the community deprived of men. What is at stake here is not the relative virtues of grandmothers and grandfathers, but the obsessive erasure of women altogether by these men.

John Redwood, too, rehearsed the Murray thesis when he cited the common prayer book and marriage as the guarantor of children's wellbeing with their fathers, grandfathers and uncles. Observers listening to his paper delivered to a 1994 IEA conference on families and crime were astonished to hear no reference to either mothers or grandmothers in his speech. Redwood had already outraged his hosts on St Mellon's estate in South Wales when he wondered rhetorically, 'Where are the fathers?' The mothers who had welcomed Redwood to their newly-built estate were astonished not only by his patronising assumption of their ignorance – they knew where the fathers were – but his insensitivity to the possibility that fatherless families might have *chosen* single parenthood in preference to life with a dangerous or dilatory man.

Crime and community

It is the crisis of crime and its threat to the public peace of pauperised neighbourhoods that sustains the communitarianism and the criminology of the new right. Neither locate the crisis in the withdrawal of both public and private capital from neighbourhoods therefore starved of access to a legal living and abandoned by a party system that blames rather than represents then.

Murray's reputation has been built on his critique of poor black neighbourhoods, informed by a confident white supremacism. He brought his contempt to Britain's poor palefaces in the municipal suburbias. I recall technicians and journalists alike looking at each other aghast during a radio

---

13.Stephen Sedley, *Report of the Public Inquiry into the Death of Tyra Henry*, London 1987.

debate with Murray in 1995 when he referred to the poor as 'sub-populations.' His British sponsor, *Sunday Times* editor Andrew Neil, revealed a similar dissociation from the *humanity* of poor people when he became puce with irritation at the suggestion that poor young men might be animated by the same pains, powers and pleasures as himself. This disconnection is embedded in the minimising of the economic and the maximising of the mothers' morals as the agent of community crisis. It thus locates it not in political strategies or social systems but in race, genes and the body. The poor are thus bestialised, represented as a class without history and without culture.

According to the distinguished sociologist of the black working class in America, William Julius Wilson, no-one has done more than Murray to encourage President Reagan's budget-cutting binges, by promoting 'the view that federal programmes are harmful to the poor.' Wilson's studies of the history of black workers in the USA shows that they have been disproportionately clustered in the workplaces that have borne the brunt of de-industrialisation. He has shown that the effect of economic restructuring has overshadowed the enactment of affirmative action programmes. Driven by the regional shift of industry away from the great Northern cities, the suburbanisation of work, and the flight of the white middle class, poor black people are quarantined in enclaves evacuated by capital, public investment and political representation. Affirmative action has this year been abolished in California; but it is the economic restructuring, rather than the failure of affirmative action per se, that explains the decline of the black working class – a theme which seems to have been enthusiastically misrepresented by the abolitionists.[14]

> 'Etzioni implicitly eschews the economic dimension by his call for a moratorium on rights'

Despite the contradictory evidence that US social security payments actually declined during the great growth in black unemployment, Murray has succeeded in importing his theory of the underclass into the UK. Indeed Murray and his English acolytes explicitly dismiss the problem of poverty. Etzioni, too, implicitly eschews the economic dimension by his call for a moratorium on rights and, by implication, a moratorium on not only the redistribution of wealth but the

---

14. Helen Wilkinson, 'Affirmative Action, Negative Effect', *Independent*, 28 July 1995.

redistribution of resources and respect in favour of the dispossessed, women and black people.

If there is a current crisis of community then it has been generated largely by the impoverishment of large swathes of the urban landscape; the growth of crime in exhausted, undefended neighbourhoods, where crime threatens public peace; and by the differential response to distress by men and women. It is a *gendered* crisis: the problem of crime is the problem of masculinity. More than 88 per cent of offenders appearing before the courts are boys and young men. And yet this has become the problem with no name: police and politicians engaging in the debate about law and order will not confront what boys and men do with their pain and their power; they will not challenge what *The Guardian* journalist Will Hutton has called a 'masculine fundamentalism' and the cult of force and coercion as a way of sorting things out. Their reluctance to come clean, as men, surely cannot be separated from their own connections to the cultural histories of gender relations which are shared by criminal coteries. The women of the community are left to manage its most dangerous elements. By refusing to name the problem communitarians and the new right alike offer no redress and no resolution.

W ithin the public and private space of the community, men's unemployment denies them the institutions that historically secured their separation from women and children: the waged workplace, the union, the club and the football terraces. This is generally represented as creating a crisis of masculinity, but this is clearly a sexist notion predicated on the necessity of male supremacy, as if masculinity is always – and only – a relation of privilege and power over women. On the contrary, it is the cultural history of masculinity that bequeaths to poor young men a cult of mastery which is dramatised in conflict over shared public space between coteries of young men and their communities. Unemployment throws men into the same time and space as women and children, the domestic and the local. Difference is reasserted among criminal cliques which take control of community space, and in the habits poor men share with their more prosperous brothers – a reluctance to co-operate in the creation of domestic democracy.

The gendered spatialisation of power which defined respectable neighbourhoods – in the polarisation of public and private – is thus re-created in the spatialisation of crime as a regime of masculine control of the community.

Charles Murray blames this crime wave that has shadowed economic restructuring on the fatherless family, on the absence of appropriate role models for boys. This has been recycled by Norman Dennis and George Erdos on the basis of a discredited study of a generation of boys born in 1947, by Israel Kolvin. Oliver James has demonstrated that it is not the *absence* of the father that causes a crisis for a boy, but the *behaviour* of the father. He reminds us that less 'maladjustment' has been found in children living alone with their mothers than with both parents, according to Eileen Crellan's study of 600 'illegitimate' children.[15] The troubled children were those who had witnessed family conflict followed by divorce. 'The most crucial problem with Dennis's misuse of Kolvin's and Crellan's data is his avoidance of the role played by the direct and indirect emotional effects on offspring of divorce or separation,' argues James. The problem for children is conflict rather than absence.[16]

> 'It is not the absence of the father that causes crime but the behaviour of the father'

Dennis's thesis blames the behaviour of boys on their mothers. 'End all support,' argues Murray, for without Social Security, 'the old reality will resurface and with it the traditional family.' And father will come home – for eleven minutes a day.

Absent activists

Etzioni extends his critique of women's flight from the family to a concomitant lament of their purported withdrawal from the stalwart work of community activism. In Britain, however, there has been not a collapse of active citizenship, but its re-orientation. It is commonplace to acknowledge that in the most impoverished neighbourhoods it is primarily mothers who have sustained new systems of self-help in rugged redoubts of community action. Single mothers' activism is clearly connected to their work of mothering. Far from fleeing their children, women have maintained the traditional work of mothering which places them at the interface between public and private. That connects them with the public institutions which often represent the only power and resources within a locality – the shops, the health service, the schools and the courts. But

---

15. Eileen Crellan, *Born Illegitimate*, National Foundation for Educational Research, 1971.
16. Oliver James, 'Vicious Outcome of the Poverty Trap', *Observer*, 23 May 1993.

it is this enduring connection between mothers, children and communities that is effaced by politicians who refuse to extend their empathy to the efforts, stamina and ingenuity of the mothers.

Appalled by politicians' malevolence towards lone mothers a Newcastle City Council committee felt impelled in November 1993 to challenge this new consensus: 'Throughout the city, but particularly in the areas worst hit by unemployment and crime, these lone parents are the most active of active citizens and are the essential glue which is holding these hard-pressed communities together. The City Council applauds their courage and commitment in working to bring safety, hope and opportunity to all who live in their communities.' [17]

Gender scepticism

The flaky father, the ghost of political discourse who is palpable and yet invisible, is for the first time in the modern era exposed to the difficulty of parenting, because he has been exposed to the demand for parental parity. The crime of the mothers is not that they have abandoned their children but that they have revealed his redundancy, the shame of his lack of reciprocity.

' "Anti-feminist" feminists have balked at the correlations between crime, community activism and gender'

Rosalind Coward and other 'anti-feminist' feminists have balked at the correlations between crime, community activism and gender. The feminist critique of these masculine cultural histories is reproached for essentialism and for lending aid and comfort to the right. 'A critique of masculinity, which was originally intended to undermine traditional claims to male power, has now become a way of attacking the least powerful men in our society,' argues Coward. In any case, 'Male behaviour cannot be understood in isolation from female behaviour. It isn't a question of blaming one sex or another, but seeing how cultural patterns arise in which the "wildness" of men often matches the demands put on them by young women.'[18]

Clearly, Coward has not consulted the poor women – and men and children – who have to put up with the 'wild men'. She repeats the tendency to explain the

---

17. *Lone Parents in Newcastle*, Report of the Anti-Poverty Sub-committee, 22 November 1993.
18. Rosalind Coward, 'Whipping Boys', *The Guardian*, 3 September 1994.

behaviour of men by reference not to gender but to class. And she has missed the point of the communitarian and new right critique. Their interest is not in masculinity but in mothers, and their stake is to disconnect 'respectable' masculinity from the masculinities that now give their gender a bad name.

'Poor young men's crime is a local piracy that is about power and control'

'There is often a curious selectivity at work in contemporary feminist criticisms of gender-based theories of identity,' warns the philosopher Susan Bordo. This is taking place in the context of a great backlash against 'changes in gender-power relations', while 'the analytics of race and class – the two other giants of modernist social critique – do not seem to be undergoing the same deconstruction.' We've been here before, remarks Bordo: the first feminist wave produced the same backlash, 'particularly among professional women, against feminist talk about gender difference.' But there is no escape. 'Like it or not in our present culture, our activities *are* coded as "male" or "female" and will function as such within the prevailing system of power relations ... one cannot be gender neutral in this culture,' no more than we can assume that the effects are *equivalent* for men and women.[19] It is the differential in effect – one of the first insights of contemporary feminism – that is erased by Coward in her coupling of culpability.

Erasure of the correlation between community, crime and masculinity cannot be achieved by excising gender, however. On the contrary, the realigned new conservatives achieve this by reassigning the crisis of community to the *other* gender. None of this is to suggest that boys are bad and mothers are good. It is simply to argue that poor young men's commitment to crime is expressed in a local piracy that is about power and control. This is what unites them with the cultural history of more privileged masculinities. This is the connection between 'respectable', mainstream masculinities and dangerous young men that is denied by the discourses of law and order, communitarianism and the new right.

Richard Collier argues that it is 'through the language of the "role model" that "underclass" theorists, be they "ethical socialist" or new right apologists, have

---

19. Susan Bordo, 'Feminism, Postmodernism, and Gender-Scepticism', in *Feminism/Postmodernism, op. cit.*

similarly sought to defend a masculinity which is, in so many other ways, now consigned to history.' He also argues that in the new rhetoric of fatherhood 'it has been necessary to render fatherhood "safe"; or, more accurately, to make a distinction between the law's construction of familial, paternal masculinities and the other "dangerous" masculinities.' The model of the family man offers a contrast between 'the benign masculinities of matrimonial law with their antithesis – the "wild" and "dangerous" masculinities of criminology'. But the cost of this bifurcation has been 'to divert attention from the problematic nature of masculinity *per se* and, in particular, from the socially destructive nature of masculinities inside the family.'[20]

This process of disconnection from the problem of masculinity, combined with a disdain for women's reality and for the miscellany of new voices that have arrived on the political stage, is now expressed in the communitarians' grandiose assertion of ethics rather than rights. It is the retreat from empathy that makes communitarianism so conservative.

---

20. Richard Collier, *Masculinity, Law and the Family*, Routledge, London 1994.

Cheddar Cross, Beauty of Bath, Cox's Lambourne, Laxtons Superb, Miller's Hambledon Deux Ans, Allington Pippin, Derby, Cornish Gilliflower, Sops in Wine, Wonder, Devonshire Quarrenden, Tom Putt, Cave, Ashmead's Kernel, Kings Acre Pippin, Albert, Brownlees Russet, Sir John Thorneycroft, Fillbasket, Tydeman's Early, Suntan, Gascoyne's Bridget, Pott's Seedling, Annie Elizabeth, Ellison's low Wonder, Rev W. Wilks, Lord Suffield, Norfolk Noble, Barnack Beauty, Bess Pool, Bramley's Seeding, Stoke Red, Yarlington Mill, Sturmer Pippin, St

Common Ground

APPLE DAY OCTOBER 21st

Orange Pippin, Beauty of Bedford, Lord Seedling, Charles Ross, Encore, Chivers Delight, Emneth Early, Lord Keswick Codlin, Forty Shilling, Newton Melcombe Russet, D'Arcy Spice, George Golden Hardy, Lord Hindlip, Lane's Prince Howgate Wonder, Isle of Wight Pippin, Kentish Scarlet, Golden Knob, Warners King, Scotch Orange, Lord Burghley, Peasgood's Nonsuch, Hounsbeefing, Norfolk Royal, Winter Coleman, Golden ling, Blenheim Orange, Lady's Fingers, Hoary Morning, Edmund's Pippin, Lady Henniker, Claygate Pearmain,

Join in Apple Day, October 21st
Celebrate a few of the 6,000 varieties of apples we can grow in Britain and the cultural richness they symbolise. Dig out local recipes, play apple games, go on an orchards walk, learn to prune and graft, identify your trees, taste a few ciders, give an apple to a friend to wish them good health. Write for ideas on how to run your own Apple Day or set up a community orchard.
For an APPLE DAY EVENTS LIST send first class SAE to:
Common Ground,
Seven Dials Warehouse, 44 Earlham Street,
London WC2H 9LA.

The politics of attachment

Lynne Murray

*The arguments put forward by Amitai Etzioni
on the so-called 'parenting deficit' are assessed
by Lynne Murray in relation to scientific
evidence. She shows that work outside the home
for mothers is usually a factor beneficial, not
harmful, to children's development. There is
no evidence, she says, to support the idea
that women's 'selfishness' is the source of
present-day parenting problems.*

We are now poised at a critical point in British politics, when the Labour Party in particular is redefining its values and agenda. There is a rare opportunity for those who work closely with families to inform the political debate; they have, after all, direct experience of the forces, both social and economic and those within the individual, that influence human conduct. This may be especially so for those who are in a clinical relationship with families. This experience is possibly unique in permitting an understanding of exactly the point at which individuals are genuinely free to make choices, and the point at which either external or inner circumstances render various options more or less possible. The clinical perspective can, for example, usefully inform decisions about the circumstances in which it may indeed be appropriate to think of taking parents of truanting children to court – when such a strategy would provide some containment and be productive, as opposed to being misplaced; or for example, where a more effective strategy would be to focus resources on providing experiences in schools that empowered young people, which could be seen by them to relate in a meaningful way to post-school training and eventual employment.

This is precisely the point of focus for current political debate: it is acknowledged by contemporary commentators of diverse political persuasions that the issue of the relationship between the individual and society is being recast. On both sides of the political divide, the individual has, in the last few decades, been taken as the starting point. On the right, embedded within an ethic of an unregulated, global, free market economy, and most clearly expressed in Thatcher's rhetoric, this has taken the form of the argument that individuals should be self-reliant and free to strive for themselves, along with a denial of the interdependency inherent in the individual's relation to society. On the left there has also been a focus on individual rights, over and above one on obligations, both from those emphasising the state's role in protecting individual rights, and from those on the neo-liberal left favouring policies of social individualism. (Strangely, both these formulations are at odds with the original philosophies of each of these movements.)

However, the tide is now turning, and the words community and communitarianism are upon everybody's lips. In recent months the topic has hit the media, and one cannot turn on the radio, watch *Newsnight* or read the broadsheets without being made aware of this formulation of the current debate. However, this apparently common agenda of the moment belies persistent fundamental divisions, in particular in the way in which community is conceived, and the way in which the individual's relation to it is formulated, with old traditions of left and right grafting onto it their own particular emphasis. One recent and influential formulation of community and the individual's place within it is that of communitarianism, as developed in the United States by Amitai Etzioni. This was spelt out in the recent publication from Demos, *The Parenting Deficit*. The argument put forward in this publication is that the ills besetting contemporary society, from delinquency to drug abuse to a general lack of moral decency, have, at their roots, a failure of adequate parenting.

In particular Etzioni frames the parenting deficit in terms of the ill effects of divorce and the fact that parents are not available for enough hours to devote themselves to their children: increasing numbers of women are in work, and they are not being replaced by the same numbers of substitute carers, therefore children are left without adequate care. (Since space is limited I shall not specifically discuss the issue of divorce; however, the arguments concerning parental working apply in a similar way in the context of divorce.) While Etzioni acknowledges that many low income couples and single parents have no choice but to seek employment, his main argument is that this *is* a matter of choice, and a moral choice at that – 'a finger should be pointed' he says 'at those who, in effect, abandon their children to invest themselves whole hog in other pursuits'… parents should consider, he argues, what is important to them 'more income or better relationships with their children'. His fundamental point is that 'at some level of income, *which is lower than the conventional wisdom would have us believe,* parents do begin to have a choice between enhanced earnings and attending to their children' (my emphasis). One would not normally wish to focus an article on just one political statement on the role of parental care, and by an American sociologist at that. However, since Etzioni's views are said to be gaining currency with New Labour, it does seem important, before policy-makers rush to take up this analysis of the fundamental causes of society's ills, to scrutinise this communitarian formulation carefully in the light of research into the determinants of poor adult outcome and difficulties in attachment relationships between parents and their children.

'The words community and communitarianism are upon everybody's lips'

In this context it is informative to look at the work of David Farrington and Donald West at the Institute of Criminology in Cambridge.[1] They and their team have conducted an exemplary study of the development of over four hundred boys growing up in a working-class area in London. The families were first assessed when the children were eight years old, and the researchers managed to follow up some 95 per cent up to age thirty-two. One fifth of the sample received criminal convictions as juveniles, one third by the time they were 25; and six per cent were chronic offenders.

Assessments included reports by the children themselves, their peers at primary

---

1. D.P. Farrington, and D.J. West, 'The Cambridge Study in Delinquent Development: A Long-Term Follow-Up of 411 London Males', *Criminality: Personality, Behaviour and Life History*, Springer-Verlag, Berlin 1990.

school, their class teachers and their parents. Even within this relatively homogeneous sample, the worst offenders differed from the rest on nearly all the variables measured. Four key factors affected outcome. The first was economic: eventual offenders were, as children, brought up in poor, large families, living in bad housing, with fathers who were unemployed. Secondly, problems were already being identified in school by the time of the first assessment when the children were only eight years old, the eventual offenders being seen at this time as troublesome and hyperactive, and having poor concentration; they also had low IQ and poor scholastic attainment. Third, delinquent or criminal outcome was associated with poor parenting, and, in particular, a combination of neglect (both physical, and poor supervision) and punitive, harsh and erratic discipline was especially pernicious. Finally, a culture of criminal behaviour in the family was influential. These factors combined to set up a causal sequence whereby parental mishandling in the context of poverty and job insecurity became associated with poor school adjustment and achievements, then truancy, followed by few or unstable job prospects, and eventually adult criminality. Notably, the particular form of parenting deficit identified by Etzioni (i.e. absence through work) was not a causal factor, indeed, maternal working was *not* associated with poor outcome, and paternal *unemployment* was predictive.

Similar complex causal sequences obtain, involving both early childhood experience of parental care and a range of social and economic factors, if one looks at the situation of women, where poor outcome, rather than taking the form of criminality, is more commonly manifest as clinical depression. Depression is a matter of considerable contemporary public interest, not least because it is costly: the mental health care costs alone for those identified as depressed in 1990 have been estimated to amount to some £333,000,000, and this figure excludes indirect costs, such as time off work, and the costs of depression that is not identified by the health care system.[2]

Some of the most important research in this area has been carried out by George Brown, Tirril Harris, and Toni Bifulco.[3] Their work is particularly notable in that it has sought to trace the pathways linking early experience to adult

---

2. R. West, *Depression*, Office of Health Economics, London 1992.
3. T. Harris, G.W.Brown, and A. Bifulco, 'Loss of parent in childhood and adult psychiatric disorder: A tentative overall model', *Development and Psychopathology*, 2, 311-328, 1990.

depression by taking account of both external or environmental influences, and also more internal or psychological processes. In order to be able to examine properly the role of early lack of parental care, this research group studied 225 women from general practice populations in Walthamstow in East London. About two thirds of the group were vulnerable in terms of having suffered the loss of their mother, either by death or separation, in childhood. Based on hypotheses deriving from their previous research, detailed interviews were conducted to obtain information in a number of areas. These included:

'The particular form of parenting deficit identified by Etzioni (absence through work) was not a causal factor'

i.   the quality of care experienced in childhood (and in particular the experience of neglect, control, and separation);
ii. the experience of premarital pregnancy;
iii. the degree to which the woman felt able to influence events or felt helpless, both as a child and in adulthood;
iv. the quality of current support.

The research also considered recent stressful circumstances, and information on social class and psychiatric state.

The results indicated that women who had lost their mother through death when they were very young (under five) were likely to have developed a sense of helplessness and low self esteem in childhood, probably because, at this age, as Bowlby first pointed out, effective mourning is just not possible. Those whose mothers died later on were rather less at risk of experiencing this helplessness, even though they did tend to receive inadequate subsequent care, and it seemed that they were protected by a previously good relationship with their mother. Girls whose mothers left them were particularly at risk: they too were likely to go on to receive less than adequate care following their mother's departure, but these children, unsurprisingly, had generally also suffered neglect at the hands of their own mothers before the separation. The helplessness and low self esteem arising from these childhood difficulties seems to launch these girls on a trajectory in which they become easily entangled in unsatisfactory, unstable relationships, often involving premarital pregnancy. This situation in itself further diminishes self esteem and feelings of control, such that, in the context of some subsequent stressful event, depression is likely.

There is now considerable evidence that depression makes it difficult for those looking after children to give appropriate and sensitive care. It is of particular interest, therefore, in thinking about communitarian concerns about the impact of mothers' working on the child's early experience of care, to explore the links between maternal depression and women's employment status. The early work by Brown and colleagues indicated that, far from being beneficial, being at home full-time when bringing up small children was associated with vulnerability to depression.[4] This finding has subsequently been replicated by this research group in a further sample, where it seemed that the lack of the independence conferred by employment rendered women more vulnerable in the face of difficulties with their partner.[5] However, this later study also indicated that full-time employment, combined with the responsibility for young children, posed a similar risk for depression to having no paid employment at all; women in this situation feel overburdened by their multiple responsibilities. The ideal, therefore, in terms of the mental health of women with young children seems to be able to work part-time. A solution that is in the interests of the mental health of parents is, as I hope now to demonstrate, also likely to be in the interests of children.

> 'A solution that is in the interests of the mental health of parents is also likely to be in the interests of children'

The remainder of this paper presents some findings from a study we have been carrying out of women having their first children. To date, they have been followed up over the first five years. A particular focus of the study is the influence of the quality of the child's early care on development, and for this reason, as well as having a number of women who were broadly representative of the local population, the study also included a group of women who, by virtue of being clinically depressed after childbirth, were at increased risk for difficulties in their relationship with their infants. (This problem is not, in fact, unusual; around 15 per cent of women experience an episode of depression at this time). The sample comprised 111 women, including 56 who had been depressed postnatally. The depressed women commonly experienced difficulties with their partners, lacked

4. G.W. Brown and T. Harris, *Social origins of depression: A study of psychiatric disorder in women*, Tavistock Publications, London 1978.
5. G.W. Brown and A.Bifulco, 'Motherhood, employment and the development of depression: a replication of a finding?', *British Journal of Psychiatry*, 156, 169-179, 1990.

support from their families and tended not to have relationships with other women in whom they could confide; they also commonly experienced financial hardship or housing difficulties. Even among those who were not depressed, however, the practical support received from others amounted to rather little: for example, the infants' fathers spent only twelve hours a week on average actively caring for their two month olds. In spite of regular contacts with the primary health care team, depression was frequently not detected, and when it was, women were generally reluctant to take the antidepressant medication that was normally prescribed. Many felt guilty about being unhappy, attempted to mask their problems, and avoided public situations where they imagined they would be seen as failing. Ironically then, the depressed women did not avail themselves of the mother and baby clinics set up by health visitors to serve their needs.

By two months, those who had become clinically depressed were experiencing a range of difficulties with their infants; for example, they found it hard to settle their infants to sleep, were more likely to have problems breast feeding, reported their infants to cry for prolonged periods, and experienced significant problems in combining household tasks with caring for the infant. A particular focus of our study was the quality of play between mother and infant: videotapes of face-to-face engagements were rated by researchers, unaware of the mother's mental health, on a series of scales assessing, for example, the mother's sensitivity to the infant's cues, her acceptance and warmth, or the degree to which she was either disengaged and remote or else intrusive and interfering. The results showed, as one might expect, that the depressed women were, as a group, less responsive and less sensitively attuned to their infants, and were more prone to be hostile and critical. However, it was not only in the context of depression that such difficulties arose: although social and personal adversity tended to stack up in the group of women who were depressed, where such difficulties existed in the absence of depression, the mothers' interactions with their infants were similarly insensitive and rejecting. It appeared therefore, that in order to be 'preoccupied' with her infant, to use Donald Winnicott's phrase, the mothers needed to be in an environment that was supportive, both personally and practically.

When the children's development was followed up at eighteen months, by which time the great majority of postnatally depressed women had recovered, continuing difficulties were still apparent: the infants of women who had been depressed were likely to be insecurely attached to their mothers, to have increased rates of behaviour problems, and were likely to fail on cognitive tasks. Where the infants were from lower social class families these problems were more marked.[6] Strikingly, the cognitive problems shown at eighteen months were strongly predicted by the quality of the mother's engagement with the infant at two months postpartum, the infants performing well where their mothers had been sensitively engaged with them.[7]

At five years the children were again assessed on a range of measures: each was observed in school during a period of free play and at a time when the teacher read to the children, and the teachers completed questionnaires on the children's adjustment once they had attended school for their first term; the children's cognitive development was also assessed, as was the quality of their friendships, and their perceptions of their family lives. Mothers were interviewed about the presence of child behaviour difficulties, family circumstances and their own psychiatric state over the intervening three years.

The mothers themselves continued to experience their children as being difficult to manage if they had experienced postnatal depression, and these difficulties applied to the behaviour of boys and girls alike. These associations with the mother's early postpartum experience were found even when taking into account current and recent maternal depression, and the presence of conflict between the parents.

At school the children whose mothers had experienced postnatal depression were reported by their teachers to show significantly raised rates of behaviour problems, and these problems were associated with insecurity in attachment in infancy. The boys were particularly likely to have difficulties, and this usually took the form of hyperactive behaviour. The girls were rated as the least distractible and the most prosocial children; although this may not at first glance seem problematic, there is independent evidence that extreme expressions of prosocial behaviour are predictive of later depression, reflecting a basic insecurity and an inappropriate concern with others' well-being at one's own expense; and

---

6. L. Murray, 'The impact of postnatal depression on infant development', *Journal of Child Psychology and Psychiatry*, 33, 543-561, 1992.
7. L. Murray, C. Kempton, M. Woolgar, and R. Hooper, 'Depressed mothers' speech to their infants and its relation to infant gender and cognitive development', *Journal of Child Psychology and Psychiatry*, 34, 1083-1101, 1993.

this interpretation seemed to be borne out by the results of the other assessments. When the children were observed during free play in school differences again emerged according to the mother's experience after childbirth: both boys and girls whose mothers had been postnatally depressed were less likely to engage in creative play than well mothers' children, and were instead more occupied in lower level, mechanical activities. The patterns of social interaction also differed between the two groups: postnatally depressed mothers' children were

> 'Without good emotional support and financial security it is difficult to provide an environment in which children can flourish'

generally less well integrated; they showed fewer positive approaches to their teachers, were approached less by other children, and when they were approached they responded less positively. (Current or recent depression in the mother and the presence of parental conflict also affected the children and particularly their being able to focus their attention and become absorbed in their play, or in what their teachers were telling them.)

Finally, the way in which the children themselves described their experience differed according to whether or not their mothers had been depressed early on: the children were invited to enact their experience in their families in a doll's house play scenario: the child was invited to choose doll figures to represent the people in their home, and they were then asked to play out what happened in four situations – a meal time, bedtime, a bad and nasty time and their best and favourite time. Transcripts were made of the children's play narratives and these were then scored using a system (a case grammar analysis) designed to describe the way in which the children constructed and organised their experience; in particular, the scheme shows the extent to which the children perceive themselves as being able to influence events, in contrast to feeling that events are out of their control. The children whose mothers had been postnatally depressed were once again at a disadvantage, being less likely, when they referred to themselves in the doll's house scenario, to describe themselves as being active agents, influencing the course of events. This lack of a sense of agency among the depressed mothers' children seemed to be specifically linked to the degree to which their mother had been critical or rejecting of the child's experience.

A number of conclusions may be drawn from these three studies: first, it is evident that, without good emotional support and security in terms of financial resources and adequate housing, it is difficult for parents to provide an environment in which children can flourish; this may be particularly hard to achieve where the parents themselves have had inadequate care in their own childhood, and have been launched on a trajectory that further compounds their initial difficulties.

Second, it is clear that, where the context for parenting is unfavourable, parents may become involved in difficult cycles of relationship with their infants that easily persist, at least into the early school years, and that have an impact on a number of areas of child functioning. These included poor cognitive achievements, and a problematic adjustment in school evident in behaviour problems, poor social relationships and an absence of creativity, all of which seem likely to relate in a fundamental way to the child's lack of a sense of agency or secure sense of self. These early difficulties observed in the children of mothers who had experienced postnatal depression were strikingly resonant of those identified in the studies of the routes to delinquency and criminal behaviour in young men (Farrington and West), and the routes to depression in women (Brown, Harris and Bifulco). Thus, the insecurities of the five year old boys of depressed women were manifested in hyperactive behaviour and poorer cognitive development, both of which are risks for future delinquent behaviour; whereas the girls' insecurity was more likely to be reflected in their extreme adaptation to others' concerns at the expense of their own interests.

'All the mothers in our research were highly motivated to do the best they could for their children'

It is important to note that the parenting problems we observed generally had little to do with women egocentrically rushing to find fulfilment in the work place: all the mothers in our research were highly motivated to do the best they could for their children; their sense of obligation to their child was strong and they needed no reminding of their duties; only a small minority worked more than 15 hours per week, as is generally true for mothers of children under two in Britain; and indeed, in this sample, there was no relationship between maternal employment and adverse child outcome. This is not to deny that prolonged parental absence through work, especially in the context of day care which provides little continuity and inadequate care, is likely to be detrimental to a child's development. However, the research suggests that, while a number of recommendations can be made to ensure that the infants of working parents have better access to parental care (including better maternal and paternal leave, better provision for job security so that parents are not impelled to go back to work prematurely, limitations on job mobility, and fiscal policies that relieve the increasing taxation burden from those with children[8]), it would be misplaced to construct a political policy principally around Etzioni's Communitarian definition of the parenting deficit.

Rather, in addition to seeking changes in the wider social agenda, such as a reduction in inequalities in education, employment and wealth, there is considerable scope for facilitating community based schemes to attend to the emotional needs of children and their parents. For example, our own research group has recently explored the possible benefits to depressed mothers and their infants of providing brief psychotherapy, over and above the benefits of routine primary care. The treatment was modelled on provision that could feasibly be provided within a health service context. From eight weeks postpartum, women received weekly, hour-long sessions in their homes over a two month period. The women's mental state was assessed immediately after treatment and at nine and eighteen months follow-up.

'It would be misplaced to construct a political policy principally around Etzioni's definition of the parenting deficit'

There were clear beneficial effects of the additional support, in terms of the women's depression remitting by four and a half months postpartum. In addition, there were significant benefits in terms of the mothers reporting fewer difficulties with the infant, both immediately after treatment and at the 18-month follow-up. And although there was no simple effect of treatment on infant attachment, the early remission from depression associated with treatment predicted more infant security at 18 months. Treatment in this study had mainly been delivered by qualified pyschologists, and following completion of the trial we extended the work to mount a local health visitor intervention that involved an emotionally supportive, counselling approach. With only six half days' additional training in

---

8. P. Hewitt, and P. Leach, *Social Justice, Children and Families*, Institute for Public Policy Research, London 1993.

the detection and management of depression, health visitors in the Cambridge district became far more effective in their work with postnatally depressed mothers. Rates of remission within a two month period doubled over those prior to the intervention; and what was particularly striking was the benefit in terms of the mother's experience of caring for her infant, with difficulties in all aspects of care, including the sense of satisfaction and pleasure in the relationship, showing marked improvement over and above the beneficial effect on maternal mood of the extra support. Similarly encouraging results occur in schemes involving the provision of additional support from the voluntary sector.

Together these findings indicate that adult experience, including issues of divorce, work and parenting, is not simply a product of rational decisions based either on a cold appraisal of self interest, or regulated neatly according to some set of moral codes: it is just as much an emotional affair where issues of attachments and interdependencies in relationships loom large; paying attention to the personal and emotional needs of children and of those who have responsibility for them, as well as seeking to bring about wider social changes in opportunity, is likely to be a far more productive and appropriate strategy for improving the outlook for children and their parents than the moralistic exhortations emanating from recent Communitarian doctrine.

An earlier presentation of this paper was given to a conference on 'The Politics of Attachment' at the Tavistock Clinic in March 1995.

Unravelling gene biotechnology

Mae-Wan Ho

In a piece of scientific advocacy, biophysicist Mae-Wan Ho examines the theoretical assumptions behind the practice and applications of gene biotechnology. She argues that the underlying paradigm on which the industry is built is fundamentally flawed. The implications of not recognising this are serious for both society and the environment.

Gene biotechnology is threatening to take over every aspect of our daily life, from the produce on sale in supermarkets to gene replacement therapy for the sick. It is hailed as the coming revolution of the twenty first century, as far-reaching as information technology has been for the twentieth. Significantly, the revolution is located (always) in the not too distant future. Gene biotechnology is big business, selling dreams and promises, none of which have yet been realised. But it is coming under increasing criticism, from many quarters, and there are growing concerns about its inherent dangers.

Many issues are raised by gene biotechnology: the ethics of genetic manipulation and the patenting of organisms; the use and abuse of genetic information; the attribution of intellectual property rights and the exploitation of the South by the North under the Biodiversity and GATT treaties; the threat posed by biotechnology to biodiversity and the livelihood of indigenous farmers; and its hazardous implications for health and the ecological environment. Gene biotechnology represents the commercialisation of science, the enclosure of the 'intellectual commons' and the exclusion of alternative knowledge systems. It is a misuse of technology, guided by a discredited genetic paradigm which epitomises the reductionist, scientistic worldview that has shaped the politics and policies of Northern countries for the greater part of the twentieth century. (For an account of the old genetic paradigm, see pp90-2.)

In the 1970s the genetic paradigm gave rise to the science of the *new genetics* as well as gene biotechnology. But – and very few people realise this – the new genetics is antithetical to every assumption of the old genetic paradigm. The new genetics is consonant with a different paradigm – the paradigm of organic wholeness and complexity that is emerging from contemporary western science. Indeed, the present wide-ranging opposition to many aspects of gene biotechnology can be seen as a concerted struggle by supporters of the new paradigm, to reclaim holistic worldviews and holistic ways of life in both North and South.

What is gene biotechnology?

Gene biotechnology, or genetic engineering, is a set of techniques for modifying and recombining genes from different organisms. It is also referred to as recombinant DNA (rDNA) technology. DNA, the genetic material, is a very long chain-like polymer made up of many, many thousands of simpler units joined end to end. The units differ in the organic bases they contain, of which there are four, represented by the letters, A, T, C, G. The sequence in which the bases occur is specific for each DNA molecule, and this accounts for its specificity as genetic material. Each DNA molecule is packaged into a linear structure, a *chromosome*. Each cell can have one or more chromosomes; for example, a bacterial cell has one chromosome, whereas the human cell has 23 pairs of chromosomes. A gene is a stretch of DNA on the chromosome, usually about 1000 units in length.

'The new genetics is antithetical to every assumption of the old genetic paradigm'

Genetic engineering originated in the 1970s as the result of the development of several techniques. The first, DNA sequencing, allows the sequence of bases in any stretch of DNA to be determined. The second technique is making recombinant DNA in the test tube using enzymes isolated from micro-organisms to cut and join pieces of DNA together. This enables geneticists to put foreign genes into *viruses* or *plasmids*, which are pieces of parasitic DNA that can infect cells and multiply in them, or insert themselves into their chromosome and replicate with the host cell. Hence, modified viruses and plasmids, carrying foreign genes from a donor species, can be used as *vectors* (or carriers) to transfer the genes to a recipient species that does not naturally interbreed with the donor species. The third technique is the chemical synthesis of DNA of any desired base sequence. A fourth technique, the Polymerase Chain Reaction, discovered in 1988, allows specific gene sequence(s) in a mixture to be rapidly amplified by many times, and is extensively used in forensic DNA finger-printing.

Genetic engineering since the 1970s

Soon after genetic engineering became possible, molecular geneticists in the forefront of developing and applying the techniques became aware of the dangers that pathogenic strains of viruses or bacteria could be created by recombination in the test tube. This resulted in the Asilomar Declaration calling for a moratorium on genetic engineering until appropriate regulatory guidelines were put in place.

Now, in the 1990s, the risks from genetic manipulation have become far greater. Genetic engineering techniques are ten times faster and more powerful, and the new breed of genetically engineered organisms (or transgenics), deliberately released on a large scale, are designed to be ecologically vigorous; they are therefore potentially much more hazardous than the genetically crippled micro-organisms engineered for contained use in the laboratory in the 1970s. Where is the voice of the scientists now? Although an increasing number are critical of gene biotechnology, there has been no equivalent of the Asilomar Declaration from molecular geneticists in the 1990s, no call for a moratorium. As Harvard biologist Ruth Hubbard has pointed out, many of the current top molecular geneticists either own biotech companies or are collaborating with, or working for, such companies. Gene biotechnology is the commercialisation of science on an unprecedented scale. The conflict of private and public interest is bound to stand in the way of proper assessment of need or benefit as against hazards or socioeconomic impacts.

The 'patenting of life' and the GATT-TRIPS

The commercialisation of genetic engineering has been growing steadily since the 1970s. The first corporation, Genentech, was formed – even as a moratorium was being debated in 1976 – by molecular geneticist Paul Berg, who signed the Asilomar Declaration a year earlier. The next milestone was the 1980 US Supreme Court ruling that genetically engineered micro-organisms can be patented. Then came the USA's $3 billion federally funded Human Genome Initiative, whose project is to sequence the entire human genome (the totality of the genetic material). This opened the floodgate to 'patents on life'. A long list of patents have already been granted, and many more are pending, on controversial 'inventions' such as transgenic organisms, human genes and gene fragments. There are patent claims for a human cell line established from the spleen of a patient removed as part of the therapy for cancer; for cell lines from indigenous tribes obtained – without informed consent – ostensibly for the study of human diversity; and for seeds and plant varieties taken by Northern 'bioprospectors' from indigenous communities in the Third World who freely provided the material as well as their knowledge. These patents go to feed the mushrooming biotech industry which is hungry for products and quick profit.

To facilitate patenting for commercial exploitation, the Trade-Related Property Rights (TRIPS) treaty was introduced in the Uruguay round of GATT. As one commentator has noted, this treaty 'effectively excludes all kinds of knowledge, ideas and innovations [from patenting] that take place in the "intellectual common" – in villages among farmers, in forests among tribals.'[1] Patenting plant varieties from Third World countries robs indigenous farmers of their livelihood, and can have widespread repercussions. An example is the neem plant in India, whose seed oil possesses insecticidal and many medicinal properties. It has been freely available for millenia, so much so that the health care system of the whole of India is dependent upon it. As soon as it was 'discovered' and patented, it became a scarce commodity. Its market value shot up 100-fold within two years, to put it well beyond the means of most ordinary people. A national health system is thereby seriously undermined.

The intellectual property right over genetic resources is emerging as a major

---

1. V. Shiva, 'Why we should say "No" to GATT-TRIP', *Third World Resurgence 39*, 3-5, 1994.

North-South issue. It began with the enactment of an International Convention – the Union for the Protection of New Varieties of Plant (UPOV) – in the early 1960s which gave property rights to plant breeders for varieties improved through human intervention. The source material, obtained freely from the biodiverse countries of the South, was considered the 'common heritage of mankind' and hence not subject to private ownership. This gave free access to corporate interests to bio-prospect in the South, and started the process of the increasingly arbitrary categorising of

> 'Northern countries are allowed to take genetic resources freely from the South as "common heritage" '

'innovation' by Northern companies, while denying the real innovative contributions of local communities.[2] Under this unfair Convention, Northern countries are allowed to take genetic resources freely from the South as 'common heritage'; the 'heritage' is then returned to them as a priced commodity. Strong protest from Third World countries led to a meeting of the FAO Commission on Plant Genetic Resources in 1987, which recognised the contribution of traditional farmers in developing the plant. But the property right was not vested in individual farmers. Instead it accrued to the farmers' governments in the form of the right to receive assistance in maintaining the genetic resources. In other words, it became translated into the obligation of the North to 'help' the South, tied into the concept of aid and dependency that has for centuries allowed the North to exploit the South. An international gene fund was set up to concretise the farmers' rights, but the lack of contributions from Northern corporations and their governments made this fund inoperative. The TRIPS proposal is generally seen as the latest attempt to formalise the continuing piracy of Third World genetic resources by Northern biotech companies.

The enclosure of the 'intellectual commons'

By defining innovation – for the purpose of financial reward through patenting – as something done within the dominant scientific tradition of Northern Europe, the TRIPS proposal effectively excludes *all* other knowledge systems, whether in the Third World, or in indigenous or folk wisdom in the North or

---

2. See G.S. Nijar, and Y.L. Chee, 'Intellectual property rights: the threat to farmers and biodiversity', *Third World Resurgence 39*, 6-12, 1994.

any other alternative frameworks. Public funding for scientific research with the US, the UK and the European Community is now disproportionately biased in favour of product-oriented biotechnology, particularly in partnership with industry. While many areas of basic science are no longer funded, disciplines ranging from embryology and ecology to psychology and anthropology have one by one succumbed to the dominant reductionist mindset of genetic determinism (which, wrongly, regards genes as the most fundamental essences of organisms). The pluralistic, open enquiry that has long been the ideal of science is fast becoming obsolete. Even molecular geneticists are increasingly disillusioned within a system that judges excellence on patents owned rather than on the advancement of science.

The commercialisation of gene biotechnology is reducing the life sciences to a monolithic intellectual wasteland of genetic determinism. It is the enclosure of the intellectual commons, and a 'de-intellectualisation of civil society, so that the mind becomes [subjugated to] a corporate monopoly.'[3]

Life as commodity and the ethics of gene biotechnology

The strongest reaction to the 'patenting of life' is often that it has turned organisms, including parts of human beings, into saleable commodities. This is morally repugnant to many indigenous cultures in the Third World, and has also united in opposition diverse groups in the North, including environmental activists, socialists, and religious organisations, as well as ordinary citizens who feel that the final frontier of human decency has been breached in the name of free enterprise.

But there are many other ethical issues raised by gene biotechnology, particularly in relation to the diagnosis of genetic diseases, and, more controversially, of more general genetic 'predispositions' to various deficiencies. For example, the diagnosis of genetic disease has led to individuals being discriminated against in health insurance and in employment. This kind of diagnosis of diseases for which no cure is forthcoming is in any case of questionable value, as even for many so-called 'single-gene' diseases, the clinical prognosis can vary widely from individual to individual.

Nonetheless, geneticists are now attempting to identify genetic

---

3. V. Shiva, *op. cit.*

'predispositions' and 'genetic propensities' for conditions such as cancer, diabetes, and schizophrenia. Worse still are the attempts to identify genetic predispositions for alcoholism, homosexuality and criminality, all of which are overwhelmingly under the influence of environmental and social factors. (Homosexuality is, of course, only a 'problem' in the eyes of these scientists.) This not only diverts attention from the real causes of illness but also increasingly stigmatises individuals, through placing the blame of society's ills on people's genes, and through the arbitrary categorisation of 'normal' versus the 'abnormal'. The identification of undesirable

'The life sciences are being reduced to a monolithic intellectual wasteland of genetic determinism'

'genetic possibilities' can further extend the scope for 'therapeutic' abortions. Such 'therapeutic' abortions of affected foetuses, together with the contemplation of germline gene therapy (i.e. genetic 'correction' of human eggs and sperm) are, respectively, negative and positive eugenics measures, and are are now 'privatised' by industry. This was prophesied by marxist geneticist Richard Lewontin ten years ago.

Eugenic movements have played a prominent role in the politics and history of much of the present century. They have played their part in the justification of the devastation of indigenous populations by colonising Europeans, apartheid in South Africa, and the genocide of Jews in Nazi Germany. Eugenic ideology is responsible for the continuing discrimination against racial minorities and all politically dispossessed groups in the world today. Major concerns about population increase are consistently directed at human populations that are non-white; whereas the real issue is the unequal distribution of resources, most of which are disproportionately consumed by the well-to-do in the predominantly white developed countries. In addition, one cannot be complacent about the dangers of state-sanctioned eugenic practice. China has just legislated for the compulsory termination of pregnancies where the foetus is diagnosed positive for conditions including schizophrenia, where the genetic etiology remains tenuous at best.

Another ethical issue is the welfare of animals used in genetic engineering experiments to improve livestock, or as living factories for drugs, or to model human genetic diseases. As the technology is very inefficient, large numbers of animals have to be experimented on before a successful transgenic is constructed, and then many turn out to be very sick animals even though they were not intended to be so.

Gene biotechnology and biosafety

At the same time that the GATT-TRIPS proposal was pushed through, a Chapter (16) was drafted for the UN Biodiversity Convention (Agenda 21, signed in Rio de Janeiro in 1992). It was entitled, 'Environmentally Sound Management of Biotechnology', and recommended that some billions of dollars of the UN budget be committed to gene biotechnology so as to increase food yield to feed the hungry, to improve human health and control population, to purify water, to clean up the environment, to reforest wasteland – in short, to solve all the problems of the Third World. *This comes at a time when no other UN project is being funded under the Commission for Sustainable Development.* Chapter 16 of Agenda 21 is generally regarded as a thinly veiled attempt to promote and subsidise the biotech industry. Moreover, as opposition to gene biotechnology has been gathering momentum in developed countries, the industry is targetting the Third World for test-sites as well as markets. Critics are justifiably concerned about the uncontrolled releases of transgenic organisms in the Third World, and people being used as human guinea-pigs for testing genetically engineered drugs and vaccines. There have already been at least 90 releases of transgenic crops in non-OECD countries and Mexico, a third of which were by multinational corporations.[4] A rabies vaccine containing a live virus was tested on cattle in Argentina without authorisation, and farm-workers who were not informed of the experiment were subsequently found to be infected with the virus.

Clearly, most Third World countries do not have the legal framework or the capacity to regulate genetic engineering. The same is true, however, of developed countries. There is at present no legal control over genetically engineered versions of drugs and chemicals already approved for the market, nor is there any legal requirement that they be labelled as such, despite the fact that, in 1989, a batch of genetically engineered L-tryptophan manufactured by a Tokyo-based company caused 38 deaths and 1512 reported cases of illness, referred to as eosinophilia-myalia syndrome.

The repeated claims by representatives of the biotech industry that genetic

---

4. I. Meister, and S. Mayer, *Genetically engineered plants: releases and impacts on less developed countries*, A Greenpeace inventory, Greenpeace international, 1994.

engineered products are beneficial, effective and safe, have not been borne out by the evidence. Over half of the transgenic crop-plants are engineered to be resistant to herbicides and other environmental poisons. Many companies are engineering resistance to their own herbicides, clearly intending to market herbicide and seeds as a package deal. These plants could easily spread as weeds or create superweeds by transferring the resistant genes to related wild-species. A genetically engineered pumpkin recently planted by farmers in the US is reported to have spread to surrounding fields and become an intransigent weed. Genetic exchanges between crop-plants and wild relatives are already well known, and have recently been documented for the genetically engineered oil-seed rape with introduced genes for herbicide tolerance. This fuels worries about secondary gene transfers to non-target species, and further diminishes public confidence in the adequacy of existing regulatory guidelines.

Another 30 per cent of the transgenic crop-plants are engineered to be insect and disease resistant. The insecticidal genes include scorpion toxin, spider venom and an extremely poisonous toxin from the soil bacterium, *Bacillus thuringiensis* (Bt). These poisons will harm non-target species as well as target species of insects. Although there is said to be no evidence that the poisons can harm species other than insects, the history of DDT is sufficient to make us wary of such claims.

A source of hazard common to nearly all transgenic plants, including some well-known brands of tomato, genetically engineered to delay ripening, and introduced to the market in the US in 1994, is the virus vector used in gene transfer, which also contains gene(s) for antibiotic resistance. This will contribute further to the spread of antibiotic resistance in disease-causing bacteria, already a major public health problem. Recent research has shown that excessive antibiotics used with intensive animal farming has caused the spread of antibiotic resistance from bacteria living in the gut of farm animals to those living in the mouth and gut of humans. Bacteria are well-known as having the capacity to pick up genes (pieces of DNA) from the environment, and to pass them onto other species of bacteria. Crop-plants are in contact with hundreds of species of bacteria both in the soil and in the air. Furthermore, plants are subject to attacks by fungi and insects, which could also act as vectors for secondary transfer of introduced genes between species that do not interbreed. In the process of such secondary gene transfers, the original viral vector could mutate and recombine with other naturally occurring viruses or pick up other genes that turn the virus into new pathogens.

Of particular significance are genetically engineered soil micro-organisms. Soil micro-organisms play very important roles in recycling nutrients for plant growth. A strain of *Klebsiella planticola*, genetically engineered to convert woody plant remains into ethanol, has been found to have unexpected effects in drastically inhibiting the growth of wheat plants. If the transgenic micro-organism were to be released, it would wipe out entire crops.

Another case in point is the engineered rabies vaccine, which has been approved for use by the European Commission to control fox rabies. It was dropped in tests as edible bait all over Europe from 1987. The vaccine has now been found to be ineffective in controlling fox rabies, and its live virus transferable to many non-target species including human beings.

What is not sufficiently emphasised is that the viral vectors used for gene transfer are deliberately constructed so as to break down species barriers and to infect a wide range of organisms. They are designed to overcome the natural checks and balances that exist in stable, sustainable ecological communities. The scenario of uncontrollable outbreaks in viral disease cannot be lightly dismissed.

Existing guidelines are clearly insufficient to guard against hazards to both ecological and human health, as detailed investigations on released transgenics are demonstrating. These valid concerns about the health and ecological implications of gene biotechnology have convinced all Third World countries (the G77 and China), Eastern European and most Western European countries that an internationally-binding biosafety protocol for the handling and transfer of genetically engineered organisms should be established as a matter of urgency. This is openly opposed by the United States (which has as yet failed to ratify the Biodiversity Convention), on grounds that it would reduce US 'competitiveness'.

Official disinformation on gene biotechnology

The official position of the US on biosafety comes from a US National Research Council report, *Field Testing Genetically Modified Organisms: Framework for Decisions*, which states *a priori*, that 'no conceptual distinction exists between genetic modification of plants and micro-organisms by classical methods or by molecular techniques that modify DNA and transfer genes.' This is obviously untrue. Recombinant DNA techniques transfer genes, on a large scale, between

species that have no probability of exchanging genes in nature. As distinct from conventional breeding methods, where different forms of the same gene (alleles) are being reshuffled between varieties of the same species or close relatives, genetic engineering transfers *novel* genes into organisms, which are facilitated by vectors. However, there is no control over where in the genome the new genes will be inserted, which makes the effects of gene transfer highly unpredictable, as demonstrated in the transgenic experiments themselves that have

'The failure of the "green revolution" is now generally acknowledged'

already created many unexpectedly sick animals. Furthermore, the stability of the transferred genes and hence their propensity for secondary mobility within the same organism or to other organisms may be enhanced relative to genes that have been introduced by traditional breeding methods.

The *a priori* assumption that there is no difference between genetically engineered varieties and varieties made by traditional breeding methods has meant that field tests are both inadequately designed and inadequately monitored for safety. (They are governed, as we are told by a defender of gene biotechnology, on the 'don't need, don't look' basis, as opposed to the 'don't look, don't see' basis.[5])

Monocultures of the mind

The failure of the 'green revolution' is now generally acknowledged. The large scale planting of genetic monocultures and the accompanying use of agrochemicals seriously eroded indigenous biodiversity and destroyed the environment; furthermore, it displaced indigenous farmers, creating wide-spread poverty. Many Third World countries have since devoted major efforts to restore the environment and to regenerate indigenous biodiversity by reviving traditional, organic farming methods which are proving to be sustainable and to have a much higher productivity than western monoculture techniques. With the hindsight of the green revolution, why is so much hope pinned onto gene biotechnology? It is the same reductionist ideology producing the same genetically uniform monocultures with the same accompanying agrochemicals. The significant difference is the added danger of genetic pollution and the

---

5. H. Miller, 'Don't need, don't look', Letter to the Editor, *Bio/Technology* 13, 201, 1995.

genetic perturbation of ecosystems, which, unlike chemicals, is a self-perpetuating, self-amplifying process that will be impossible to recall.

Sustainable agriculture is increasingly practised also in Northern countries as decades of mechanisation and heavy dependence on agrochemicals have led to declining soil productivity, deteriorating environmental quality, reduced profits and threats to human and animal health. The 1989 report of the National Research Council of the US Academy of Sciences has emphasised the development and use of alternative farming systems as a means to increase productivity and decrease environmental damage, and estimates that pesticide use could be reduced by 75 per cent in ten years.

'With the hindsight of the green revolution, why is so much hope pinned onto gene biotechnology?'

There are many variants of sustainable agriculture, using a combination of modern and traditional methods, all characterised by a holistic, systems approach to understanding the complex interactions within agricultural ecologies. According to the recent surveys in the United States, sustainable agriculture not only overcomes all the problems of conventional, mechanised farming, but is also more profitable('profit' defined as income relative to input costs).[6] As ecologist Cavalieri concludes, 'Sustainable agriculture is an essential goal for a viable future. It's time to put the emphasis on the real means that will get us there.' Despite that, the US Department of Agriculture currently provides less than $5 million to research in sustainable agriculture compared to the $90 million it has allocated to gene biotechnology.

Vandana Shiva, theoretical physicist turned political activist, has been in the forefront of the Third World's struggle (with the Third World Network, TWN) against the exploitative and destructive policies of the North. In the process, she came to realise the pervasive influence of the reductionist ideology – 'monocultures of the mind' – in shaping the policies of the North. In particular, she sees 'redefining' the life sciences as an important part of the struggle. She and Martin Khor (Malaysia), with the help of Tewolde Egziabher of Ethiopia and Brian Goodwin (Open University, UK), organised a conference on 'Redefining the Life Sciences' in Penang in July, 1994, involving scientists, social scientists,

---

6. J.P. Reganold, R.I. Papendick, and J.L. Parr, 'Sustainable agriculture', *Scientific American*, 72-78, June 1990.

diplomats, and political activists from 15 countries. It was an exciting and eye-opening event. A consensus among the 50 or so participants was reached by the second day. The scientists who were there took part in drafting a *Scientists' Statement on The Need for Greater Regulation and Control of Genetic Engineering*, which was published by the TWN and distributed at the Conference of the Commission on Sustainable Development at the United Nations in April 1995, where a number of us also had the opportunity to speak to policy-makers and UN delegates.

The genetic paradigm and gene biotechnology

The real irony is that there is a deep contradiction between the rational (scientific) message of the new genetics, i.e. genetics since the 1970s, and the outmoded ideology of the old genetic paradigm which continues to inform the practice of gene biotechnology, shaping its goals and aims and serving to manipulate public opinion in its favour. The new genetics makes it possible to modify genes and genomes. But it also overthrows every single assumption of the old genetics. However, the old, discredited paradigm is pressed into the service of selling gene biotechnology, and to formulate policies on gene biotechnology. Paradoxical as it may seem, gene biotechnology is possible precisely because the old genetic paradigm is widely recognised as invalid. Thus, many of the promises of gene biotechnology can never be fulfilled because the genetic paradigm is an erroneous, reductionist representation of organic wholeness and complexity. The many problems which have arisen with gene biotechnology are indicative of the fundamental error in judgement on the part of those who see gene biotechnology as the solution to all the problems that humanity faces today. If further evidence is needed, biotech stocks are currently in the doldrums. According to a report in *Business Week*, 'The industry is still peddling dreams… From Wall Street's perspective, "the industry hasn't worked, and the likelihood of success is lower".'[7] A long list of products have failed clinical trials, and even the remaining handful that have got through are not without problems.

Financial ruin is perhaps a small price to pay for misjudging gene bio-technology, when the future of the planet and all its inhabitants are at stake. The

---

7. J.O'C. Hamilton, and J. Carey, 'Biotech. An industry crowded with players faces an ugly reckoning', *Business Week*, 66-72, 26 September 1994.

dangers of the mismatch between a powerful set of techniques and an outmoded, discredited ideology guiding its practice should not be underestimated. This mismatch also constitutes the major stumbling block to a rational debate on gene biotechnology and its legitimate spheres of application. With that in mind, let us look at the genetic paradigm and the new genetics in turn.

What is the genetic paradigm?

A 'paradigm' is a comprehensive system of thought and practice developed around a key idea or theory. A scientific paradigm is obviously built around scientific theories, but it can be so pervasive that it spills over into all other disciplines, and permeates the popular culture at large. The genetic paradigm is of this nature. It portrays genes as the most fundamental essences of organisms. It supposes that while the environment can be molded and reshaped, biological nature in the form of genes is fixed and unchanging and can be sorted from environmental influence. Further, it assumes that the function of each gene can be defined independently of every other. It is on such a basis that the Human Genome Project promises to unveil the 'genetic programme' for making a human being. James Watson, the first Director of the Human Genome Organisation (HUGO), set the tone, 'We used to think that our fate was in the stars. Now we know, in large measure, our fate is in our genes.'

The twin pillars of the genetic paradigm are Darwin's theory of evolution by natural selection and the gene theory of heredity as developed by Mendel, Weismann, Johannsen and others. Darwin proposed that evolution occurs by natural selection, in which nature effectively 'selects' the fittest in the same way that artificial selection practised by plant and animal breeders ensures that the best, or the most desirable, characters are bred or preserved. The ideology of natural selection is clear: those that survive to reproduce, those that do well, are naturally favoured with superior qualities that can be passed on, like a legacy, to the next generation. In the same way, those with inferior qualities are eliminated. Darwin's theory lacked a mechanism of heredity and variation. This was supplied by Mendel, who proposed that the (Darwinian) qualities inhere in constant factors (later called genes) which determine the organisms' characters, which are passed on to the next generation during reproduction, and variations are generated by rare random mutations in those genes. The combination of Mendelian genetics and Darwinian theory resulted in the 'neo-Darwinian' synthesis.

The demise of the genetic paradigm and the new genetics

The genetic paradigm today is neo-Darwinism writ large. Thus, everything from IQ to philandering in human males can be explained by invoking a gene or genes responsible, which can be selected for or against. And so geneticists can hunt for them in the genome.

There are three basic assumptions of the genetic paradigm:

1. Genes determine characters in a straightforward or additive (i.e. noninteractive) way.
2. Genes and genomes are stable, and except for rare random mutations, are passed on unchanged to the next generation.
3. Genes and genomes cannot be changed directly by the environment.

All three assumptions have been demonstrated to be false.

Assumption one contradicts everything that is know about metabolism and genetics for at least 40 years. Organisms including human beings have tens of thousands of genes in their genome. Each gene exists in multiple variants. One of the main functions of genes is to code for the thousands of enzymes catalysing thousands of metabolic reactions in our body which provide us with energy to do everything that constitutes being alive. These metabolic reactions form an immensely complicated network in which the product of one enzyme is processed by one or more other enzymes. Thus no enzyme (or gene) ever works in isolation. Consequently, the same gene will have different effects from individual to individual because the other genes (in the 'genetic background') are different. So-called 'single-gene defects' – which account for less than two per cent of all human diseases – are now proving to be very heterogeneous. Many different mutations of the same gene, or of different genes, may give the same disease, or not, as the case may be. This has been known for sickle-cell anaemia, common in in people of ethnic African origin, and more recently, for cystic fibrosis, common among Northern Europeans, and for a conglomerate of 'craniofacial syndromes' which includes achondroplastic dwarfism. All this has provoked a geneticist reporting in *Nature Genetics* to declare that there is 'no such thing as a single gene disease.'[8]

The extent to which the effect of single genes is entangled with that of all the

8. J.J. Mulvihill, 'Craniofacial syndromes: no such thing as a single gene disease', *Nature Genetics* 9, 101-103, 1995.

other genes really comes home to us in the findings of the new genetics. These findings not only further discredit assumption one, but also fatally undermine assumptions two and three – that genes or genomes are unchanging and do not respond directly to the environment.

The picture unveiled by the new genetics is an incredibly complex and dynamic catenation of cellular and genetic processes, many of which serve to destabilise and alter genomes within the lifetime of the organism. This is in direct contrast to the static linear conception of the 'Central Dogma' of molecular biology that previously held sway. The Central Dogma states that the genetic material DNA makes RNA in a faithful

'The genetic paradigm today is neo-Darwinism writ large'

copying process called *transcription*. (RNA is ribose nucleic acid. It is similar to DNA except for the extra oxygen atom in each of the units making up the polymer.) The RNA then makes a protein by a process of decoding called *translation*. There is strictly a one-way 'information flow' from the genetic message coded in the DNA to RNA to protein, and no reverse information flow is possible (Fig. 1a). In other words, proteins cannot determine or alter the transcribed message in RNA, and RNA cannot determine or alter the genetic message in DNA. We shall see that such reverse information flow not only occurs, and in a wide variety of forms, but is, furthermore, a necessary part of how genes function within a metabolic-epigenetic supernetwork (Fig. 1b).

The Fluid Genome and the New Genetics [9]

A complicated network of feed-forward and feedback processes has to be traversed just to express one gene or to make a single protein. Genes, especially of 'higher' organisms, are found to exist in bits, and the bits must be correctly joined together to make the 'messenger' RNA. Numerous other proteins take

---

9. Details are to be found in the following publications: J. Pollard, 'Is Weismann's barrier absolute?', in *Beyond Neo-Darwinism. Introduction to the New Evolutionary Paradigm*, M.W. Ho and P.T. Saunders (eds.), Academic Press, London 1984; M.W. Ho, 'Evolution by process, not by consequence: implications of the new molecular genetics for development and evolution'. *Int. J. Comp. Psychol 1*, 3-27, 1987; J. Rennie, 'DNA's new twists', *Scientific America*, 88-96, March 1993; E. Jablonka, and M.J. Lamb, *Epigenetic Inheritance and Evolution: The Lamarckian Dimension*, Oxford University Press, Oxford 1995.

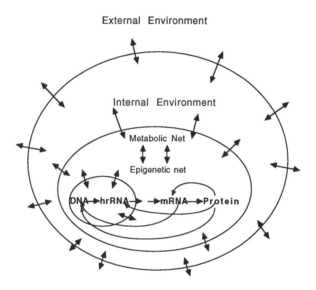

a. The Central Dogma

DNA ——→RNA ——→Protein

b. The New Genetics

External Environment

Internal Environment

Metabolic Net

Epigenetic net

DNA→hrRNA→ →mRNA→Protein

Figure 1. Genetics old and new

part in making every single protein in chopping and changing, editing and recoding in a complicated *epigenetic* network which interposes between the genes and the metabolic net, and interlocks with it, forming an epigenetic-metabolic supernetwork. *It becomes increasingly difficult to define and delimit a gene, as the metabolic-epigenetic supernet ultimately connects the expression of each gene with that of every other.*

The genome, embedded as it is within the epigenetic-metabolic supernet, is far from stable or insulated from environmental exigencies. A large number of processes appear to be designed especially to destabilise and alter genomes during the life-time of all organisms, so much so that molecular geneticists have been inspired to coin the descriptive phrase 'the fluid genome'. Genes can be marked by chemical modifications, base sequences can mutate, stretches of DNA can be inserted, deleted, or amplified thousands, and tens of thousands, of times. The sequences can be rearranged or recombined with other sequences, genes can jump from one site to another in the genome, and some genes can convert other genes to their own DNA sequences. These processes keep genomes in a constant state of flux in evolutionary time. Genes are found to have jumped between species that do not interbreed, being carried by mobile genetic elements, viruses or micro-organisms, which can exchange genes at a prolific rate, as witnessed by the rapid horizontal spread of antibiotic resistance in bacteria. Parasites that infect more than one species are also vectors for horizontal gene transfer. A particular genetic element – the P-element – has spread to all species of fruitflies in the wild within the span of less than 50 years, probably carried by a parasitic mite. Jumping genes, viruses and vectors for gene transfers are all related genetic parasites. They can help one another jump or mobilise, mutate, exchange parts and infect each other's hosts as a result. As I have already indicated, the vectors used to transfer genes are designed especially to overcome species barriers and to be used for a wide range of hosts, which would speed up and amplify the process of genetic exchange enormously. The genetic perturbations from large scale environmental releases of transgenetic organisms are therefore orders of magnitude greater than those normally experienced in ecological communities. Ecological systems are stabilised by a complex of natural checks and balances, of positive and negative feedback interactions, which, when sufficiently perturbed, will break down in a catastrophic manner.

'Ecological systems, when sufficiently perturbed, will break down in a catastrophic manner'

The fluid genome processes in the living system are likewise subject to physiological and cellular regulation, which can also be disrupted by the gene transfers, leading to highly unpredictable effects, as we have seen with transgenic plants and animals. On the other hand, gene jumping, recombination and other alterations of the genome have been found to be also part of the normal physiological response to environmental stress or starvation. Thus, transgenic crop-plants and other organisms will be much more prone to mobilise their transferred genes in the event of drought and other environmental stress, increasing the likelihood that they will spread to non-target species.

Most provocative of all, there is now abundant evidence of (previously forbidden) reverse information flow in the genomes of all higher organisms. Predictable and repeatable genetic changes have been found to occur simultaneously and uniformly in all the cells of the growing parts in plants exposed to different fertilisers, and the changes are inherited in subsequent generations. Similarly, plants exposed to herbicides, insects to insecticides, and cultured cells to drugs, are all capable of changing their genomes repeatedly by mutations or gene amplifications that render them resistant to the noxious agent, which is why resistance evolves so rapidly, even without the help of transferred genes introducing the resistance. And as long as high levels of herbicides are used with the herbicide-resistant transgenic plants, or high levels of insecticides are expressed by the insect-resistant crops, then some weeds and some insects will be bound to evolve the appropriate resistance, rendering the transgenic plants useless – and with disastrous ecological consequences besides.

As a final blow to the genetic paradigm, starving bacteria and yeast cells are now known to respond directly to the presence of (initially) non-metabolisable substrates by mutating the genes required to use the substrate. The genetic responses are so specific that they are referred to as 'directed mutations'.[10] In summary, genes are neither stable nor immune to environmental influence. On the contrary, they mobilise and mutate as part of the physiological response of the organism to environmental change.

Implications of the new genetics for heredity and evolution

The genetic paradigm has collapsed under the weight of its own momentum in the findings of the burgeoning new genetics. The genes are far from being the constant essences of organisms, whose effects can be neatly separated from one another or from the environment. There is furthermore, no constant genetic programme or blueprint for making the organism, for the genome can also change even as the organism is developing. How should we see heredity in the light of the new genetics? If the genome itself is so dynamic and fluid, where does heredity reside? It is clear that heredity does not reside solely in the DNA of the genome. In the first instance, it resides in an epigenetic cellular state – a dynamic equilibrium between interlinked genic and cellular processes. But even that is an

---

10. See note 9, p92, for details.

abstraction and reification. It cannot be assumed that heredity is exhausted at the boundary of cells or organisms. For as organisms engage their environments in a web of mutual feedback interrelationships, they transform and maintain their environments which are also passed on to subsequent generations as home ranges, cultural traditions and artefacts. It is this whole complex of dynamical interrelationships that gives rise to the stability and repeatability of the developmental process, which we recognise as heredity.[11] The fluidity of the genome is *necessary* to the dynamic stability of the system, for genes must also adjust as appropriate to the whole.

What implications are there for evolution? Just as interaction and selection cannot be separated, so neither can variation (or mutation) and selection, for the 'selective' regime may itself cause specific variations or directed mutations. The organism experiences its environment in one continuous nested *process*, adjusting and changing, leaving imprints in its epigenetic system, its genome as well as on the environment, all of which are inherited by subsequent generations. Thus, there is no separation between individual development and the evolution of future generations. In that respect, our fate is neither written in the stars nor in our genes, for we are *active participants* in the evolutionary drama.

The new genetics that underpins gene biotechnology belongs with a paradigm of organic wholeness and complexity which is emerging in many areas of contemporary research in the west, which is reaffirming the universal wisdom of traditional indigenous cultures all over the world.[12] However, the new genetics can give no justification to *simplistic* ideas on the capacity of organisms or ecosystems to adapt to any and all new circumstances. Organisms and ecosystems are complex dynamical systems with positive and negative feedback mechanisms that make them resilient as well as resistant to change. However, as mentioned above, these same mechanisms will also cause them to break down when the disturbance is large enough. And when they break down, they tend to do so in

---

11. Directed mutation is now accepted even by some of its former strongest critics, for example, N. Symonds, 'Directed mutation: a current perspective', *J. theor. Biol. 169*, 317-322, 1994. However, some committed neo-Darwinists still will not admit it exists.

12. This ideal is satisfied when the system is *coherent*. For the biophysics of coherence, see M. W. Ho, *The Rainbow and the Worm: The Physics of Organisms*, World Scientific, New Jersey 1993; also M.W. Ho (ed), *Bioenergetics, S327 Living Processes*, Open University Press, Milton Keynes 1995.

a catastrophic, spectacular fashion. The appearance of novelties and of mass extinctions alike in evolutionary history are but two sides of the same coin; we cannot be complacent about the capacity of organisms or ecosystems to adapt to any and all environmental insults that are perpetrated. The challenge is to chart the safe and sustainable uses of gene biotechnology within the new holistic paradigm.

The struggle to reclaim holistic ways of life

The collapse of the genetic paradigm is both symptomatic and symbolic of the collapse of the reductionist worldview. The implications for gene biotechnology and biosafety are clear. The reductionist aims and assumptions in the current practice of gene biotechnology are misguided. The promises can never be fulfilled because they are built on false and discredited premises. Many of the products are not only useless but are bad for health and dangerous. They are made on the erroneous assumption that genes are stable, that their effects can be localised and specifically targetted in the tangled web of living processes.

The Harvard Working Group on New and Resurgent Diseases has just presented fresh evidence that diseases such as tuberculosis, malaria, cholera and yellow fever are still a major cause of death in many parts of the world, and that these diseases are returning to regions where they were on the decline. New diseases also continue to emerge at unprecedented rates, from social conditions and environmental disturbances that enable pathogens to gain access to new host populations, or to become more virulent in immunologically weakened human hosts that suffer from poverty and malnutrition. Many of the agents of infectious diseases rapidly develop resistance to drugs and chemicals, and new variants continue to arise that escape the protection of vaccines – as we would expect, from what we know of the fluid genome. The Harvard Group's conclusion is that, 'Disease cannot be understood in isolation from the social ecological, epidemiological and evolutionary context in which it emerges and spreads. Indeed, if one lesson has emerged from the spectacular failure of western medicine to 'eradicate' certain diseases, it is that diseases cannot be reduced to a single cause nor explained with the prevailing linear scientific method: complexity is their hallmark.[13]

---

13. The Harvard Working Group on New and Resurgent Diseases, 'New and resurgent diseases. The failure of attempted eradication'. *The Ecologist 25*, 21-26, 1995.

In opposing the patenting of life, French geneticist Daniel Cohen, a prominent figure in the Human Genome Project, made the unprecedented move of offering a wide range of DNA sequence data obtained in his laboratory to the United Nations as the property of humanity to use freely for any appropriate purpose. Another hopeful sign is that in early 1995 the European Parliament has voted against patenting life, at least in principle, by a substantial majority.

The debate over gene biotechnology is not about disembodied, objective, ivory-tower scientific knowledge. Knowledge is what people live by. The western ideal of being 'objective' is misplaced, for it implies that one must be a completely detached, unfeeling observer outside nature. Within the participatory framework of other knowledge systems, the ideal of objectivity in knowledge is to be maximally communicative and connected within the nature that is the object of our knowledge, which we, as both knower and actor, participate in shaping. The present opposition to gene biotechnology is thus a concerted struggle to reclaim holistic worldviews and holistic ways of life, which are spontaneous, pluralistic, joyful, integrative, constructive and life-sustaining.

I wish to thank Martin Khor, Vandana Shiva, Gurdial Nijar, Chee Yok Ling, Ruth McCoy, Vicky Tauli-Corpus, Tewolde Egziabher, and many other members of the Third World Network for ideas that are contained in this article, and for their constant support and encouragement. I am also grateful to Brian Goodwin and Peter Saunders for helpful discussions and key references and to Doreen Massey for suggestions to improve the manuscript.

Environmental images and imaginary landscapes

Lola Young

Lola Young *discusses the work of photographer Ingrid Pollard, and looks at the extent to which environmental issues are racialised.*

As an accomplished photographer, and as a founder member of the Black Environmental Network (BEN), Ingrid Pollard has produced a body of work which encourages a reconsideration of certain assumptions about the relationship between humans, the land and the environment.[1] But before I discuss her images in detail, I want to raise some points about links between black immigration, national cohesion and identity, and discourses on the environment. Contemporary fears about the state of the environment tend to focus on a number of basic assumptions that often include the following: the havoc wreaked by the presence of humans; the dehumanising effects of living in industrialised societies; the malevolent advance of technology; and crucially, in the context of this essay, the belief that population needs urgently to be controlled.

---

1. The Black Environmental Network (BEN) was formed in order to encourage black people's participation in activities and debates about environmental issues.

This issue of population control and environmental degradation is very much linked to 'race' and immigration and has been for some time. In 1968, Paul Ehrlich's *The Population Bomb* tapped a rich vein of anxiety within the USA about the growth of urban (black) ghettos, and the deterioration of the Californian wilderness. These fears grew in the context of the demands for equality expressed by the civil rights movement and emergent Black Power activists, and what was seen as a proliferation of

'The degradation of the English countryside is seen as analogous to the alleged deterioration of the nation itself'

urban civil disorder. In Britain, Edward Goldsmith's *Blueprint for Survival* (1972) opened up the debate about the use and conservation of the countryside from being a parochial concern to wider issues of environmental management, and in doing so posited a radical approach. Like Ehrlich, Goldsmith found the main problem to be one of excessive population, and again it should be noted that at the time that Goldsmith's book was published, ferocious debates, and discriminatory legislation concerning black immigration into Britain were underway. As is the case in recent Green Party campaigning material, an ideal population for Britain is deemed to be 30 million – approximately half of what it is currently. Goldsmith's utopian proposal was to construct small group settlements of around 500 people which would be part of larger communities of some 50,000.

Central to these propositions for developing small communities is the notion that cities are by definition inferior places to live in, in comparison with the countryside. Cities are represented as breeding crime, disease and alienated subjects. The issue of population (its size, composition and location) provides much of the focus for what is sometimes termed 'eco-racism', which is a loose collection of ideas claiming that migrants and 'aliens' exacerbate environmental problems by their very presence, contributing significantly to pollution through their lifestyle, especially through their rate of reproduction. Additionally, these people (principally referring to those from Africa, Asia and countries like Turkey) are accused of diluting the sense of 'natural' national cohesion, leading to crime-infested, conflict-ridden, run-down ghettoes.

In Britain, the degradation of the English – rather than 'British' – countryside is seen as analogous to the alleged deterioration of the nation itself: the land is held up as a repository of values, culture and heritage which transcend class or gender interests, all of which should be subordinate to the nation. So how is membership of the nation defined? In the 1993 Schumacher lecture, the financier James Goldsmith stated that:

> You can't bring together all sorts of people from all sorts of cultural and ethnic backgrounds and create a nation... It is the common culture, identity and traditions which create a nation's heritage and constitute a vital pillar of its stability. That stability takes a long time to develop.[2]

In Goldsmith's account, a multi-racial/multi-cultural country, which would be a falsely created nation according to his criteria, leads to the breakdown of the social structures which make a society stable and precipitates 'misery and ethnic conflict'.[3] Goldsmith gives an apocalyptic version of future events in which 'mass movements of peoples... will engulf those nations too weak to protect themselves.' Goldsmith's pronouncements are particularly interesting in the context of his daughter's subsequent, much publicised conversion to Islam and marriage to Imran Khan.

More recently, the questioning of allegiance of black British players in the English cricket team (in an article published in *Wisden*), and the desire for a national curriculum which promotes a sense of national cohesion dependent on 'traditional' British values, evidence the continued unease about what constitutes 'Britishness'. These anxieties can be detected in the subtext of the words of a plant ecologist:

> Perhaps dislike of alien species is indeed similar to racial discrimination – wanting to preserve the culture and genetic integrity of one's own stock (a natural human failing). Alien species are welcome in strictly defined areas (gardens) but must not be allowed to pollute the native culture (the wider countryside).[4]

The use of language here is highly suggestive in its echoing of racist discourses: indeed, it is difficult to locate precisely where the discussion is concerned with plants and where with people. The garden/countryside split and the phrases

---

2. James Goldsmith, 'Superstate of Europe', in *Resurgence*, July/August 1993, No. 159, p1.
3. *Ibid.* p10.
4. J. Fenton, 'Alien or Native?' in *ECOS*, 1986, Vo.7, No.2 pp20-30 (quoted by Julian Agyeman in an unpublished paper, 'Heritage in Multicultural Society', May 1993).

'alien species' and 'must not be allowed to pollute the native culture' are particularly significant. In human terms, this passage may be interpreted as meaning that migrants may be just about tolerated in the cities because they provide a pool of cheap labour, but in the heartland, the countryside, they are invasive predators who have exceeded the spatial parameters set for them.

What about black peoples' participation in green politics? Such involvement is fraught with anxieties and difficulties. Freedom of movement, space and territory were problematised for colonial subjects in their own countries, and on their arrival in Britain restrictions on movement became even more emphatic. The organisation of space and territory meant that black people who came to settle in this country lived and worked most frequently in major conurbations. Generations later, this recent history of urban settlement, together with the *volk*ish correlation of conservation and heritage, the white, middle-class image of green politics and its lack of engagement with racial issues, have resulted in many black people thinking that the countryside and the environment have nothing to do with them. It was the recognition of a need to address this situation which provided the impetus for setting up BEN.

Imaging the Landscape

Crucial to an understanding of Ingrid Pollard's work is the recognition of her perspective as a black photographer working in a society where images of black people invoke a different history from those of the white population. Although the range of locations and occupations in which black people may be found has expanded over the years, old stereotypes persist.

Images of the countryside have come to represent a rural idyll signifying space, freedom, health and community. But views of the landscape are, in part at least, constructed for us through a familiarity with a particular descriptive language and imagery that informs 'ways of seeing' the land and being in it. It is this set of common-sense ideas about the countryside that Pollard's past work has sought to critique. Much of her previous work has been concerned with the effect of inserting black people into what have hitherto been portrayed as quintessentially 'white' English landscapes where they become immediately visible 'outsiders'.

Pollard's photographic work on the Lea Valley in East London testifies to the complexities of the assumptions embedded in apparently obvious, apparently natural oppositions, such as old/new, nature/culture, country/city, natural/

artificial, traditional/ technological and so on, and broadens the scope of her earlier visual critiques of Lake District landscapes. In the Lea Valley project, Pollard's photography seeks both to extend and to redefine some of her previous perspectives through a different look at those oppositional couplets. This time her object of study is the 'country within the city' and since the city, and especially the 'inner city', is defined in terms of confinement through fear of crime, ill-health due to pollution and isolation because of the lack of a sense of community, linking the city with the country seems like a contradiction in terms.

Much of the disquiet about cities and the countryside, has to do with what is perceived as the rapid rate of visible, radical change: the intrusion of unsightly buildings, structures incompatible with the 'natural' landscape, and excessive motor traffic with its smells, fumes and noise pollution. (None of these problems are new: there have been references to smog, pollution and crime since at least the 16th century.) Yet, looking at the panorama (a section of which is shown on p105) which Pollard has constructed – the long views with sheep, cows, sheds, lorries, telegraph poles and pylons – I was struck by how harmonious the elements of the images are and how, in the future, new generations would not necessarily see the man-made structures as architectural 'scars'. This may indicate the extent to which dissent about the trappings of modern life is partly engendered by what these structures signify – the meanings which have become attached to them – rather than what they actually are. They keep reminding us that there has been change, some of which is unsettling and disruptive: pylons, for instance, are not inherently 'ugly', but they remind people of the differences between an imaginary ideal past and a demonised present.

Of course, many of the eulogies about the ways of life prior to industrialisation and the modern city depend on the suppression of knowledge about the endemic poverty of life in the 'golden age'. Their rhetoric also relies on the notion of the 'naturalness' of the countryside: there is an unconscious idea that somehow the land was not *worked* on but was just there, providing sustenance for its contented inhabitants. Of course this is not true and the triptychs constructed by Pollard subtly question such myths through the juxtaposition of the traditional tools, the rangers posed in their working environment, and the close-ups of fragments of 'nature': the presence of the rangers indicates the extent to which these 'wild' landscapes are the result of the labour of women and men who rely on a range of tools to assist in keeping the surroundings looking 'natural'. Pollard's of hand colouring emphasises the constructed character of *all* images and leads us to question the ways in which the eye of the photographer intervenes and constructs the way in which the spectator approaches the image.

Finding a black person in an historical setting outside of images of slavery is still unusual. The long history of black people's presence in Britain is most frequently ignored in favour of a myth which says that black people first came here in the 1950s. The placing of a black man in a nineteenth-century industrialised setting is just as unsettling as the image of the black person in the countryside: 'they' don't 'belong' in these contexts. Whether or not there *actually* was a black man working in the mill is largely irrelevant: this is not a documentary-style reconstruction. Again, the image serves to remind us of the partiality of official historical accounts and the unreliability of the photograph as a window on 'factual truth'.

There is much pleasure to be had from picking out details and constructing your own interpretation of this body of work. I have not covered all of Ingrid Pollard's images here: what I've tried to do is to suggest that there is both simplicity and complexity in her images and that her work functions to undermine the certainty of the unthinking assumptions which underpin a certain view on the world.

Material in this essay was drawn from two previous publications: 'National Selection? Ideology, Environmentalism, "Race" ', in *Cultural Studies from Birmingham*, 1994, No.3, pp151-169), and 'Looking at Ingrid Pollard's Images' for the exhibition 'Hidden Histories; Heritage Stories' at the Lea Valley Leisure Centre, London, September 1994.

Bibliography
A. Bramwell, *Ecology in the 20th Century: A History*, Yale University Press, New Haven 1989.
A. Dobson (ed), *The Green Reader*, Andre Deutsch, London 1991.
R. Williams, *The Country and the City*, Paladin, St Albans1975.
J. Young, *Post-Environmentalism*, Belhaven Press, London 1992.

These photographs are part of an exhibition called *Hidden History: Heritage Stories.*
Anyone who would like further information can contact Debra Reay at Lea Valley Park on
01992 717711.

Mountain bikes in them there hills

Is it about a bicycle?

Maggie Mort

Are mountain bikes green? Maggie Mort
*reports from the Yorkshire dales on conflicting
demands for access to the countryside.
She analyses mountain bikes as postmodern
fashion accessories for the rich, and questions
the attitude to nature which their current
form entails.*

I magine you're out walking to the pub. Not 'rambling', not kitted out with hiking boots and waterproofs and bars of Kendal Mint Cake, just a brisk trot over the bridleway to the next village for a pint, maybe before Sunday lunch. It's a couple of miles.

Next thing you know, there's a sort of hissing noise behind you. Turning round you see an advancing clutch of helmets, Dayglo and fat wheels. They've left their cars at the bottom of the track and mounted their expensive new 'hobbies'. You flatten yourself against the dry stone wall and the hawthorn hoping not to get spattered with mud. The posse passes by. You regain the track for a while until the next wave. This is the Yorkshire Dales.

There is currently a battle being played out in some of the most sensitive parts of the countryside over the issue of access for off-road vehicles. At its most extreme and emotive there is the four wheel drive lobby, then there is the trials bike lobby and then comes the mountain bike lobby. While these groups may have little in common, all are trying to increase rights and access to bridleways, 'white roads' and undesignated routes. What they all want is to ride/drive their vehicles where none have gone before – before the technologies became available that is – such as up, down and round parts of Ingleborough in the Three Peaks of Yorkshire.

This struggle involves residents, farmers, ramblers, landowners, the tourist trade, the National Park authorities, cycling clubs and mountain bikers, among others. But while there might be little sympathy for those actually attempting to drive motorised vehicles over bridleways, or for Byways Open to All Traffic (BOATS), the mountain bike has an aura, derived from the bicycle, of being environmentally friendly, harmless, a mode of green transport. But this image completely ignores the relationship between the mountain bike and the car, and it also belies a darker side of the activity – an off-road biking culture which is increasingly aggressive and macho.

Take the recent spring 1995 event which was held in the Dales to the horror of the National Park authority and many locals. The eighth POLARIS International Challenge described itself in its publicity brochure as 'The Ultimate test of all round MTB skills. Called by many the toughest MTB event ever, the POLARIS CHALLENGE tests riders of all abilities to the full over all types of terrain.' In this highly competitive event, 500 teams of paired riders – that's a potential of 1000 mountain bikes – set off on a two day challenge which included an overnight stop at a 'wilderness campsite'. The idea is for competitors to collect the highest number of points by visiting as many checkpoints as possible. The teams are given the grid references of the checkpoints, but must plan their own routes along bridleways and unclassified roads.

The Yorkshire Dales National Park Committee advised the Polaris promoters that the event was unsuitable because of the impact on the surface conditions in spring, because of local opposition and because some of the checkpoints were in ecologically sensitive places, or in places where rights of way were unclear. However, even though the National Park has an overriding duty to protect the environment, the committee recognised that it was ultimately powerless to prevent the event from taking place.

Mountain bikers claim that tyre marks in soft soil do no more damage than boot soles. They believe the main opposition to mountain biking in the countryside comes from 'ramblers' whose objections are primarily 'aesthetic'. One commentator writing in the access column of *Mountain Biker* magazine in May this year put it like this:

> We need to remind ourselves that we are the visitors and should respect local views – but not to the point that we see our biking rights undermined, particularly if we are unsure whether or not the opposition comes from a 'not in my backyard' attitude… Despite the hassle which thorough consultation is almost bound to produce, our only way forward is to fight our battles in a professional and up-front way, even if we have to make irksome concessions to protect our long term future.

Events like Polaris are a sell-out. And they obviously enable mountain bike technology, which has fostered a 'conquering of nature' mentality, to be tested and developed. On the face of it it is this new technology that is opening up frontiers in the 'wilderness'. But it's no good simply blaming the technology. Technological artifacts do not *determine* our behaviour and the development of technologies does not follow some inevitable trajectory; it should not be seen as an unstoppable force. On the other hand, once created and used, technologies have the potential to promote destruction and become the carriers of social and political upheaval. They can form the stage on which human battles get fought. What mustn't happen is that we become passive witnesses to technological change.

Mountain bikes have travelled far from their Californian 'hippie' origins in the 1970s. Then a group of people who wanted to race down Mount Tampalpais built 'clunkers' out of frames and components found lying around in backyards. The descents attempted became more and more daring as these devices evolved. During the 1980s there was a massive commercialisation of the bikes, but even since then the design of mountain bikes has constantly shifted.

The mountain bike has not yet become a stable technological artefact. There are still new frontiers to be driven back. Its constantly changing, flexible and increasingly individualised technology, produced by fragmented multinational workforces, represents for some an example of post-Fordist, postmodernist society – but at the same time it draws on modernist images of nature and technological progress and innovation. (It's interesting to note here the role played by mountain bikes in inner-city drug dealing or as the focus of much profitable urban theft because of their high resale values.)

B ut for some of us, who live and work in the countryside, our living space is being consumed. We see the rich arriving in flash cars and 4WDs, kitted out in fluorescent gear. And then they unload these hugely expensive fashion accessories on which they set out to be consumers of the dales, the fells, the rights of way. They are of course superfit, because they pursue physical perfection. But by moving through the landscape at speed, they lose touch with it, so that it becomes something to be used up, rather than something which can be observed/contemplated. Even the gear they wear drives away nature. Whoever would go birdwatching in Dayglo, or climb the fells clad only in figure-hugging Lycra? It all assumes you're going to get home – fast – after a rather narcissistic display.

These are the trappings of the mountain bike. But it is, itself, essentially a post- rather than pre-internal combustion technology. Secondary, rather than primary, transport. Cycling clubs used to visit the Dales from home, sticking to the country roads. That was primary transport and because it was primary, it had built-in limits. These users, however, use cars to carry their bikes to their chosen venue. Where mountain bikes are used as primary transport, they probably cause less damage and arouse less hostility.

But even if mountain bikes are symbols of postmodernity, the breaking down of old modes of production and the birth of flexible technology, that isn't much consolation if you're having a peaceful walk ruined, or if you can see under your very nose the erosion of the landscape, and its colonisation, aided and abetted by merchandising. (In some small Dales villages there are now two or more shops selling sophisticated outdoor gear but none selling even the most basic food.)

The National Park authorities do not have sufficient powers to curtail off-road vehicles, even though the spirit of the law would seem to encourage restriction. But if our paths and tracks have to give way to frontier freaks it would be a cruel irony if this was to be done in the name of sustainability and green transport.

I am grateful to Paul Rosen for some of the information in this article, and have, in particular, found very useful his article 'The Social Construction of Mountain Bikes', in *Social Studies of Science*, Vol.23, Sage 1993.

Containing the car

Returning the streets to the people

Kerry Hamilton, Max Dixon
and Graham Smith

*Can the car be dislodged from its dominance
of the street?*

G rowth in car ownership has been relentless over the last thirty years. Currently 24 million people have a driving license and there are 21 million cars on British roads. The authorities forecast a doubling of this number by 2025.

We are finding it nearly impossible to live with the rate of current car use, yet for many people the ambition to own and drive a car is unaltered.

It is traditionally argued that the decision to get a car is based on an individual judgement about the need for mobility, access and status. In reality, this individual choice is one shared with millions of others. Together, these choices have fundamentally shaped our environment and changed our world.

The spiral of dependence starts with the calculation that if most other people travel by public transport, you can get there first on most short-medium length trips by using a car. Soon, however, enough other people also have one to cause

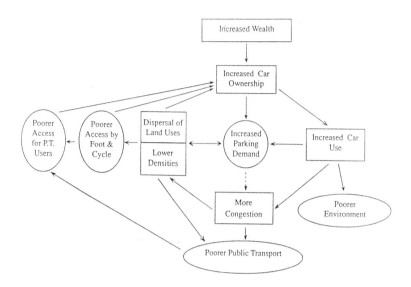

traffic congestion. The bus service not only loses passengers and becomes less economic, but becomes less reliable because of the traffic congestion.

More people desert public transport for the car. Congestion becomes worse.

Some people drive to facilities outside the most congested areas. Congestion is one of the reasons some people move house or job, usually outwards to less congested suburbs, or villages outside the town. Shopping, employment, hospitals, leisure facilities are established in less congested areas on cheaper land.

The city as a whole becomes more spread out. Facilities become more dispersed, rather than being concentrated in town centres. Trips to reach facilities become longer. It is harder to combine several functions in one trip. More people find it harder to do the things they used to do by public transport or on foot.

More people acquire and use cars. Congestion spreads.

The highway authorities implement, one way and another, traffic management schemes to squeeze more vehicles through existing streets. Drivers find their own rat-runs through formerly quiet residential streets to try to avoid congestion. The urban environment deteriorates, providing another incentive for people to move outwards from the most congested inner areas. The authorities succeed in building a few new urban roads, but at such cost in environmental degradation that they eventually have to admit that they cannot conceivably meet the demand for everyone to drive.

So far in the UK governments have either actively supported the adaptation of the whole society towards the car, or have talked about (and occasionally even actually introduced) the occasional palliative. No major politician has pointed the way towards a policy environment that could begin to really free us from increasing car dependence. At least, perhaps, until former European Commissioner Carlo Ripa di Meana launched *Car Free Cities* in 1992, with a report *Villes sans Voitures*. This estimated that it would cost between two and five times less to live and work in car-free cities because of the savings people could make in not having to buy, park, insure and maintain cars.

But are car-free areas a pipedream?

In countries such as Germany and Holland attitudes to the car have shifted, allowing for a concentration on the car as a problem. The resulting changes to street design aimed at countering the car have humanised the environment and are a demonstration of the exercise of local choice over local environment.

Durener Strasse, Köln (Cologne) PARKING
Main road parking in Köln calls for a balance between functions. In this mixed use shopping/residential street the car is given a place, but only a small space. Its presence is softened by generous planting. The angled parking spaces leave the car's back-end poking into the traffic, which is obliged to proceed more carefully as a result. Pedestrians have a wide space and cycles are conveniently accommodated inboard of the parking.

Aachen, SE GREEN SPACE
An important concern in Germany has been 'unsealing the street' – breaking up the waterproof tarmac and allowing the ground to breathe. The addition of trees helps, looks good, and legitimises carriageway narrowing, calming traffic, even in this busy local centre.

Kalker Hampstrasse, Köln SITTING SPACE ...
This street includes parking and loading but also generous sitting space in the busiest locations. The large store has a serving hatch to sell food.

Venloer Strasse, Köln SPILL-OUT SPACE
This street had four traffic lanes, train lines now underground and parking on both sides. Only two traffic lanes are in use. The widened pavement supports a safe cycle lane and spill-out space for the shops, at the expense of moving traffic which is often impeded by frontage loading.

Venloer Strasse, Köln LOWER SPEED

The central shopping area of this street has a block-paved surface and a 30 kph (18.6 mph) speed restriction, which enables crossing at will. A genuine mixed use space.

Frankfurterstrasse, Hennef (North East of Bonn) CANALISING OF TRAFFIC

This busy four lane street has been restricted to two lanes with over-taking prevented by lamps in the centre. Passing of stationary vehicles is possible only when no on-coming vehicles are present. Cobbles at the road-side squeeze cyclists onto the smooth tarmac and when they reach the long canalised section they become 'humanisch-hindering' or a form of mobile traffic calming. Traffic proceeds gently even when cycles are not present. Less bold cyclists are 'invited' onto the footpath but at pedestrian-friendly speeds.

Amsterdam, SE EASE OF CROSSING FOR PEDESTRIANS
The motor lanes have been narrowed to restrict car speeds and volume and are easily and safely crossed. Two vehicles cannot easily pass and concrete bollards deter uncontrolled behaviour.

Damrak, Amsterdam
This central major street has cars reduced to one traffic lane, with some parking. A generous footpath, cycle lane and public transport fill the rest. Vigorous bollard/sculptures convey protection and enjoyment.

Biaritz
BEFORE
Like most other towns Biaritz had to be viewed through a mask of cars.

Biaritz
AFTER
More recently cars have been banished.

Balancing act
Personal politics and anti-roads campaigning

Heather Hunt *was involved with the recent Claremont Road protest against the building of the M11 link road through Hackney in East London. Here she talks to* Doreen Massey *about the experience of that campaign, and compares it with others, such as Greenham, in which she has been involved. But Heather is also a consultant psychologist. Like many public sector and professional employees, she is over-worked. How can we get a better balance in our lives, between formal work and more personal and political concerns?*

Getting there, being there: Claremont Road

What was the campaign at Claremont Road like?

We would be phoned up, at night usually, to say can you come? There's going to be an eviction early, tomorrow; could you come? There'd be a red alert or an amber alert, or whatever. And you make your decision. Is this something I can do or not? You make your decision – can I get to work by nine thirty? – today, can I put myself in a position where I might get arrested? And I always remember that I am not a main, core, person, I am a campaigner on a phone-tree. I'm thinking now of the last one. It was an eviction on a road parallel to Claremont Road. Part of it is arriving at 5.30 a.m. or that sort of time, after a 30 minute bike ride through dark streets, and being aware of who *are* the occupants of Claremont Road – they are the main core group. There were people sleeping out on the road, on settees; there were all the sculptures – one aspect of the occupation has been a visual campaign, trying to create symbols that are about what the campaign is about – communities.

On this occupied street, where people are living in the houses, they have made the street itself a community area, and it is amazing. There are the most beautiful sculptures, some of which are very funny. One simple symbolic one is an old car painted green, with grass around, and it just says 'Rust in peace'. That is a nice one. And then there are others down the street, which turn things inside-out. They were like delightful living rooms, out on the street. Or strange constructions of, say, a tropical cocktail bar. People's living areas on the streets.

So you are very aware, when you arrive at 5.30 in the morning, that these are living spaces, for the people that are involved in the campaign. And you aren't part of that. And you are aware that these people have been extraordinarily imaginative and inventive. Expressing what *can* be: communities not commuters.

So how do you feel when you walk into a place, which you know you are not part of, but which you are a linked-in member of?

It is dark, and dawn is breaking. And I think this is where I do get excitement, because I do enjoy being connected – that is me. I feel a buzz. I feel so clear about everything, it is so polarised. The campaign is about protesting against knocking down the houses so that commuters can take eight minutes off their journey into the city. These are terraced houses in a working-class area in Leytonstone, in a part of East London where there is an enormous housing shortage. It doesn't make sense in human terms. And it is also very, very clear that the whole campaign is committed to non-violence. So I know that the method of campaigning is what I believe in, and the issues are very clear. So there is a strong feeling for me of being pleased to be there, of knowing that this is where I need to be.

Then, obviously, there is the whole business of uncertainty and fear – what is going to happen. Security guards can be very rough. So I am always happier to be there with at least one other person whom I know well, a friend, to look out for each other. We learnt this at Greenham, to handle fear by psychologically preparing yourself with one other woman. In action, keeping a focus on another's well-being gives a connection which inhibits the paralysing effects of fear.

Central to the campaign at Claremont Road are the people who live there. Young men and women who have squatted the houses and live the campaign. The parallel is the women who made Greenham their home. I'm interested to see parallels and differences between the politics of the women's peace movement, which I was very involved with, and the current

'Knocking down houses so commuters can take eight minutes off their journey into the city'

anti-roads campaign. One similarity is the life-changing commitments people have made, which are inspirational to others. Young men and women have squatted houses in the path of the link-road and they live the campaign. In the 1980s, women left their homes to make Greenham US base a women's peace camp. Other parallels are the commitment to non-violence and to direct action. The obvious difference to me is that the anti-roads campaign involves both men and women.

There is enormous hopefulness for an old-time feminist campaigner like me to see so many young men committed to non-violence ('Keep it fluffy' is what is urged as the bailiffs move in and the adrenaline surges.) And the anti-roads people are making their campaign into a positive campaign, with the sculptures on the street, and the 'inside-out' idea, having a community, a street for people not roads for cars. And defending local people from eviction is a very direct way of emphasising that houses are needed as homes not as hard core for motorway tarmac. And then last summer, through to the autumn, every Sunday night, there was a street party, and musicians came and folk-singers came, and there was dancing on the street.

Greenham Common

Did you take part in that, in spite of the twenty year age gap you've mentioned?
Yes, any chance for a dance; it was great! And although the people who were living there were mostly younger, there was a spread of people. There were other people like me, middle-aged, middle-class – drop-outs we have been termed, which I am proud of – who are still part of it all. I don't think it is dropping-out, it is trying to promote alternative ways of being, that keep visions alive about what things should be, enjoying that connection with younger people wearing three T-shirts and dreadlocks. I'm not part of that uniform and I would look silly if I tried to conform with that image. But what was lovely about those parties was that they were welcoming to the range of people. It seems to be a culture which is very accepting and welcoming of difference. So that is the sort of politics I want to be part of – campaigning in ways that promote a vision of what can be.

I wasn't at the centre of that community but as I passed through there would be people I would recognise and there would be some acknowledgement. I was not a part of developing the creative force there. The community was really the people who lived in the road, to defend it. People who had made major changes in their life, to be part of that campaign, some by virtue of being there; 90-year old Dolly refusing to be evicted from a terraced house in Claremont Road where she'd lived all her life; the local lollipop lady who is committed to the campaign

Greenham Common

to keep the streets safe for children. And younger people who would either move down there from another campaign, or had given up what they were doing to live there, like many women had done for Greenham.

What I find interesting is how gender issues are reflected in this mixed campaign. I've seen both men and women engaged in brave and creative activity and in ways that challenge conventional gender roles. 'Green Dave' doing the cooking for the community, women padlocking themselves high up on cranes. Patsy and Becky, local women who have lived the campaign for 2 years, barricaded themselves with concrete into a first floor room of a house to be demolished. 90 year old Dolly being an eloquent spokesperson. And the images too. 'Union Jill' – a criss cross purple, green and white flag flying high from the rooftops, campaign photos of men campaigners erecting scaffolding on rooftops in skirts. But looking on it is apparent it is not a 'unisex' way of working. Two things stand out for me: roles are not equally taken on between the sexes and men have developed their own way of acting non-violently which is distinctly different from women's.

Through my gender lens I see a lot of the physical construction done by men, building tree houses, erecting scaffolding on roofs; activity that is related to the traditional male trades really, climbing, physical strength and skill.

Claremont Road, 1994

Can I give you an example about erecting big nets from the tops of these three-storey old Victorian houses to the trees on the other side of the road. The nets came from circuses – I was there shortly after they were erected, and it was the men that had erected them. I was there one morning up on the roof and it was clear that the police and bulldozers weren't coming after all. And I do like climbing and being up high...

So it is not just men who do climbing after all?
No, no but they erected all the ladders and they got the nets up. I was helped by men. There is no problem – it isn't 'men-only land' at all – it's just that there is something about the way that things happen 'naturally' in this culture. Women aren't excluded. In fact men are encouraging.

Anyway I climbed up there one morning, and there were a couple of men who were crossing the nets. It was scary but not dangerous, so I felt I would like to have a go. And they said, 'Go on have a go'. So there was me at 47, about 20 feet above the ground, on a circus net. I had never done anything like this in my life before, and it is quite scary, because you leave the roof and you are suddenly on the rope with nothing below you before the tarmac road. I was given quite a lot of encouragement from everybody, and I did it. I got across in the end. And I was

Claremont Road, 1994

told I was the first woman to have done that, so I was quite chuffed. But also disappointed really, that it should be me at my old age. To be truthful I did it partly because I thought 'hah, it is just men out there'. The other part of me said that I do like doing things like this. But it was notable that in the two days before then there hadn't been other women who lived there, who had thought 'I want to do this'.

I was nostalgic about the women's peace movement. If there was physical work to do we developed ways to do it. We learnt ways to climb over high barbed wire fences, we taught each other to use heavy bolt cutters, we carried our own home-made 30 foot maypole into a silo in a Nato airbase. The array of women-made 'benders' was an exhibition of designer self-build sustainable houses.

But as a woman friend in the anti-roads campaign and co-protester Di Manning reflected, perhaps these areas of male prowess are not challenged because younger women feel they have nothing to prove. Perhaps the gender issues are being worked through in a different way and there are many other areas where women are developing their strength and sense of power. I'd like to have these conversations with younger women.

I will give you another example about the strengths of the non-violence and the imagination but also about the maleness. This is what happened. Last summer the government announced that pollution levels were very high, and people were advised to stay at home. There was no statement that *cars* should stay at home. *People* stay at home, but it is *cars* that make the pollution. Anyway, I was involved in Hackney Friends of the Earth in wanting to protest to the Minister of Environment and Transport, that *cars* should be restricted not people, and I had agreed to go with a person and a letter and a petition to the Ministry of Transport, to say what was happening in Hackney. I had also been at Claremont Road at the weekend, and they were painting a wonderful enormous banner, which said, 'M11 link road, you must be choking'. It was enormous. And I knew that they'd been saying they would take it to 'a position of power', and that they were thinking about taking it down to the Department of the Environment, because part of the Claremont Road demonstration has been about taking the issues of Claremont Road to where the centres of power are. Everybody knows the houses are going to go, so there is no point in just having the campaign to save Claremont Road and then feeling defeated.

> 'There was a wonderful banner, "M11 link road, you must be choking" '

Well, we were at the Department of the Environment in our official guise – we had rung up, properly, very properly, as Friends of the Earth, with me saying I am a Hackney consultant community psychologist (you can *use* your formal status, you see) and we are coming to make our case. And so there we were in the Department of the Environment, and we were greeted by the assistant, and we made our little speeches and presented our letters. And suddenly outside, up the scaffolding, came all these young men, with their dreadlocks and whatever else, and the two of us – two women – were kept inside the building. The police came, and there were tannoyed messages for the civil servants telling them to 'stay calm'. We knew what it was, it was Claremont Road people, scaling up 20 floors. And they unleashed their wonderful banner, saying, 'M11 link road, you must be choking'. And they fixed flares all around it, releasing smoke.

It was coincidence that we were inside just at that moment, doing our formal bit, and that outside there was this direct action. I was delighted it had happened. But of course we said 'this is totally separate, nothing to do with us'. We wanted the connections to be made, but we felt it was stronger to say that we were people from different walks of life, who were protesting about the air pollution and roads. It was strategic really, to keep our distance, although we knew everybody.

But we hadn't planned it together. When we went outside there was the banner, and it was the Claremont Road people, with tv cameras and reporters. There were quite a few young women who had been down there with the men, and had been involved in the making of the banner and the planning, but it *had* only been men that climbed up that tower.

Can I tell you now about ways men resist non-violently in different ways to women. I was on another site where the link road is bring built, and I was there with women friends from our choir, *Raised Voices*. The choir has been a great source of strength: singing is a very powerful thing to do against feelings of your own powerlessness, and also, in a way, it is a challenge to people who are behaving so mindlessly, and it can have a calming influence when levels of provocation are high. Me and my friends were singing. We were trying to prevent trees from being cut down. It was only men who were in the occupied area – there weren't any women there – and the men were being chased by the security guards. It seemed like quite high spirits on both sides, but the kind of thing that would traditionally end up in a tussle. When men get cornered, they don't want to be seen as beaten. It was very interesting to watch: when they were caught, they would often both laugh, but the protester would also stay very rigid, tensing his muscles, so it made the job of pulling him away harder. This is very different from us women at Greenham, or on other peace demos or road demos that we have been on. My experience has been about learning to allow yourself to relax to be pulled away, on the one hand so it doesn't do any damage, and on the other hand because it isn't confrontational. When you are a dead weight you can keep your spirit and soul and your voice, but by relaxing you are not offering physical opposition. It was interesting seeing the men *not* doing that, but keeping physically very tense – not fighting, but *looking* strong.

And that wasn't confrontational either?
It was interesting, because it wasn't *seen* as confrontational; and I thought it might have been. But the demonstrations have been going on for a long time, so the security men and the police probably know now that strong muscles do not mean that they are going to get a fist in the mouth.

Do you think those men are in some ways trying to challenge the masculinity of the security guards and the police, the macho kind of masculinity?

Well, that's what I hope for, and I can see, symbolically, that to me that is the picture. I have not had a chance really to be able to have those discussions. My connection isn't that close.

But it seems a possibility. On the sit-downs on the roads, we would be pulled away and we would link arms, and go physically limp – though keeping mentally alert and strong. But seeing men being pulled away was a hoot really. There they are sitting cross-legged and cross-armed, and they are picked up. They won't be pulled along, because they are staying cross-legged and cross-armed, which means it takes an awful lot of strength to pick them up. So I do think it is a way – and it looks to me a very effective way – of men saying we're not going to go limp because that's a bit soft, and we are not soft men, we are strong men, but we are committed to non-violence, and we are showing our strength not our aggression. So we are confronting might by showing our alternative strength. But I haven't had conversations with the men about this.

Making connections: the local and the global

Let's turn to the politics of it. There is a way of referring to things like anti-roads campaigns as single issue campaigns; I just wondered what is the politics that leads you to go there? Does it link into other things, or does it matter that it is a single issue?

I don't see it that way really. I have lived in Hackney for 13 years, and I am committed to issues about people's well-being, and addressing inequalities. I work in Hackney too, in the child health department, in a job which aims to prevent distress in children and families. In Hackney a major issue for child health is respiratory distress. And there is the issue of poor housing – one in 20 people are homeless in Hackney. Old people and children's health, particularly, are affected by polluted air. Only 40 per cent of the people in Hackney have access to a car, yet we have air pollution which is above the world health level, and it is caused by commuters. I don't see it as a single issue. I think it is to do with the relationship of issues. So the issue about the M11 link road coming into Hackney and funnelling its traffic through Hackney is one which will affect the well-being of poor people particularly, although it will affect everybody. It highlights the limits of ballot box democracy in Britain. We have just had local council elections. The majority Labour council opposes the M11 link. Both our Hackney MPs are committed to opposing the M11 link. But decisions on trunkroad building are taken by central government. It seems they are more influenced by the funds coming into the Tory Party coffers from the road construction and haulage companies than by the views of the majority of people living in the area affected. So you see I think it raises a central issue – how decisions are made that affect our lives, and the need for 'extra parliamentary' activity to draw attention to the fact that our consent is not being given.

Another way people might try, in part, to belittle such campaigning, would be to say it is local, and in a sense you are making the same point. Here you are struggling locally, but not even the local members of parliament can do anything about it. How do you respond to that 'It is only local'?

We *did* respond to it at a local level but in many different ways. We increased the information available to local people, and engaged the high ups in the health authority. I made connections through my work. The child health services wrote to the Public Health Department expressing our concern about the effects on child health if the road is built. Public Health is part of the Health Authority and has responsibility for ensuring adequate health care is provided, and that diseases

' "We are not soft men, but we are committed to non-violence" '

are prevented. In the past, Public Health has made a greater contribution to our health than any high-tech medicine – a classic is the discovery that cholera is spread by contaminated water. Contemporary research is very convincing that traffic-exhaust air pollution is a major exacerbator of asthma and respiratory distress. We are suggesting that just as fresh water was seen as a major health issue a century ago in the UK, now clean air needs to be.

Anyway, the consultant in Public Health took on the issue and surveyed the research and agreed that traffic-based air pollution was a major health issue and agreed to address a public meeting. A small Hackney 'No M11 link' campaign group, which I am involved in, which also involves a local GP, held a public meeting in a health centre about the effects of traffic on health. 60 local people came and many have taken on the issue in schools and community organisations. Information can be empowering. People attending knew air pollution was bad for them and their children, but to hear the reasons why and to learn about the projected M11 link – and coming from respected authorities – was catalytic in getting a local campaign going.

Subsequently the Hackney 'No M11 link' campaign has involved a very broad cross-section of the community to campaign against a Sainsbury's hypermarket proposed to be built off the link road on Hackney marshes. The local council supported the proposal. The campaign co-ordinated inputs from local traders, schools, mother's groups, churches, to a public

'Earlier, fresh water was seen as a major health issue, now clean air needs to be' planning enquiry putting forward evidence on adverse health effects of the projected increased traffic flow and on the effects on the local economy. We have just learnt that planning permission has not been granted! This is an enormous victory for local people against the might of Sainsbury's and the local council.

So it is a local issue, yes, and one which can engage a lot of people in diverse ways that feel compatible to them, and in ways they want their voices heard. From direct action to letter writing to campaigning in schools. I think this is very valid politics in a country where many people feel disempowered.

We can congratulate ourselves on three things: on a successful local campaign to prevent the building of a hypermarket, changing the government view because of public pressure and the expense of the protest, and on the major change there has been in *public* views about roads and cars. It is now much more mainstream, not just to be against cars, but to recognise the need for public transport, and for an integrated public transport policy.

Thinking globally now – traffic exhausts are a major cause of global warming. And of course the wealthy northern hemisphere countries are responsible for the majority of pollution. The multinational car manufacturers are building demand in southern hemisphere countries at the same time as exploiting cheap un-unionised labour in their manufacture. Campaigning locally to stop the road and for public transport is part of that process of change and making connections.

So those are the ways in which you would say the campaign at Claremont Road, or similar campaigns, could be a success, has been a success.
The particular fact that that road is being built, those houses got demolished, isn't the measure of the success of that campaign. The day Claremont Road houses were demolished a campaigner remarked, 'we've lost the battle but we've won the war'.

And look at the change in the Labour Party – I think that is more significant than the change in the Tories, because Labour at the last election was still supporting the car industry, and using car-ownership as an index of growth and well-being. I think cars are a symbol of a lot of things which are not healthy – pollution, individualism… So the Labour Party hadn't really grasped that nettle.

It was there in their transport policy but it wasn't there in their industrial policy?
That's right, but they have changed their policy. They are committed to review every major road building programme.

I think they would still find it hard not to defend the car industry.
I think that is work still to be done. But I think that after the conversion of the arms trade, the next struggle is about the conversion of the car industry. That's why it is not a single issue. The campaign stimulates a need for a radical rethink of employment strategies, socially constructive ways of using human skills, and public transport as a necessary infrastructure for a sustainable egalitarian society.

Politics and time
A number of times you have referred to yourself during our talk. You began by calling yourself 'a middle-aged, middle-class drop-out', and then you said 'well no, not quite', and then you said, 'I am a consultant community psychologist'…
Doesn't sound very drop-out?

Put it together for me.
Rather than being a 'drop-out', 'opting in' would be more appropriate. Choosing a sustainable lifestyle is unconventional and seen as eccentric for a middle-aged woman in a professional job. It's about trying to keep a balance between working within the mainstream structures to influence change and keeping engaged with creative direct action which keeps me vital.

And you have made major changes in your life to try and do that?
There was a time when I made much more significant shifts. I cut down my time at my job. I went from five days a week to two-and-a-half. That was about ten years ago, in 1983/4. I had been engaged in Greenham since 1982. I worked at Great Ormond Street Children's Hospital, and I'd been involved with the left and the women's movement for a long time. So that wasn't new. Nor was it new

to think critically about clinical psychology, to question the old individualistic assumptions, and to argue that the social context and power relations were crucial to an understanding of human distress. So I was in a dilemma about how to integrate these things: I wanted to change the

'After the conversion of the arms trade we need the conversion of the car industry'

'external world', not just to recognise the effects, working with people's individualised distress. I was at Great Ormond Street and also at Greenham. And I basically decided not to put so much energy into work. It wasn't any great kind of heroics. It was a sense of wanting to be able to have energy left for creative, life-enhancing ways of doing politics and of being. I had been working very hard as well, and blaming myself for not keeping up to tight time-boundaries. People were expected to work late and had to write their reports and lectures outside their work time. So there was all that really, and wanting to be conscientious. And also I wanted to do my political bit in work too, and in the union, and the joint shop-stewards committee. So reducing my hours was like being given an opportunity, knowing that there were more creative things to do, to be engaged in, to be honest.

But still it was a big decision.
Well it did mean that there was some negotiating to do, and that is useful to think about. The assumption if you go part-time is that it is either because you are pregnant or you want to do a PhD. And I didn't want to do either of those things. I wanted to have more time to be political and creative. And it caused quite a lot of commotion, because it didn't seem to be quite justified: 'why should people be able to change their terms and times and become a part-timer, if they didn't actually *need* to be part-time?' And I reckon there might have been another issue. People were complaining, which we all do when we work full-time, because it is taking up all our lives. And so going part-time, for something which was not a 'serious' issue, was quite a challenge to other people, really; that was interesting.

And was it a challenge to you? Although you are making quite light of it, it sounds like a big decision to make.
Well it was more the negotiating of it. And I had to give up my tenure, so I no

longer had job security. I had no dependents, so it wasn't a disaster. I'd stopped smoking, I sold my car and took to a bike. I lived a bit more simply and healthily. It was to be a two year job-share. But I knew I needed a kick up the backside, because I didn't want to continue my life at Great Ormond Street. I had been looking at ways to develop a community psychology, which would address the political as well as the personal, and which could be part of fostering healthy communities. I think that is a theme running through what I do, linking the political and the personal – and that includes environmental issues as well as structures of inequality. So I was looking for ways of doing that, but jobs like that just aren't around. I didn't know what I was going to do, so having a two year deadline at Great Ormond Street was a necessity. I think it was a very healthy decision, and it did spur me on to leaving Great Ormond Street, and to developing other work. I applied for jobs as a part-timer.

And that is what you are doing? Your current job is quite high-powered?
Well that is a problem. I have got myself into a muddle. The job is a consultant post to develop a new service. When I was offered it as a full-time job four years ago, I said I only wanted to work three days a week, and they said, 'Fine'. Of course it saved them money; it meant that I was prepared to do a full-time job in three days. I was naive really. And then I went up to four days because I needed to do that to be able to do the job. This job is the best opportunity to integrate my psychology and my politics in the community I've lived in and been active in for many years. The job is

'I sold my car and took to a bike. I lived a bit more simply'

to develop a psychology service in Hackney dedicated to preventing distress in children and families in ways that address the psychological impact of racism, sexism and socio-economic disadvantage. That is amazing scope, and as a small team we've created some models of good practice and raised difficult questions, but the pressures and contradictions are enormous... which might be another conversation – the public sector in a business culture in a social context of increasing health and wealth divides. It is highly destructive at so many levels. So it isn't just about pressure of work. It is now also the culture. The contradictions are very great. Yet we know that survival strategies have to be about solidarity *and* connections. And it can be very hard to maintain that in the current business atmosphere.

Do you think all those pressures together mean that the kind of decision you took way back then is now more difficult for people to take?
Yes I do, because I think that people's sense of insecurity has increased and there is an ethos of competition which inhibits collaboration. And the cuts are real, jobs are harder to get, and the sense of competition is higher.

But are you happy with the decision that you made, over the long term?
It was the right decision at the time, but the conflicts with the culture in the health service are now exacting too much of a personal cost. I would much rather be able to do something that is constructive and creative, in a realistic part-time way, and to keep the energy. I have always worked, for 23 years I have always worked, within the main structures of education, health or social services, because I have felt they impacted on everybody. And the public sector was a valid place to work with others committed to locally accountable democratic services. I *used* to be against being part of a drop-out alternative culture. I felt we had to alter the main structures. I don't feel that now. I do feel now that there is a need to provide alternatives. So I might be changing my practice. For me, now, to be innovative and creative about community-based ways of addressing inequality might mean being outside the main structures and outside the public sector. I have two complementary motivations; to be part of the process of making changes in the society we live in and to maximise opportunities for being constructive and creative.

'Linking the political and personal includes environmental issues as well as structures of inequality'

138

William Cobbett and the invention of popular radical journalism

Michael Rustin

Soundings *should have regard for the great*
models of popular journalism of the past, says
Michael Rustin. *He shows in his article how many*
of the techniques of popular polemical writing
were invented two hundred years ago by the
great advocate of the rural working class,
William Cobbett.

Soundings

Here are two characteristic passages from the writings of the radical journalist William Cobbett (1763-1835):

To the labourers of England, on the projects for getting them out of their native country

My Friends,

The London newspapers tell us, that the newspapers in the country are full of 'forebodings as to the designs of the labourers!...'

I, however, want no information on the subject, for I know your designs, and I highly approve of them; namely, *first*, to secure for yourselves, in return for your labour, a belly-full of meat and bread; and *next*, to obtain some good wholesome beer, to wash them down; and also to obtain good and decent clothes, and clean bedding, as your grandfathers had. These are your designs, and God send that they may be accomplished, instead of being a subject of *'ominous forebodings.'* But now, upon these projects for getting you out of the country... (p2)

I have frequently told you, that there is a man of the name of Malthus, who is a church parson, who was the great inventor of the doctrine, that it is your breeding so fast that is the cause of your misery. This man has long been a great favourite with the greater part of the law-makers and ministers, and it has recently come to light that he has been and is in the pay of the government, and that he has been receiving and is receiving a hundred pounds a year for his literary services. That which he has received would have wholly maintained nine or ten labourers' families. Such transactions as this form part of the cause of your misery; but though this is as clear as daylight to me, and to every man of sense in the kingdom, still the schemers are at work to get some of you away; to get some of you out of the country in which you were born... while they suffer swarms of Italians, Jews and Germans, hurdy gurdy grinders, broom-sellers and Scotch pedlars, to swarm over the land, like lice on the body of a diseased animal... (p3)

But, you will say, what have we to do with this Right Honourable WILMOT HORTON? Why, you have a great deal to do with him: he is the head emigration schemer; and he has just now been made the governor of an island, a post which, they say, is worth eight thousand pounds a year; and who is it that pays it, I need not tell you. However, he has schemed, it seems, pretty well for himself; but, my friends, look only at this thing! a board of commissioners, established by the King, to collect information for persons who may wish to get out of the country! a board of commissioners, with a Duke at the head of it, to show people how they may carry away out of England that which constitutes England's strength. A board of royal commissioners to get the king's subjects out of his kingdom... (p14).

Two-Penny Trash, July 1831

To the Yeoman Cavalry: On the Fires

I cannot call you *friends*, and I will not call you *gentlemen*. This plague of the country is now raging with greater fury than ever, and I think it proper to address you on the subject. You are called *yeoman cavalry*; though perhaps more than half of you are loan-mongers, tax-gatherers, dead-weight people, stock-jobbers, shag-bag attorneys, bailiffs (mostly Scotch), toad-eating shopkeepers, who are ready to perform military duty towards the 'lower orders' in order at once to give evidence of your gentility, and to show your gratitude towards your rich customers for their paying your long bills without scruple. A very great part of you come in under one or the other part of this description; but to those of you who are farmers; that is to say who have land in your occupation; and who grow corn, and rear cattle, and who have barns, ricks and other things, liable to be set fire to; to you only do I address myself upon this occasion, being well aware that my arguments would produce no impression whatever upon your comrades above-mentioned. First of all, call the roll of your corps over, and see how many of them there are who are not interested in the taxes and the tithes, either immediately or through their relations, landlords or somebody else. When you have called the roll, and have separated yourself from the rest, get into a plain room, pull off your hairy caps, your parti-coloured jackets and your Wellington-boots; put on your own Christian-like clothes, your high shoes well-nailed; and then pick out someone with a good strong voice to read to you that which I am about to write. (p145-146)

Two-Penny Trash, January 1832

Cobbett was one of the inventors of popular radical journalism in Britain, and it is appropriate therefore to remind readers of our new radical journal, *Soundings*, of the example of his work. In one way, reminders are scarcely needed. Several of the major socialist writers of this century have written about him – a full-length biography and various reprints of his work by G.D.H. and Margaret Cole, virtually a chapter devoted to him in Edward Thompson's *The Making of the English Working Class*, and more references to him in its index than to anyone else, a short book on him by Raymond Williams. (Ian Dyck adds Karl Marx, Matthew Arnold, G.K. Chesterton, Michael Foot, A.J.P. Taylor, Asa Briggs and Richard Ingrams to this list of admirers.) Yet of Cobbett's huge amount of writing, only *Rural Rides* has remained consistently in print, and this probably more for its topographical interest, and as a classic kind of 'travel writing', than for its politics. Or perhaps one should say that its ever-present politics has been tolerated for these other merits. It is extraordinary that there has never been an accessible paperback compendium of Cobbett's political writing, drawn from the *Political Register*, *Peter Porcupine* (his writings in America) and the *Two-Penny Trash* (priced to evade the stamp duty), even though good scholarly work on him continues to be published.[1]

These extracts show two aspects of Cobbett's identity as a popular journalist. On the one hand, he speaks to his readers; hails them, whether as friend or foe; shows in his writing that he *knows* them, is identified with them. On the other hand, Cobbett faces up to the powerful, observes and reports how *they* regard the people, and discloses their material interests in so doing. Cobbett creates a space for himself between the people, as he conceives them, and their political masters. He establishes himself as a representative voice, speaking to the powerful on behalf of the weak.

Cobbett came from the rural and small-town world of southern England in the eighteenth and early nineteenth centuries. Most of his *Rural Rides* are journeys across these southern counties, even though it was for the industrial constituency of Oldham that he was elected as a Member of Parliament after the Reform Bill in 1832. He writes with deep knowledge and affection of this countryside, his

---

1. Two good biographies are George Spater, *William Cobbett: the Poor Man's Friend* (2 Vols), Cambridge University Press, 1982; Ian Dyck, *William Cobbett and Rural Popular Culture*, Cambridge University Press, 1992. A collection of Cobbett's writings, *Cobbett on Ireland*, edited by Denis Knight, was published by Lawrence and Wishart in 1984.

chief pleasure being in its cultivation, and in the harmonious relationship, where he found it, between the land and its occupants. (This is a quite different view of nature from some of his Romantic contemporaries' pleasure in wild, mountainous places, devoid of human habitation, the location of the sublime.)

I have now seen (for I have, years back, seen the Vales of Taunton, Glastonbury, Honiton, Dorchester and Sherburne) what are deemed the richest and most beautiful parts of England; and if called to name the spot which I deem the brightest and most beautiful, and of its extent, best of all, I should say the villages of North Bovant and Bishopstrow, between Heytesbury and Warminister in Wiltshire; for there is, as appertaining to rural objects, everything that I delight in. Smooth and verdant downs in hills and valleys of endless variety as to height and depth and shape, rich corn-land, unencumbered by fences; meadows in due proportion, and those watered at pleasure; and lastly the homestead and villages, sheltered in winter and shaded in summer by lofty and beautiful trees; to which may be added roads never dirty and a stream never dry.

> *Rural Rides*, Burghclere, Hampshire, 2 October 1826
> Everyman edition, Vol. 2, p135

This was a stratified and paternalistic society, in which most significant relationships were of a face-to-face kind.[2] But it was a society in transition. The growth of London – the Wen, as Cobbett usually called it – was already having great effects on agriculture and trade, and Cobbett spent his political life campaigning against the abstract financial systems of public debt, borrowing, taxes, and the printing of paper money which were the inflationary means, as we would now say, of paying for the wars with France. The political life of this pre-Reform Bill society also took place on a face-to-face scale, not least because of the central role of small numbers of aristocratic families and their clients at the heart of this system.

Cobbett insisted on individual voice at a moment when the more impersonal and large-scale society which would submerge such voices into anonymous

---

2. Harold Perkin's *The Origins of Modern English Society, 1780-1880* (1969) describes this paternalistic order.

aggregates was coming into being. His own highly-recognisable voice was one element of this insistence on the actual individual experience, as he presented his own observations, encounters and feelings to his readers in his efforts to inform them. He also addressed his opponents as named individuals, in the open letters to the powerful (members of the government, dukes, rival leaders of opinion like Wilberforce and Malthus), which was one of the main rhetorical devices of his journalism. For example:

To Parson Malthus

On the Rights of the poor and on the cruelty recommended by him to be exercised toward the poor.

PARSON,
I have, during my life, detested many men; but never anyone so much as you. Your book on POPULATION contains matter more offensive to my feelings even than that of the Dungeon-Bill. It could have sprung from no mind not capable of dictating greater cruelty than any recorded in the history of the massacre of St Bartholemew. Priests have, in all ages, been remarkable for cool and deliberate and unrelenting cruelty; but it seems to have been reserved for the Church of England to produce one who has a just claim to the atrocious pre-eminence. No assemblage of words can give an appropriate designation of you; and, therefore, as being the single word which best suits the character of such a man, I call you *Parson*, which, amongst other meanings, includes that of Boroughmonger tool…

In your book you show that, in certain cases, a *crowded* population has been attended with great evils, a great deal of unhappiness, misery, and human degradation. You then, without any reason to bear you out, predict, or leave it to be clearly inferred, that the same is likely to take place in England. Your principles are almost all false; and your reason, in almost any instance, is the same. But it is not my intention to waste time upon your abstract matter. I shall come, at once, to your practical result, to your recommendation to the Boroughmongers to pass laws to *punish the poor for marrying* …

The bare idea *of a law* to punish a labourer and artisan for *marrying*: the bare idea is enough to fill one with indignation and horror. But when this is moulded into a distinct proposal and strong recommendation, we can hardly find patience sufficient to restrain us from breaking out into a volley of curses on the head of the proposer, be he who he may...

But, before I proceed further, let us have your proposition before us in your own insolent words; first observing, that, at the time when you wrote your book, the Boroughmongers first began to be alarmed at the increase of the *Poor-rates.* They boasted of wonderful *national prosperity*; wonderful ease and happiness; wonderful improvements in agriculture; but still the poor-rates *wonderfully increased.* Indeed, they seem to increase with the increase in the Boroughmonger's *national prosperity*; which might I think very fairly be called the eighth wonder of the world.

Being in this puzzle, the Boroughmongers found in a priest the advocate of a method to rid them of their ground of alarm. You, overlooking all the *real causes* of the increase of the paupers, assumed, without any internal proof, and against all experience, that *the giving of relief* is the cause of the evil, and then you came to your proposition of a *remedy*. The words, the infamous words, are as follows:

To this end I should propose a regulation to be made, declaring that no child born from any marriage taking place after the expiration of a year from the date of the law; and no illegitimate child born two years from the same date, should ever be entitled to parish assistance. After the public notice, which I have proposed, had been given, to the punishment of nature HE should be left; the punishment of severe want; all parish assistance should be rigidly denied him, HE should be taught that the laws of nature had doomed him and his family to starve; that HE had no claim on society for the smallest portion of food; that if HE and his family were saved from suffering the utmost extremities of hunger, HE would owe it to the pity of some kind benefactor, to whom HE ought to be bound by the strongest ties of gratitude...

You talk of the '*punishment of nature*'; you talk of the '*laws of nature* having doomed him and his family to *starve.*' Now in the first place, the laws of nature, the most imperative of her laws, bid him *love* and seek the gratification of that passion in the way that leads to the procreation of his species. The laws of nature bid man as well as woman desire to produce and preserve children. Your prohibition is in the face of these imperative laws; for you punish the illegitimate as well as legitimate offspring...

Your muddled parsons's head has led you into confusion here. The *law of nature* bids a man *not starve* in the midst of plenty, and forbids his being punished for taking food wherever he can find it. Your law of nature is sitting at Westminster, to make the labourer pay taxes, to make him fight for the safety of the land, to bind him in allegiance, and when he is poor and hungry, to cast him off to starve, or, to hang him if he takes food to save his life! That is your law of nature; that is a parson's law of nature. I am glad, however, that you blundered on the laws of nature; because that is the very ground on which I mean to start in endeavouring clearly to establish the *rights of the poor*; upon which subject I have, indeed, lately offered some observations to the public, but on which subject I have not dwelt so fully as its importance seemed to demand; especially at a time when the poor ought to understand clearly what their rights are. (pp1-2)

Political Register, May 1819

Readers will note the similarity between Malthus's thinking, and Peter Lilley's proposals for limiting benefits to single mothers. Lilley's ideas did not, however, bring forth quite such a ferocious reaction as Cobbett's. It may signify progress of a kind that it is not now just HE who is being held responsible by the present government, but SHE.

The *Rural Rides* are full of love for the fertile land and its people, as well of hatred for the powerful whom Cobbett sees as parasitic upon them:

Beyond the garden is a large clump of lofty sycamores, and in these a most populous rookery, in which, of all things, I delight. (Vol 2, p32)

A very fine morning; a man, *eighty-two years of age*, just beginning to mow the short-grass in the garden; I thought it, even when I was young, the *hardest work* that man had to do.*To look on*, this work seems nothing; but it tries every sinew in your frame if you go upright and do your work well.This old man never knew how to do it well, and he stoops, and he hangs his scythe wrong; but with all this, it must be a surprising man to mow short-grass at *eighty*. *I wish I* may be able to mow short-grass at eighty! (Vol 2, p33)

It is part of our system to have certain *families*, who have no particular merit, but who are to be maintained, without why or wherefore, at the public expense, in some shape, or under some name, or other, it matters not under what shape or what name. If you look through the old list of pensioners, sinecurists, parsons and the like, you will find the same names everlastingly recurring. They seem to be the sort of creatures that have an *inheritance in the public carcass*, like the maggots that some people have in their skins. This family of Dampier seems to be one of those. What, in God's name, should have made one of these a bishop and the other a judge! I never heard of the smallest particle of talent that either of them possessed. This rector of Wyly was another of them. There was no harm in them that I know of beyond that of living upon the public, but what were their merits? They had none to distinguish them and to entitle them to the great sum they received; and under any other system than such a system as this they would, in all human probability, have been gentleman's servants or little shopkeepers. I dare say there is some of the *breed* left, and, if there be, I would pledge my existence that they are, in some shape or other, feeding upon the public. However, thus it must be , until that change come which will put an end to men paying *fourpence* in tax upon a pot of beer.(Vol 2, p62)

Malthus's proposals aroused Cobbett to such fury because they abused what he saw as the fruitful, natural order of life.

Whilst Cobbett addressed his opponents as named individuals, he usually appealed to those whom he defended in their collective identity. This was often in the conventional form of 'to the Electors of Honiton', and other places, but he also, more radically, conjured up entire social classes or their sub-sections, as 'To the Journeymen and Labourers of England', or 'Address to the Country Gentlemen'. Social classes were being constructed and defined as their members were invited to recognise themselves in these terms. Cobbett devoted particular efforts, as is shown in the second extract above, to maintaining or achieving an identification between the farmers and the labourers, against the corrupt system which, he believed, was oppressing both. He did this by evoking their common interests, and the farmers' natural sense of obligation to their employees, but above all by continually reminding them of the vileness of their common oppressor:

To the Working People of England, On the Emigration that is
now going on

Then, as to the *fact*, if there be *too many working people in England*; and let
me stop to observe that it is only the *working people* that these tax-eating
vagabonds say are *too numerous*. They do not say that the pensioners, the
sinecure folks, the grantees, the allowance-folks, the half-pay-folks, the
military academy folks, *the poor* parsons (whom we are taxed to relieve), the
placemen, the taxing people, the fundholders, the swarms of clerks in
offices; they do not say, that these endless crews of idlers, all of whom live
on the fruits of the people's labour; the tax-eating vagabonds do not say, that
these are too numerous! (p231)

Two-Penny Trash, May 1832

O ur modern placemen (they still seem mainly to be men), the new
millionaire directors of the public utilities enriched at the public
expense, and the much larger numbers of those who have benefitted
from the huge tax concessions to the rich in the past sixteen years, seem to be
less tellingly characterised in print than their equivalents were in Cobbett's day.
The conversion of the heads of our former public suppliers of necessities like
water into monopolistic capitalists reminds one of the conversion into
entrepreneurs of the former state industry and party bosses of Eastern Europe.
One is curious to know how large the donations to the funds of the hard-up
Conservative Party will be from the grateful recipients of these expropriations of
the public wealth. One aim of the National Lottery must have been to create the
general illusion that anyone can now become a millionnaire overnight, though
the chances given by a lottery ticket are rather than less than come from a seat
on one of these Boards. Of course the new profits from the utilities also come at
the expense of the present-day labourers who have been made redundant and
early-retired in order to improve the company balance-sheets.

Cobbett also appealed to his audience's common identity as citizens of a
particular place ('To the People of Hampshire') and above all as citizens of their
country ('Letter to all True-hearted Englishmen, on the Suspension of the
Habeas Corpus Act, the Sedition Bills, etc.'). Cobbett, in his campaigns against
state oppression during the counter-revolutionary wars, is one of the main sources

of the rhetoric of the 'free-born Englishman' which Edward Thompson celebrated in his writing. The various discursive constructions of collective identity in Cobbett's writing would be a rich field of study in themelves.

Cobbett, however, consistently sought to root these new collective identities in particular experiences. This is one reason for the extraordinary and delightful oscillations in *Rural Rides* between topographical description, agricultural notes, denunciation provoked by some place (for example 'the Accursed Hill' of Old Sarum, the most notorious rotten borough) or by arriving near the property of some notable, encounters with individuals met along the way, and political reflections. Often these topics touch each other off, for example after he has ridden up the 'Accursed Hill' and on the way instructed an unfortunate passer-by on the reasons why times are so hard for him:

> The hill is very steep, and I dismounted and led my horse up... It was impossible to stand on this accursed spot without swelling with indignation against the base and plundering and murderous sons of corruption. (Vol 2, p57)

Cobbett has a different tone for his different audiences, as he himself explains. The contents of the *Trash* 'are to be pithy; they must consist of opinions shortly stated, of striking and useful facts, and of narration at once brief, clear and interesting.' ... 'I shall... NUMBER THE PARAGRAPHS, to make them of easy reference.' The *Register*, on the other hand, 'must be devoted to essays of considerable length, to subjects for *discussion*. *Rural Rides* was perhaps addressed mainly to his more prosperous farmer readership, the very people whom he describes as coming to his meetings, and putting him up for the night on his journeys. But he knows that his writings will often be read aloud, to groups assembled to hear them, and this influences his style.

But he had another way of rooting his agitation in individual experiences, and that was through publicising the cases of victims of oppression by the law, and of making sure they were known and commemorated. There were three of these cases in particular – 'HENRY COOKE of MICHELDEVER (who) was *hanged* for striking BINGHAM BARING without doing him any harm at all' (here is an early appearance of the Baring family perhaps), and Joseph and Robert Mason, who were sentenced to death and subsequently transported for 'taking the mildest and most inoffensive part in these risings' (Captain Swing). 'He little thought,' said Cobbett of Joseph Mason, 'that being one of a crowd who extorted a few shillings from a farmer or a parson, and of which he neither extorted nor took any part, would be to commit an act of '*highway robbery*,' for which he should be dragged from his wife and child, condemned to death, and sent into slavery for life.' 'If the people at MANCHESTER, or any other place,' wrote Cobbett in 1832, 'shall think fit to put me into Parliament, I pledge myself that is not the last that shall be heard of JOSEPH and ROBERT MASON, and of HENRY COOKE.' Cobbett thought that the Mason brothers were in reality being punished for Joseph's role in a petition he had delivered to the king, that 'the infamous *Times* newspaper, which from first to last sought the blood of these people', falsely claimed had been instigated by Cobbett himself. He felt a good deal of responsibility for the fate of these men, as a result, and often referred with affection thereafter to the 'ten hard parishes' from which the men had come.

T he broader issues behind these cases were the desperate straits into which the labouring poor were being placed by scarcity, and by the harsh enforcement of laws – both the strengthened game-laws, defending the privileges of land-owners, and the many measures to put down protests – deployed against them. Cobbett wrote with great sympathy of the protests of the rick-burners and rioters of Luddism and Captain Swing, holding that men had a primary entitlement to avoid starvation, and arguing that these protests should be seen not as a revolutionary conspiracy, but as spontaneous, understandable and natural protests, which should be taken as a signal that reform was urgently needed.

In writing about Henry Cooke and the Masons, Cobbett is the forerunner of contemporary writer-advocates of the cases of the harshly-treated – one thinks for example of Paul Foot, encouraging his readers to bring instances of injustice to his attention, and then using his newspaper columns to seek remedy for them.

All these forms of writing – the constructed personal 'voice' of the columnist, the open address to the named public figure, the taking-up of the cause of an unknown victim of injustice – are of course now everyday devices of newspaper and broadcast journalism. But with the difference that few contemporary journalist voices stand in a representative relationship to any definite public. It is unfortunately part of the dominant code of radio and television journalism that such voices should *not* be partisan – that is to say, speak from any particular political location. Jeremy Paxman, Kirsty Wark, or Jon Snow can be and are independent, irreverent, tough-minded, and intelligent, but they are not allowed, in their public roles, to uphold any consistent or coherent point of view. I suppose one has to add that this convention of impartiality does spare us, in Britain, the right-wing talk-show hosts who have apparently been so influential in the rise of the Republican Right in the United States. But Cobbett was one of the main inventors of the signed newspaper column, and of the Parliamentary report.

Cobbett had to work hard to establish and maintain this 'voice'. One of the purposes of the journeys he reported in *Rural Rides* was to investigate with his own eyes what was happening to the people, in order that he could write with authenticity about it. These were also, as IanDyck, author of the most interesting recent book on Cobbett, has said, the lecture-tours of a political organiser and speechmaker. Cobbett's political work on behalf of the agricultural workers was thus analogous to that of a modern trade union organiser. He went from place to place, doing meeting after meeting, often staying, as he tells us, in the homes of 'friends', whom he has never previously met. He went around as a public figure, always pleased to tell his readers when it turns out that his reputation and that of the *Register* have preceded him. Cobbett did not lack self-esteem. In a society in which power and status belong to notables, Cobbett was clearly quite a notable himself, but one who positioned himself on the side of the people, against 'the Thing,' or the system.

Cobbett's credibility as an antagonist of the powerful required him to put himself in jeopardy and endure hardship. He was imprisoned in Newgate for two years from July 1810 for a seditious libel in an article in which he had protested against the flogging for mutiny of soldiers in the militia at Ely. During his imprisonment, he continued to bring out his *Political Register* with the byline, 'State Prison, Newgate'. Fearing that he would be prosecuted and imprisoned again he fled to America in 1817, and brought out the *Register* from there for over two years until his return to England. This flight did him some political damage, showing how important it was that a radical spokesman should be willing to share the risks of those he represents.

Cobbett was an agent of modernity, in several respects, even though his objective was to defend and restore an earlier England in which the labourers had bread and meat:

To the Labourers of England

All of you who are sixty years of age can recollect that bread and meat, and not wretched potatoes, were the food of the labouring people: you can recollect that every industrious, labouring man brewed his own beer, and drank it by his own fire-side; you can recollect that, at every wedding, and every christening, such labouring men had a barrel of ale in the house provided for the occasion; you can recollect when the young people were able to provide money before they were married, to purchase decent furniture for a house, and had no need to go to the parish to furnish them with a miserable nest to creep into... (p3)

Two-Penny Trash, March 1831

He achieved a weekly sale of 50,000 for the *Political Register* in the 1820s, in a population of eight or nine million. He published numerous books, marketing them as 'Mr Cobbett's Works,' through the pages of his newspapers. These were pioneering works of popular education; *Cobbett's English Grammar* – which sold 100,000 copies in its first 15 years, and gave as examples of its nouns of number 'such as Mob, Parliament, Rabble, House of Commons, Regiment, Court of King's Bench, Den of Thieves, and the like'[3] – *The English Gardener*, and *Cottage Economy*. In the *History of the Protestant Reformation*, Cobbett traced 'the Thing' and the privileged position of the aristocracy back to the expropriation of the monasteries in the sixteenth century. He argued that the numbers and size of parish churches proved how much more populous the countryside had been in the past, and that the monasteries had taken their obligations of charity much more seriously than the modern clergy. His farming at Kensington must have been for the London market which he disliked so much. He was a seed-distributor, and an importer of new crops from his days in America – 'Cobbett's Indian Corn', and locust trees, for example. One of Cobbett's most modern inventions was his marketing of himself as a public institution, just prior to the time when more representative collective organisations developed.

There is, from a modern point of view, a less admirable side to Cobbett's

---

3. This is quoted in Spater, *op. cit.*

powerful persona. He is persistently and offensively racist, towards Jews, 'the Scotch' and the Quakers, whom he associated with the parasitic financial system, and whom he thought lived off the labour of others, and towards 'Negroes'. The former hostility belongs to his generic hatred of the city and its ways, in particular the ways of gaining wealth without apparently producing anything useful. The second form of racial abuse in part came from plain prejudice, and in part because he saw the contemporary anti-slave trade agitation as a moral rival of his own campaigns to defend the English labourer. The same William Wilberforce who led the anti-slavery campaign was a supporter of the government's repressive legislation at home, and was hated above all as a hypocrite:

To William Wilberforce, on the State of the Cotton Factory Labourers, and on the speech of Andrew Ryding, who cut Horrocks with a cleaver.

WILBERFORCE,
I have you before me in a canting pamphlet; upon your conduct and character, as developed in that pamphlet, it is my intention to remark fully, at some future time. At present, I shall use it only thus: to ask you what need there was, or what propriety there was, in spending your time in writing and publishing 'An Appeal to the religion, justice and humanity of the Inhabitants of the British Empire in behalf of the Negro slaves in the West Indies'; to ask you what propriety, what sense, what sincerity, there could be in your putting forth this thing, in the present state of the country? It is to the inhabitants of the *British Empire* that you appeal, in this heap of shameless cant. *Empire* in your teeth, you retailer of bombast! The French do not call their country an *Empire*. They, possessing real wealth and strength, are content to call their country what it was always called, that is to say a Kingdom... (p1)

Political Register, August 1823

Cobbett's aggressiveness here (apart from its habitual quality) is provoked by Wilberforce's apparent indifference to the condition of the labouring class in Britain, which Cobbett holds (hardly convincingly) is worse than that of the slaves in the West Indies. And by Wilberforce's being on matters affecting public order a supporter of the government. Cobbett's position on these issues, according to his biographer George Spater, is in fact less appalling than appears from this passage. Cobbett asserted that 'I hold all slavery in abhorrence', and he never used coffee, sugar or rum because they were the products of slavery. He shows great hostility in his writings to those who seek to profit from the colonies, 'negro slave-drivers' and others. His chauvinistic point, however, was that problems at home should come first.

Cobbett's construction of 'Englishness' does at times come near to rant (Raymond Williams described him as 'this attractive old roaring man'), though mostly he is saved from this by his hatred of suffering, his love of life, and his courage in fighting the powerful. Now that we know how potentially multivalent any form of discourse always is, it is not difficult to see right-wing, as well as left-wing, denunciations of public expenditures, nest-feathering, and job-creation spinning off from Cobbett's rhetoric. One can hear other more reactionary tones – even the patriarchal sermonising of Johnny Speight's Alf Garnett – in Cobbett's voice, as well as those of an exemplary democratic populist. But he was something of a one-man institution – this is probably what it took to be a pioneer of democracy before the Reform Bill – and some of his failings of prejudice, repetition, and self-assertiveness are to be explained by this.

None of this justifies the neglect of Cobbett as a contributor to both democratic and socialist political traditions in Britain. This neglect derives from the fact that he wrote largely for popular audiences, and not as a formally-trained scholar or philosopher. Tom Paine has until recently suffered a similar though lesser neglect in academic philosophy (John Keane's recent biography is another important step towards changing this situation). Thus it is the case that the major agitations for democracy, and some of the most cogent and powerful statements of democratic principles, preceded by fifty years the canonical philosophical texts by John Stuart Mill through which the idea of democracy has been most studied in English universities. Something similar can be said about Cobbett's ideas on the moral entitlements due to labour.

To the Journeymen and Labourers of England, Wales, Scotland, and Ireland

Whatever the pride of rank, of riches, or of scholarship, may have induced some men to believe, or to affect to believe, the real strength and all the resources of a country, ever have sprung, and ever must spring, from the *labour* of its people… and hence it is that this nation, which is so small in numbers and so poor in climate and soil compared with many others, has, for many ages, been the most powerful nation in the world: it is the most industrious, the most laborious, and, therefore, the most powerful. Elegant dresses, superb furniture, stately buildings, fine roads and canals, fleet horses and carriages, numerous and stout ships, warehouses teeming with goods; all these, and many other objects that fall under our view, are so many marks of national wealth and resources. But all these spring from *labour*. Without the journeyman and the labourer, none of them could exist; without the assistance of their hands, the country would be a wilderness, hardly worth the notice of an invader. (p1)

Political Register, November 1816

This is something like the discovery of socialism, even if a very particularly British socialism. But it is the vehemence and vigour of Cobbett's radical writing that is most missed today.

156

Six Poems

Growing up German

Growing up when the killing was over,
the dead tidied away, we knew our history
as electricity is known, by its effects:
fathers reduced to photographs,
dud bombs, American soldiers, refugees.
The rest came from books, much later,
and it didn't add up. So we asked.

When our fathers died defending murder,
how shall we remember them?
Where shall we shelve the pastoral
haywagon and willow pipes?
What are we to live by if we dare not
trust even your button collections
or the way you folded the sheets?

Susanne Ehrhardt

Selfdefence

Wishing for balm oil baths
he comes shielded with knives

Wishing for kisses
he comes cloaked in abuses

Wishing for learning
he comes in shouts of all-knowing

Hearing he is humbled
he comes in noisiest fanfare.

James Berry

Parousia

I could imagine a biblical presence:
a darkening of matter like this charged
sky, before the coming of the storm,
the lime trees around the station
streaming with rain,
a stiffening, a scab of pus and blood,
a wound on the air, a voice above the rooves,
– but I think, if it came, there would be
something more subtle:
a blur at the corner of vision, a trick of the light,
or the notion that things have shifted
closer: streetlamps and walls,
privet hedges, trees, the neighbour's door,
intimate, all of a sudden, and out in the dark
the animals defined and understood
– vixen and weasel, barn owl and pipistrelle –
granted their privileged moments to sleep and kill.

John Burnside

Poetry Course

Shaun doctored the Spaghetti Bolognese
with Dettol. It was just a gesture.
He didn't have much subtlety with words.

The rest of us cooked omelettes instead
but Shaun had second helpings. 'Disinfectant's
great, try it!' he said. He puked all night.

A self-announced Punk-Fascist-Socialist, did he think
we'd try to wash his mouth out with daffodils?
(His mum had sent him on the poetry course.)

'Cunt', 'screw' and 'fuck' were clearly meant to shock
but sounded quite Romantic, even Rousseauesque.
We lingered with the melody of 'Rivers of Shit'...

It makes you think of rustic innocence –
a paradise of celandines and sprouts
before low-level radioactive waste

meandered through the meadows of organic verse.
Shaun was treading water like a kingcup,
his hair still golden, somehow, at the roots.

Sylvia Kantaris

The children's assault

Robins and blackbirds and thrushes
at four and five.
Your drawing-room was a mess, trashed
by Linda and Lucy,
those dear little girls.
The curtains were a rag mess, half off,
and vests, sheets dragged in, rucked
into pretend hideouts by the radiator,
your rugs driven into wigwams,
your china dismembered on the carpet,
white arms, heads rolling here, there,
the skins of party balloons
littered like so many pursed lips –

But here you stand telephoning, unblinking,
waiting to be straightened out,
calm as cucumbers –
Nothing to be done but to catch
that Lucy, that Linda and the rest of the children –
screw them into understanding –
They walk insouciantly over the lawn's curve,
cheeking each other, falling over their socks,
cheerful as tomatoes.

Remember me who became
saddled with the duty of the room,
powerless in changes.
Your eyes glide past my hands,
broken, my broken arms, my head…
How I have kept it neat for you two,
don't I glue your good room together again…
But each night those children
turn it over in terrible song.

Judith Kazantzis

Death of an Afternoon Woman

('Something is pushing them
To the sides of their own lives.' *Afternoon*, Philip Larkin).

A hand, was it? Or something heavier,
Swooping with the down-swing,
Its shoes packed with meat
And little bones chipped from my own?
I didn't try to resist.
I'd be kicked anywhere,
Sit smiling on the one-plank seat.
Was life mine to be lived?
Almost unwillingly,
As each bright load fell up,
Fell back, strengthening, laughing,
Separable, I could feel
The rush of another weather,
The verse-horse tugging me
Against the slowing strokes
Of iron on sky.
And I was realigned.
My life? Thanks. I'll keep it.
Keepers, losers, they whispered.
Then I woke up.
If this is my house, it's mist.
If this is my land, water,
Constantly traversed
By floating heels, child-hands,
Wide open, chainless.
The force I feared is so small
I could catch it in a caress
And run with it to wherever
It tells me our home is.

Carol Rumens

Consuming in the face of hatred

Lifestyle and the gay advance

Simon Edge

The lesbian and gay movement has emerged as a major political force. But it has done so at a time when male gay consumerism seems to signal – as elsewhere in society – the triumph of market alienation and depoliticisation. Simon Edge explores this conundrum and argues that the visibility of positive lifestyles engendered by consumerism can be an integral part of the political process.

It has become fashionable to talk of one-issue movements as the basis for activist politics in the 1990s. The unremitting onslaught of the Tory years has left the old-fashioned political protestor looking like the breed of a bygone decade, and small wonder. The chant 'Maggie Maggie Maggie, out out out!' had become an ingrained cultural ritual by the time the invocation finally seemed to work. Euphoria turned to numb shock as Thatcher's departure yielded something more terrible – an administration whose brutality and petty-minded vindictiveness increased as its competence and moral authority ebbed. For the dissenting, the Major years have brought the awful realisation that none of the marching, campaigning or badge-wearing made a jot of difference. For better or for worse, grand catch-all schemes of ideology have become the exclusive preserve of Tony Blair and the shadowy Peter Mandelson, and the alternatives are either to get on board or to stand muttering about Clause IV on the mesozoic sidelines. On an individual level, the possibility of making a difference and effecting real change has become restricted to tiny little pocket-handkerchief areas of the political map. These seem unimportant until national politicians are caught out by them, like the siting of a motorway extension or the export of live animals.

The emergence of effective activism in unexpected political domains has been exemplified by the muscle-flexing of two interest groups which previously seemed too peripheral to merit much outside attention: the disabilities lobby and the lesbian and gay movement. This article is concerned with the emergence of the latter group as a mainstream political force.

Only a few years ago it would have been inconceivable that the pros and cons of lesbian and gay rights should be the centre-stage preoccupation they have become today. Whereas in the 1980s the merest hint at support for gay issues was enough to guarantee a Labour politician or local authority an eternal 'loony left' label, sixty-odd Tory MPs can now vote for an equal gay age of consent with apparent electoral impunity, and the Archbishop of Canterbury can appoint a self-declared 'sexually ambiguous' bishop to the number two spot in the Church of England without any great fuss. (Dr Carey's mind-boggling declaration this February that homosexuals are made in God's image caused barely a ripple.) The last two years have brought Britain's first gay law reforms since 1967, with minor changes to the draconian anti-gay laws in the military and the merchant navy as well as the 'compromise' reduction of the age of consent from twenty-one to eighteen (compared with sixteen for heterosexuals). Furthermore, the disgraceful retention of an unequal age of consent should not be allowed to obscure the fact that the campaign for outright equality by the lesbian and gay lobby group Stonewall came within an inch of success – a dozen or so changed votes would have swung it. The campaign drew in a host of national organisations and public figures, including politicians previously known as dyed-in-the-wool homophobes, and won the support of traditionally gay-baiting papers like the *Evening Standard* and the *Daily Mirror*. The Home Office minister in the House of Lords warned peers off reversing the 'compromise' reduction, saying the Commons might go the whole hog if the debate were re-run, and Tory opponents of equality, including the mover of the 'eighteen' amendment, have privately admitted that sixteen will be a dead cert next time round.

So after years of being hushed up as too much of a political liability to mention, lesbians and gay men have suddenly found ourselves a safe political issue whose rights are conceded by most liberal decision-makers and opinion-formers (although there are shameful exceptions). The phenomenon can seem bizarre. For example, Tony Blair believes he should move away from the trade unions, ditch Labour's paper commitment to public ownership and perform extraordinary somersaults over education policy in order not to upset Middle England voters, but he was prepared to take an unprecedented stand against homophobia

'The love that dared not speak its name is now the love that won't shut up'

in his first party conference speech as leader, with the Tory press hanging on his every word. Within weeks of election to the top job, he also attended Stonewall's annual fundraising extravaganza at the Albert Hall – and his casual attitude to the event appeared to rub off on the tabloids, which reported an unfortunate attempt at a joke by film actor Richard Gere but passed no adverse comment on Blair's presence. The question of lesbian and gay equality is, it seems, no longer a hot potato. The shadow cabinet member who voted against an equal age of consent apparently out of concern for her slender constituency majority has been rightly criticised for her cowardice and lack of principle — but her Labour colleagues chiefly derided her stupidity for thinking the issue would matter to the electorate.

Just as gay issues have emerged into the political mainstream, leaving their advocates unscathed, so have gay people begun to step more confidently centre-stage. High-profile figures like actors John Sessions and Nigel Hawthorne, comedienne Sandi Toksvig, pop singer Neil Tennant, Tory MP Michael Brown and Bishop Derek Rawcliffe (not to mention the haplessly 'ambiguous' Archbishop-elect of York) have all stepped unharmed from the closet in the last year. Rumours fly around the Tory party that a serving minister is contemplating joining them. The right-wing academic and broadcaster David Starkey makes no effort to hide his gay activist record, but avoids being typecast; no-one bats an eyelid. Gay politics, culture, fashions and lifestyles appear to be endless subjects of press interest. The BBC runs gay radio and TV magazine shows. And woe betide the soap opera which does not feature a confident, attractive lesbian character. As the nervous hate-mongering columnists in the tabloids rightly put it, the love that once dared not speak its name has become the love that won't shut up.

If the blossoming of the gay agenda has come as a surprise to the heterosexual world, it has been a bolt from the blue for the traditional gay activist. For the last five years or so, two apparently connected processes have been at work in the gay community: a breakneck growth in the commercial gay 'scene', which has in turn fostered an explosion of so-called 'pink' services and consumer marketing; and a diminution of overt political consciousness within that scene and the wider lesbian and gay community. Of course, neither process is particularly surprising. Market orientation and depoliticisation are what we have come to expect in the post-Thatcher years. What *is* surprising is that the gay cause seems to be doing so well out of it.

The processes of commercialisation and depoliticisation are real enough. The expansion of the gay scene, exemplified by the development of Old Compton Street in London's fashionable Soho, has been quite extraordinary. Five years ago, this unremarkable thoroughfare contained a solitary gay pub. This is still thriving, but the street now also boasts a continental-style gay café/bar, a gay restaurant, an all-night gay coffee shop, a gay hairdresser, a gay cab company, a gay tanning salon and two gay retailers, one stocking pornography and sex aids as well as mainstream gay fashions and books, the other carrying more upmarket designer gear. It also hosts an annual 'queer' street carnival. Within two minutes' walk are another two large café/bars and a second gay cab firm. This relatively small area has become the commercial hub of the gay community, both in London and in the country as a whole. Its emergence has not undermined gay businesses elsewhere in the capital – Old Compton Street is simply the most concentrated example of a wider phenomenon. Although some gay and straight entrepreneurs have fallen prey to the get-rich-quick hype peddled by enthusiasts of the 'pink economy', the number of venues all over London has steadily increased, and more and more gay establishments are springing up outside the capital. London has eclipsed San Francisco, New York and Amsterdam as a gay tourist destination, which means Old Compton Street can reasonably claim to be the centre of the gay universe (although the fact that a handful of small shops and bars can merit such a description says more about gay oppression than the street itself).

As the social centres have multiplied, so has the number of spin-off services aimed at gay people. There are now three paid-for glossy magazines aimed at the lesbian or gay communities, compared with a single title just two years ago, while the free press is increasingly used by advertisers and promoters as a marketing instrument to access 'pink' spending. Gay people in the capital can use gay solicitors, mortgage brokers, therapists and dating agencies, which they can locate using a glossy directory of lesbian and gay services, updated on a regular basis and distributed free at gay venues. A major national publishing house has its own lesbian and gay department, issuing forty to fifty new non-fiction titles a year. Three all-gay video companies produce soft-core pornography, sex manuals and lesbian and gay films, and a London local radio station broadcasts a nightly gay music-and-chat show.

In this flurry of consumerism, politics seems to have been left behind. Where once the out lesbian and gay community was so small that its members inevitably needed some kind of political armoury just to get by, and political expression was part of the mortar which held the community together, the commercial flowering of gay-oriented services has provided a wealth of other ways for gay people to make positive expressions of their sexuality. Political activism, focusing on the injustices and discrimination gay people constantly face, inevitably has a negative aura. In contrast, gay-oriented consumerism offers gay people positive ways of *flaunting*, rather than bemoaning, their sexuality. The pursuit of a young-at-heart hedonism, increasingly elusive for heterosexuals of a certain age as they grapple with the pressures of childrearing and conjugal convention, is *de rigueur* for the modern urban homosexual. If affirming your sexuality comes down to a choice between (on the one hand) wearing badges, carrying placards, talking about gay oppression and getting arrested, and (on the other) mincing up and down Old Compton Street, drinking pavement-café cappuccino and wearing skin-tight lycra T-shirts to show off carefully worked-out or pool-toned physiques - the second option is quite simply more fun. Since fun is a commodity on which many gay people feel short-changed if they spent vital teenage years suffering the misery of the closet, it is barely surprising that hedonism should prove the more popular option. Once upon a time, 'glad to be gay' was a political slogan; now it's a lifestyle.

Arguments over strategies for liberation or reform of course rumble on within the gay community – there are as many opinions about the rights and wrongs of Peter Tatchell's recent 'outing' campaign as there are out gay people. And the community cared enough about the age of consent campaign to lobby MPs up and down the country, to rally in Trafalgar Square and to riot outside Parliament on the night of the vote. Nevertheless, gay activists are a diminishing breed. When the direct action group OutRage was formed in 1990, it generated large meetings and mounted a wide variety of well-attended 'actions' from one week to the next. It was at the centre of resistance when the government attempted

'Many gay activists bewail the political decay of the gay community'

to increase the penalties for gay sex offences, leading a demonstration of 10,000 people through central London. It built on the activist fervour of the Clause 28 era, and drew large numbers of young gay people into political activity. Now, the group is largely a rump around Peter Tatchell, frequently involved in messy rows with Stonewall and carrying out increasingly ham-fisted stunts. History alone will tell whether Tatchell's exhortations to bishops and MPs to come out constitute a useful contribution to the quest for gay rights, but whether they do or not, the strategy is a far cry from leading political activity in the streets. Gay activist politics are not completely dead. For example, the women-only group Lesbian Avengers, formed in 1994, bears a strong resemblance to OutRage in its early days. But the popular lifestyle paper *Boyz*, distributed free in gay venues throughout the country and glanced at by virtually every gay man using the commercial scene, sets the tone when it apologises for making the occasional editorial point which could be construed as political. It is also instructive that in the year of Stonewall's major age of consent campaign, readers of the gay press all cited HIV/AIDS groups when asked to name their 'voluntary organisation of the year': responding to the AIDS crisis is evidently considered a more appropriate and laudable focus for voluntary efforts than working for gay law reform or liberation.

Many gay activists, particularly those who identify with the left, look at both the rise in consumerism and the decline in overt political consciousness, blame the one for the other, and bewail the political decay of the gay community. 'The growth and development of a lesbianandgay (*sic*) commercial scene built on Pilsner and porn and now diversifying into financial services has overwhelmed collective endeavour and replaced it with individual consumption,' writes a trade union activist in the gay left magazine *Rouge*.

Being able to draw up a will, arrange the buying of a house etc through a firm of solicitors who are 'gay friendly' is very good and I don't mock it. The Pink Pound has got *Gay Times* and other lesbian and gay literature into mainstream retailers such as W H Smith, increasing their visibility and accessibility for lesbians and gays in the process of coming out. But to confuse this with liberation is a fundamental mistake... You cannot 'consume' yourself out of being sacked purely because of your sexuality, being demonised because you are a lesbian teacher or being jailed for having sex at the age of seventeen.

This analysis is palpably mistaken. A knee-jerk rejection of consumerism because it makes a fat profit for someone is no bad instinct, particularly given the speciousness of some of the claims made by gay entrepreneurs about the purity of their communitarian motives. Furthermore, the decline in political consciousness is indubitably linked to the establishment of hedonism as a gay totem for the 1990s: a lifestyle press which tirelessly promotes the notion that it is unfashionable or 'naff' to care about anything other than the price of sunbeds, the latest dance mix, or the quality of the current batch of Ecstasy tablets clearly has something to answer for. Nevertheless, an outright rejection of mindless consumerism does not explain the social and political gains which the gay community appears to be winning at a rate of knots. It relies on the mistaken assumption that activism is the primary motor of political change. In reality, there is a far greater force at work, which is intrinsically tied up with consumerism and the creation of positive lesbian and gay lifestyles: visibility.

The cornerstone of gay politics, and the feature that distinguishes oppression on the grounds of sexuality from any other form of discrimination, is the need to 'come out'. Coming out to ourselves and those around us is for most gay people the first step on the path to the rewarding social and sex life which is usually impossible in the closet. For many it is a terrifying prospect, with fears of ridicule, rejection, ostracism, violence, sacking or eviction looming large. Some or all of these fears may turn out to be justified, but however painful the process is, few try to go back in the closet once they have come out.

But vital though self-fulfilment is, coming out represents something further.

The closet is the crutch which props up anti-gay prejudice. The recent upsurge in support for outing is a symptom of gay frustration at the hypocrisy of closeted public figures who uphold homophobic laws or traditions, and there is no doubt that the world would be an easier place for gay people to live in if such high-profile closetry did not exist. It would be harder for Tory MPs to sustain anti-gay legislation if the public knew what some of them got up to in private. The same goes for senior bishops who preach fire and brimstone in public (and sack junior gay clergy) while leading active gay lives in private; or for closeted gay judges and magistrates who hand down stiff sentences to hapless gay souls convicted of 'crimes' which would have been quite legal had the perpetrators been heterosexual. The world would also be an easier place for us if the heterosexual in the street had any conception how many of his or her idols and role models are lesbian or gay - and it would certainly be harder for writers in the tabloid press to make such a handsome living out of ridiculing homosexuality. Knowledge of how many red-blooded Hollywood heart-throbs are gay might (heaven forbid) encourage the subversive notion that a man can love another man and still be masculine. The teenage girls who hold up placards at boy-band concerts inviting the singer with the big smile to do his worst with them might be a little miffed if they knew what *really* made him smile – but would they really find his condition a ridiculous, disgusting or pitiful one?

But gay men and lesbians in positions of authority or influence who hide their sexuality from the general public are a distraction from the real 'enemy' – the closet which imprisons thousands and thousands of ordinary homosexual men and woman, perhaps for their entire lives. Drawing these people out should be the primary aim for anyone who cares about gay liberation – not to mention about those individuals themselves – for the simple reason that strength lies in numbers. On the most basic level, Stonewall could lead a tough campaign over the gay age of consent in 1994 because tens of thousands of lesbians and gay men up and down the country were prepared to write to their MPs and say 'I'm your constituent, I'm gay, and I want you to listen to me' – a resource denied to the handful of brave fighters who pioneered gay law reform in the 1950s and 1960s. Perhaps more importantly, confident, out, gay people play a major role in breaking down prejudice in the rest of society. Every opinion poll ever carried out on attitudes to homosexuality has shown that people are less likely to hold homophobic views if they know an openly gay person. Large numbers of gay people who haven't the slightest intention of ever returning to the closet often have no choice but to confront prejudice wherever they find it – and the more of us who do it, the less the vocal homophobes find they can get away with it. The disco bunny who can give as good as he gets to the drunken old bigot on the late-night London tube train is a better foot-soldier in the struggle to overcome homophobic prejudice than armies of banner-waving Trots – even though he may consider himself fundamentally apolitical and eschew overt political discourse.

In 1972, 2000 lesbians and gay men walked down Oxford Street in London's first official Gay Pride march. Twenty-two years later, in 1994, the number attending the Pride Festival had risen to 150,000. This exponential growth in lesbian and gay visibility has created the conditions for immeasurable improvement in the quality of gay life – for those who are able to take advantage of it, at least. The ever-growing number of lesbians and gay men prepared to stand up and assert that homosexuality is something to be proud of rather

'People who live openly gay lives which appear to be worthwhile and happy act as a beacon'

than to hide, whose self-respect is increasingly reflected in positive commercial and media images, are helping create more and more areas of society and/or parts of the country where homophobia is being pushed to the margins. You can still be sacked for being gay, but it happens to fewer people because more people, gay and straight, will make a fuss if it does. Many gay people still face intense prejudice from families, neighbours, colleagues or bigots in the street, but the fact remains that today more people are likely to come out, because fewer people are likely to bat an eyelid when they do, or because they can move to a part of the country where being gay is no big deal. Whilst homophobia is undoubtedly alive and well in far too many walks of life (often dwarfing in intensity and acceptability the other 'isms'), gay people are much less vulnerable in the Britain of 1995 than we were in that of 1970.

If visibility undermines prejudice, it also hacks away at the closet. The more people who live openly gay lives which appear to be worthwhile and happy, the more they will act as a beacon to entice others out of the closet. When my contemporaries and I were first realising we were gay, in the late 1970s, the most obviously identifiable homosexuals (I use the word advisedly) were Larry Grayson and the John Inman character in the sitcom *Are You Being Served?*. We sure as hell knew we didn't want to be like *that*, so we slammed the closet door shut again, gritted our teeth and desperately tried to convince ourselves we were heterosexual. Times have changed. The tabloids may insist that our social lives take place in a 'twilight world', but teenagers do not have to search too far to detect a confident, glamorous community, proudly boasting it has the best-looking people and the most 'happening' nightlife, and smugly

'The discovery that a particular type of gay-identified man has a consumerist herd instinct is an entrepreneur's dream'

congratulating itself on being the most sexy – and sexed – subculture in society. For some, the reality may not always measure up to the sales pitch; but our visibility nevertheless gives young gay people an inkling that there is something out there worth leaving the closet for.

That the process is exponential should be clear to see. The willingness of large numbers of gay people to leave the closet behind and forge positive and open lives for themselves has the effect of undermining prejudice. Their openness encourages others to leave the closet too. They, in turn, lead open and happy gay lives, further undermining homophobia and nailing their own standards to the mast of lesbian and gay visibility. Thus, in the best bit of good news lesbians and gay men have had in years, the process becomes a virtuous circle, gathering its own momentum and greatly strengthening our position in society.

If the main route for undermining prejudice and for boosting the resources available to political lobbyists is the creation of an attractive gay community which closeted people want to join, the modern gay male lifestyle, with its huge emphasis on consumerism, is clearly crucial. But tolerant of diversity it isn't. Largely created by the anti-political lifestyle press, with its minimal distinction between advertising and editorial, the 1990s metropolitan culture dictates to young gay men the clothing, cosmetics, hair salon, designer drug, music, novels, videos, holiday destination, taxi firm, mortgage broker, alcohol brand and even coffee (anyone not ordering cappuccino does so at their own risk) they must choose to qualify as authentic members of the urban gay ghetto. (So far, lifestyle identities have achieved less of a stranglehold in the lesbian community, partly because it is smaller and partly because women's lesser spending power makes it appear a less attractive market to the pink promoters.) The discovery that a particular type of gay-identified man has a consumerist herd instinct and the ultimate label fetish is an entrepreneur's dream, and the pink poundsters are exploiting it for all it is worth. But the herd mentality is not the *creation* of those who stand to gain by pushing notions of a pink economy. The gay market is only such a pliant one because it is full of individuals who have grown up feeling isolated and different, from their families as well as their peers, and are yearning to develop a new sense of identity in a community where they feel comfortable. The membership badges they sport cost money, which is a boon for those with something to sell; but concomitantly, the wearing of *any* gay badge, whatever form it takes, is a shot in the arm for gay visibility, legitimacy and pride, which cannot but have a positive effect on those who are still not convinced it is worth leaving the closet.

This is not an abstract blueprint for building the community or for fighting homophobia. It is a simple description of what is actually happening. It enables us to see consumerism not as something antithetical to the achievement of lesbian and gay political gains, but as an integral part of the very process through which these gains are slowly but surely being made. This does not mean accepting the self-serving and offensive claims of gay entrepreneurs that we will be permitted to play our proper role in society once the market economy realises how much double-income-no-kids cash we have to spend. Predicating human rights on spending power is a distasteful and potentially counter-productive project. But it does involve recognising that the commercial scene has become the necessary locus in which lesbian and gay visibility and pride is being realised, and that it is proving to be the best vehicle for undermining the closet.

The commercial lesbian and gay scene undoubtedly has its shortcomings. It is clearly a problem that people may feel excluded on the grounds of looks or age, and that the 'pink' explosion has far more to offer men than women. Participation in the scene also requires a degree of disposable income – although the claim that the gay social life costs more than the heterosexual one is an outdated myth, largely peddled by Trotskyite groups which are fundamentally opposed to gay single-issue politics. But if our aim is to empty the closets, both for the sake of those who are in them and for those who are already out, lifestyle proselytising must be at least part of the way forward.

Are you concerned about genetic engineering?

In the 1990s a revolution is taking place. The incredible speed of advances in genetics is making the debates over genetic engineering increasingly central to anyone concerned with the environment, food politics, gender issues, health, civil rights or Third World development. Concern over the safety and socio-economic implications of genetic engineering, and the domination of the technological agenda by multinational corporations has already led to protests in many countries.

GenEthics News is your guide to the politics and the science of genetic engineering.

Each issue:
* reports on what industry, government and campaigners are doing
* gives clear and jargon-free information on the latest developments in genetics
* analyses the debates and provides a critical perspective on the way the new genetics is being hyped

> *Totally indispensable in an increasingly important field.* John Vidal, Environment Editor, The Guardian.
>
> *GenEthics News fills a long neglected gap.... its literate non-technical reporting is a wonderful resource for academics, activists and plain concerned citizens.* Professor Sheila Jasanoff, Department of Science and Technology Studies, Cornell University.

For subscription details and a free sample issue of GenEthics News, write to Dr. David King, GenEthics News, FREEPOST (LON 6013) PO Box 6313, London N16 0DY.

The echoing corridor

Music in the postmodern East End

Andrew Blake

Andrew Blake *argues that one can 'read' a geographical region through its popular music. The place in question is East End London, and its music reveals a vibrant and creative intermixture of ethnic subcultures.*

Music surrounds us so thoroughly that we hardly ever ask what it means. Part of the answer is that it helps to give a sense of place. It is time to explore this geography of sound, the relationship between sound and space. Listen to your environment. You'll hear some or all of: birdsong, wind, traffic, office or domestic equipment such as fans or kettles, and music. Music from cars, out of doors and windows, from your own radio, television, walkman or hi-fi. Most people choose to structure their places of work and relaxation with particular musical sounds. We associate music with places, often enough we quite deliberately make music to fit them. So we can *hear* places (rooms, buildings, areas) as well as see them. Listening to East London through the music which is made there, we can see as well as hear more clearly.

We can hear what is happening, how people have moved through the area and changed its culture. In his recent book *Dangerous Crossroads: Popular Music, Postmodernism and the Poetics of Place*, George Lipsitz has argued that 'while the nation state recedes as a source of identity and identification, popular culture becomes an ever more important public sphere.'[1] Lipsitz claims that transnational capital has worked both with and against patterns of migration; thanks to the development and use of new technologies of communication, and the creation of new multilingual spaces and continuities, not only the nation state but the 'country' may be obsolete as a way of forming identity. Instead of conceptualising countries, Lipsitz remarks (with acknowledgement to the work of Arjun Appadurai), we should think about 'ethnoscapes, mediascapes, technoscapes, finanscapes, ideoscapes: through which we can all inhabit many different "places" at once'. Music is a constantly present aspect of this multiscape. This is, in other words, one way of addressing the vexed question of the global and the local, of seeing them, or rather of hearing them simultaneously. The global availability of musics such as rai and reggae have meant *not* the presence of a series of universal signs or the creation of universal cultures, but their incorporation into syncretised local cultures. This article celebrates these cultures, and asks how public policy can and does encourage their creation and growth. Looking at the influences of American and more recently Asian music, and at the traces of English musical history (e.g., music hall) present in late twentieth-century music made in East London and its extended 'suburbs', I will comment in particular on the location and development of musical forms, and examine the nature and extent of music provision by the music business, by educational institutions and local government.

By approaching music this way we can see the lines of cultural gravity holding the East together. One of London's many contemporary troubles is a crisis of spatial/geographical identity. The shambolic, unplanned development of the metropolis has often caused problems (for example, of access) for people living to the east of the City; to the aggregate shambles of the centuries has been added the twentieth-century gifts of the bomb and the overflow town, to produce an 'East London' whose boundaries are limited neither by the conventional postcodes nor by the more recent physical limit of the M25 motorway. Parts of

---

1. G. Lipsitz, *Dangerous Crossroads: Popular Music, Postmodernism and the Poetics of Place*, Verso, London 1994, p.5.

Essex are, no doubt, rural, agricultural and as traditional as any country farmed by the descendants of recent Scottish immigrants may be. Many urban areas of Essex, on the other hand, are parts of London; and this does not just apply to places which are contiguous with or actually part of London boroughs such as Barking and Dagenham, Havering and Redbridge. Basildon, Southend and so on are not only parts of the East Thames Corridor; they are parts of London.

For all its insights, the recent work on the city in postmodernity has not paid much attention to this phenomenon of displaced urbanity, of commuter-distance areas which are themselves parts of the urbs, rather than the suburbs, of the city. Whatever their differences, common constructions of the

' "East London" is an urban entity which extends certainly as far as Southend'

postmodern city (the work of Harvey and Jameson among others on the spatialisation of postmodernity, and Davis more specifically on the most thoroughly imagined postmodern city, Los Angeles,[2] substantiate the fluidity of the city, its continuing developmental crisis. Work on London has noted the consistent underdevelopment of the East, its lack of infrastructure, and the comparative isolation, therefore, of many of its communities. By contrast, through the technologies of postmodernity, cultures may be drawn together, held together, created and recreated through music.

East London has been spatially extended beyond geographical integrity, but continually recreated through music. The growth of holiday resorts in the late nineteenth-century, the ribbon-development expansion until the 1930s, the development of the new towns from the 1950s, the continuing suburbanisation of Essex, and the developing commuter culture of the M25 hinterland, have all impacted on the idea of East London and the affiliations and identities of people who live outside the greater London postal area. London as an idea, an imagined space, and a source of identity, has grown and continues to grow. Musicians originating in various parts of Essex such as Southend and Canvey Island (pub rockers Dr Feelgood), Chelmsford (witty songsmiths Blur), as well as Grays (classical composer Mark-Anthony Turnage), Romford (live-techno band Underworld) and Dagenham (the Dagenham Girl Pipers), use the relatively

2. D. Harvey, *The Condition of Postmodernity*, Blackwell, Oxford 1989; F. Jameson, *Postmodernism, or, the Cultural Logic of Late Capitalism*, Verso, London 1991; M. Davis, *City of Quartz*, Verso, London 1990.

undifferentiated mode of pronunciation known as Estuarial English, and claim or have claimed London as their focus of identity. 'East London', therefore, should be read as an urban entity which, through cultural, transport and communication links, extends east certainly as far as Southend.

This should not be taken to indicate the imposition of a grid of cultural coherence. It is not easy to align age, gender, ethnicity and cultural allegiance. A paradox typical of postmodern cultural politics underlines the point. As the above identification of the extended East End indicates, 'Essex Man', and 'Essex Girl', (both of whom were the butt of much anxious, reactionary humour in the late 1980s) are a particular form of East London identity – but such an identity is not simple or uniform. This overwhelmingly white grouping is partly responsible for the introduction of a great deal of black-influenced dance music to the ears of the nation. At the high moment of late 1980s 'enterprise culture', under the very brief apparent hegemony of Thatcherism, the sound systems of Ford XR3i's being driven around Essex London were annoying older residents with the soul/dance music mix which was then being provided by illegal, 'pirate' radio stations, but not by the official national broadcasting networks of BBC radio. As the government began to offer new licenses for local and national radio services, one station seeking legitimacy, the former London pirate Kiss FM, actually boasted that it would have access principally to the young C2s of the area. Kiss FM's PR exercise argued to potential advertisers that this group – usually mortgage-free pre-mid-20s marriage – had as much disposable income as people higher up the social-scale alphabet, and a greater willingness to spend it. Advertisers were impressed; Kiss FM was duly licensed; and the pattern of officially sanctioned broadcast music changed, with mainstream BBC Radio 1 reacting to the presence of Kiss by increasing its output of dance and black-influenced music. (In January 1995, for example, Radio 1 appointed black MTV VJ Lisa L'Anson to a daytime slot aimed at precisely the young, fun-seeking C2 Kiss audience.)

The general point is that the musics of this wide area (what might be called the greater East Thames corridor) must be analysed as evidence of East London's cultural diversity – both of the affinity of certain musics with certain specific ethnic groups and cultures, and but equally of the ways in which barriers cannot hold and musics have influences well beyond their points of origin.

The location and development of musical forms

Any survey, however brief, must start with music hall. There are certain continuities and developments in staged variety entertainment by and for East Londoners, from the beginnings in the 1840s, through the mid-twentieth-century heyday of Flanagan and Allen, to the 291 Club, an all-black variety show which was held at the Hackney Empire (and televised) in 1991. This theatre was built specifically for music hall in 1901, and still hosts regular Old Time Music Hall shows aimed at older residents.[3] Music Hall also remains in a more portable form. The borough of Redbridge and the London Boroughs Grants Committee support the work of Gilt and Gaslight, a small company which provides music hall style entertainment for people in residential homes and day centres for the elderly, working all over East London.[4]

Music hall began in pubs; the connection between drinking and leisure in the East End was continued in the development of Southend as a bank holiday resort for the East London working class. It was these seaside resorts which, as White and Stallybrass claimed in their rather naive celebration of the uninhibited side of popular culture, *The Politics and Poetics of Transgression*, saw the last vestiges of the early modern festival which reversed the social order, the carnival.[5] Here in the early 1960s mods were threatened by rockers, to the prurient delight of the national press. And here, a decade later, the most important of the proto-punk pub bands, Dr Feelgood and Eddie and the Hot Rods, thrashed around in an ostentatiously semi-pro answer to pomp rock's concert-hall respectability (including that of Southend's very own progressive rock band, Procul Harum, whose greatest success, the single 'Whiter Shade of Pale', had brought Bach to the Top Ten in 1968). The pub bands' national success was based on working a circuit of Essex and London pubs; but when the Dr Feelgood album *Stupidity* headed the charts in 1976, it heralded the breakthrough of the punk ideology of autonomy, manic energy and lack of respect for major-label rock. This moment underlined again the importance of Southend and Canvey Island as centres of carnival, of the reversal of order, of

3. I am grateful to University of East London Cultural Studies graduate Helen Noake for permission to use material from her 1991 dissertation on local music hall.
4. My thanks to Havering Arts Officer Chris Cole for this information.
5. O.Stallybrass and A. White, *The Politics and Poetics of Transgression*, Methuen, London 1987.

East London on holiday; it was also a reminder of the connection between the public house and other aspects of popular culture.

There are times when popular culture's oppositional tendency is more explicitly political than mere carnivalesque celebration. In a similar musical configuration to the R'n'B-based success of the Feelgood-type pub bands, the charismatic Ian Dury began to explore his Upminster inheritance, working with pub bands like Kilburn and the High Roads and (with Chaz Jankel) the Blockheads. Dury's staples have included such militantly East London songs such as 'Billericay Dickie', 'Plaistow Patricia' and 'Upminster Kid'. Dury's 1981 album *Lord Upminster* was made with Jankel, again, but also with the innovative backing of Sly and Robbie – a West Indian rhythm section much in demand in Thatcher's early years as attempts were made to counterpose, and sometimes to combine or fuse, the musics of the oppressed (punk and reggae) in the interests of left politics. Dury's political astuteness has remained part of his appeal. Rock Against Racism, and its politicised detritus (notably Red Wedge's attempt to market the Labour Party to young people through music) also helped to throw up the rather more aggressive singer-songwriter Billy Bragg, a denizen of Barking and reliable supporter of left causes.

'In the early 1980s Depeche Mode demonstrated the alienation of Basildon man'

One could, in a more general sense, form a history of British post-war popular music from the contributions of East London and its environs. In the late 1950s Joe Brown attempted both to play rock'n'roll and to find a slot in the fading light music/music hall scene which has more recently been reoccupied by heritage culture cockneys Chas'n'Dave. At the same time trumpeter Kenny Ball (born in Ilford) helped launch the trad jazz revival in pre-Beatles Britain, while from nearby Romford Graham Bond was one of the leaders of the British blues scene which eventually, through the Yardbirds and then Cream, saw the beginnings of British rock. While during the mid-1960s Chris Farlowe effectively aped black American soul singers, another Romforder, Chris Andrews, wrote bubblegum pop for Sandie Shaw. A couple of years later Procul Harum's pomp rock was followed by the heavier offerings of Uriah Heep, one of the very few successful heavy rock/heavy metal acts from London and its environs. When all this became too much, the pub bands anticipated punk, and Billy Bragg kept its aggression going into the 1980s.

In the meantime pop made a comeback. With the gloomily robotic, underproduced synthesiser sound of the early 1980s, Basildon-based Depeche Mode demonstrated the alienation of Basildon Man. The gradual disappearance of first the drummer and then other live performers (replaced by drum machines and synthesisers, and later by tapes, samplers and sequencers) is an interesting analogue of the replacement of skilled East End labour such as typesetting (with the concomitant breaking of the unions which had dominated Fleet Street). It mirrors the Essex turn to consumerism, self-employment and individual ownership. There was nothing very dominating about synth pop, though when Depeche Mode's founder, Vince Clarke, got bored with the band and went back to Basildon to search for something different, he found the imposing musical and physical presence of Alison Moyet, whose wonderful voice illuminated Clarke's electronic doodlings in the bizarre but successful Yazoo. (Moyet's career quietened after two goodish solo albums, though the recent *Greatest Hits* album is a portent of a return; Clarke's later outlet, the splendidly camp Erasure, features a vocalist, Andy Bell, whose talents match Clarke's more aptly.)

To interpret this outline: what we have here in microcosm, from the late 1950s on, is an important aural history of British post-coloniality, in two directions. Throughout the post-war period there has been increasing cultural interaction with the USA, and especially with American music. American products have inspired British popular culture, to the resentment and hostility of many on the left who, for all the xenophobia of a reaction such as Richard Hoggart's diatribe *The Uses of Literacy*, could at least see that this was a power relationship. Elsewhere American music was welcomed and emulated: Brown, Ball and Bond each worked with a different aspect of American jazz and popular music. But it is not a simple story of cultural imperialism muscling in on 'indigenous' music. The Andrews/Sandie Shaw material, for instance, was less reliant on American models, and Procul Harum were at first part of progressive rock's engagement with European classical and folk musics (though in later incarnations their sound became more Americanised). The pub bands, for all Dury's local humour, were musically back in the territory of R&B and American rock; synth bands such as Depeche Mode qualified the Americanism once again.

British musical culture has been formed in part through this narrative of engagement, rejection and incorporation of American musics. But this is not the only story of British music, which has also been formed through a corresponding relation to the former colonies, their people and musics. The arrival in Britain since 1945 of many musicians and musics from the former colonial and imperial territories, including the West Indies, India and South Africa has produced moments of cultural miscegenation which have been enormously creative for the development of British music. (It was partly because of this that Jimi Hendrix came to London in 1966, to forge a new expressive language of guitar playing within a song-writing context which did not rely merely on blues harmonies or the controlled rhythmic repetition of R&B or soul, but also paid respect to white popular musics.) The saxophonist Joe Harriott was one of the first wave of Caribbean immigrants to Britain. As well as playing in the accepted styles of the late 1950s and after, Harriott attempted in the mid-1960s to create a specifically post-colonial music using Indian musicians and instruments as well as Caribbean and white musicians and styles; the result he called 'Indo-Jazz Fusions' – releasing an album by that title at the same time as the exposure given to the sounds of sitar and tabla by the Beatles' *Sergeant Pepper*, and batter drums and bamboo flutes by the Rolling Stones' *Their Satanic Majesties Request*. Again, it was through London that this postcolonial interaction took place, as it was from London that white Jamaican entrepreneur Chris Blackwell's Island label launched reggae as a worldwide musical form, principally through the elevation of Bob Marley as a 'rock' superstar.

The examples of Joe Harriott and Bob Marley point to the reason for the importance of Britain as a site for the transformation of pop musics – the nature and extent of post-war, post-colonial immigration. While there has been a black presence in Britain since at least as far back as the sixteenth-century, and while there have always been musical cultures associated with black people in Britain,[6] the concentration of migrating peoples in the last fifty years has created new markets for musical forms developed by and for specific ethnic groups, causing the interaction of these with existing forms and the consequent hybridisation of musics. Reggae, for example, was re-created in Britain partly because there were substantial numbers of British people of West Indian origin prepared to buy concert tickets and albums. But reggae did not remain a specifically West Indian form; it was used in other music. Important points of

---

6. P. Fryer, *Staying Power*, Pluto, London 1984; P. Gilroy, *There Ain't no Black in the Union Jack*, Hutchinson, London 1989; P. Oliver (ed), *Black Music in Britain*, Open University Press, London 1990.

crossover include the moment of punk in 1976, and the subsequent infusion of reggae in the Rock Against Racism movement of the late 1970s, and the continuing importance of dance music of all kinds to the pop charts. In particular, the astonishing success in Britain of House music since 1988 is due partly to the presence of a reggae aesthetic which makes bass and drums the most important part of the mix. (The archetypal House band name Bomb the Bass, and seminal Acid House track title 'Bass: How Low Can You Go?' emphasise this, while the revival of dub reggae in 1993 was often led by white DJs fascinated by the possibilities of detuned bass guitars, rather than young blacks who tended to dismiss it as 'parents' music.' The summer of 1994 saw the growing commercial popularity of Jungle, a hybrid reggae/ragga/rave music, in which techno drum patterns, dub and techno bass lines, and soul samples interact in a music claimed by its innovators to be specifically a London product; several point to the impossibility of such open black/white cultural interaction in New York, for example.

This perception by practitioners suggests a qualification to the arguments put forward in Paul Gilroy's book *The Black Atlantic*.[7] Gilroy claims that music has a particular importance to African-American and Caribbean people because of its power to go beyond the verbal and express the black experience of modernity in ways unavailable to language. Gilroy's argument is signalled by his subtitle, 'Modernity and Double Consciousness'. The legacy of slavery, and the continuing pervasiveness of racism, mean that feelings of placed identity are both local and African, mediated by the Atlantic as both the historic site of the middle passage and the current site of cultural exchange between the Americas, the Caribbean and Europe. Music is one of the crucial registers of this double consciousness.

> 'Americanised culture is the only way British popular culture has experienced modernity and post-modernity'

I want to make two points in relation to this very important argument. First, African-American music has a commanding place in popular culture; it is continuously available as a marker of the black presence, even taking into

---

7. P. Gilroy, *The Black Atlantic*, Verso, London 1993. For a broader version of my argument about modernity and consciousness see A. Blake, 'Listening to Britain', in A. Blake, M.Nava,B. Richards and I. McRury, *Advertising and Consumption*, Routledge, London 1996.

account the relative absence of black faces from mainstream visual culture in film and television. This relative absence from visual representation, together with the expressive power of the music, underlines the alternative, even the subversive status of black cultures in such a way as to attract many white people who wish to reject the dominant values of their societies, whether young white Americans who buy rap records or the young white Britons who, according to Dick Hebdige, have engaged in a 'phantom dialogue' with black American and Caribbean cultures since the 1950s.[8] The ethnographic work of Simon Jones, and the chart success of such cultural hybrids as Apache Indian's Handsworth-originated dancehall/ragga-with-Indian-percussion, have indicated the availability of a *performed* black identity to young British whites and Asians, in the inner cities at least. This could also be theorised as a form of double consciousness.

Second, there is more to American culture than popular music. Hebdige's classic work on subcultures was followed by *Hiding in the Light*, in which a broader view is taken of the Anglo-American relationship.[9] Cars and other products, films and film stars, the whole panoply of American culture is present in this latter text – not just African-American culture. British culture is thoroughly imbricated with American products and values. There is a White Atlantic, through which both the present and future are visualised, and heard, in Americanised terms. Indeed, it can be argued that this Americanised culture is the only way in which British popular culture has experienced modernity and experiences postmodernity. Except for those on the fringe of the extreme right, any notion of indigenous white culture is consigned to the heritage past.

Having said that, African-American music remains the single most important part of this affiliation. The Kiss FM C2s with their House-derived dance music, and the pub rockers of the Dr Feelgood era, are part of this continuing 'phantom dialogue', though it should be recognised that in the case of dance music, there is also a phantom dialogue with Europe and an envisioned European future.[10]

8. The classic text here is of course D. Hebdige, *Subculture: the Meaning of Style*, Methuen, London 1979.
9. D. Hebdige, *Hiding in the Light*, Comedia, London 1988.
10.Much dance music is European (German, Belgian and Italian especially) in origin; the use of gregorian chant in the very successful first Enigma album, and the quite casual comparison made between the work of ambient techno wizard The Aphex Twin and the German avant-garde composer Karlheinz Stockhausen, e.g. on BBC Radio 3, 18.10.1994, signal, I suspect, an attempt to distance this music from its American heritage.

We should, then, go beyond the Atlantic in assessing the sense of place available in the postmodern East End. Musical fusions made in Britain have involved many different cultural interactions. Presently, one of the most successful of these is Bhangra, a development of a Punjabi folk idiom which has kept its drums, its basic rhythms and the language and intonation of Punjabi in its songs, while incorporating Western pop, and African-American and African-Caribbean harmonies and instruments. Bhangra

'We should go beyond the Atlantic in assessing the sense of place available in the postmodern East End'

is a nodal point in a large bilingual (occasionally non-English-speaking) Asian commercial culture, in which flourishing record labels and all-day parties rival the sales of English monolingual urban culture. While Bhangra may be said to be principally a north and west London development, it is also popular in the Asian communities of East London. But it is not the only syncretic Asian pop performed here. Members of the Bangladeshi community in Tower Hamlets have produced 'Joi-Bangla', a music which, like Bhangra, blends traditional instruments and performing styles (played mainly by older people) with high technology instruments played by youngsters. In this case, unlike Bhangra, there is also an obvious inflection from rock music which, as the success of the pub bands and Uriah Heep suggests, is arguably more important in the east than elsewhere in London. The venue for this music remains a point of concern, especially since the takeover of the Tenor Clef, a small venue in Hoxton which had provided a regular public outlet for this music, by the proprietors of the Acid Jazz label which was set up in Hackney. (Newham local authority's widening of their provision for music education, which will for the first time in 1995 include funding for community-based ethnic musics, may begin to make good this deficiency).

The 'Greater East End' has also played a part in the continuing transformation of the British music scene. One important tendency should be noted. Proclamations of the death of rock'n'roll have often based their verdicts on the impact of new technology. The 1980s hegemony of first the drum machine and synthesiser, then the sampler and computer sequencer, have apparently made live-performance popular music a thing of the past, or will do so imminently. Not so; from the land of the pub bands has come music which uses new technologies to transform and extend the possibilities of live performance, not to replace it. For example, Disco Inferno (a trio from Essex, currently based in West Ham, whose voices betray the usual estuarial characteristics) use samplers not to provide endless drum loops but new banks of sounds which can be triggered from the fretboards of their guitars or the skins of their drums. The result can confuse the onlooker, since the common expectation is that bass guitars will produce bass guitar sounds and not those of the bass drum, the horn section, well-known television tunes or the building site. Their music often, however, reverts to its roots: a version of the jangly-guitar 'indie' music beloved by the students of the late 1980s, the journalists who wrote for the inkies and hardly anyone else, but which might claim spiritual kinship with the Seattle grunge sound and its derivatives.

Currently in vogue are the computerised samples and sequences of the broad genre which can loosely be called Dance Music. This too can involve the use of live instruments in recording and even, occasionally, in performance, though it is basically a music of the shortlife white label mix and the club – and therefore a music which, like pub rock, tends to subvert the conventional, deeply overcapitalised music business. One of the best known of these is the Essex outfit The Prodigy, whose success has crossed over into mainstream sales. A more typical, low-budget, East London example is Medium High, a partnership between Georgina Dark and Kristian Rutter, whose work is typically programmed at home, recorded and mixed in professional studios, and then transferred to white label 12" vinyl discs for use in clubs.

But it is the story of Underworld, a band based in Romford, which embodies the present and predicts the future rather more than the pseudo-cockney impishness of those lovable creatures of Colchester art college, Blur. Like Disco Inferno, Underworld incorporate live instrumental performance into the manipulation of high technology samples and sequences. Starting in the late 1980s as a funk/blues/rock outfit, the band has been joined by a DJ and is associated with video and multimedia production facilities (which have produced television advertisements for Nike among other things). Like Disco Inferno and a few other acts such as Bark Psychosis and Ultramarine, Underworld have combined mixed and layered samples with live instrumental performance, thus keeping in touch with the audience interaction and unpredictability which have always informed popular entertainment. Underworld's 1994 album *Dubnobasswithmyheadman* reflects this interest in all modes of performance and composition.[11]

The nature and extent of music provision

Interactions with America and the former colonies have produced changes at every level of British musical life. The continuing presence of pop music, and the music of the Asian and Caribbean communities, on radio and in record stores, and the presence of the children of Commonwealth immigrants in the schools of British urban centres, have led gradually to the reformation of senior school music teaching away from music appreciation, classical composition and instrumental technique, and towards the technologies and practices of popular music. The GCSE syllabuses introduced in 1985 stressed the learning of compositional and performance skills, including the use of synthesisers, samplers and recording equipment. More recently the Interim Report of the Working Group on the place of music in the national education curriculum was published in March 1991. Enthused with its multicultural brief, the committee's report assumed the equal value in education of musics as different as reggae and ragas, sambas and serialism. The skills of performance and composition were stressed rather more than the critical appreciation of the work of previous generations. Again, the use of synthesisers, computer-based composition packages and multi-track tape recorders, African drumming techniques and jazz improvisation were placed alongside baroque counterpoint and sonata form. The only composer from the European tradition mentioned by name was Mozart. There followed a

'In Tower Hamlets, schools with a majority Bengali population usually provide lessons in tabla, tanpura and harmonium'

predictable furore in the pages of the broadsheet newspapers. The Working Group was harangued for betrayal of the classical music tradition, and a series of letters and articles rallied the intellectuals of both old and new right in defence of 'traditional' musical education (i.e., the appreciation of the techniques and achievements of previous generations of male Europeans).

In most East London schools, however, this battle had already been decided in the interests of multiculturalism. In Tower Hamlets (and from September 1995 in Newham), music teaching is provided on the basis of relevance and interest. Peripatetic instrumental tuition is available in Western, African and Asian

11. I am indebted to Underworld's publicity agent, Robin Turner, and to Sophie Zante, a University of East London Cultural Studies undergraduate who interviewed Underworld for her final year dissertation in 1994.

musics. In Tower Hamlets, schools with a majority Bengali population will usually provide lessons in tabla, tanpura, harmonium and other South Asian instruments; all children are taught to sing the work of Rabindranath Tagore, the Nobel Prize winning writer (and composer of the Indian national anthem among other things), in a popular Bengali style known as 'Rabindrasangheet'. Most of the children who take to these musics, however, have ambitions beyond the classical or folk styles they are taught: they want to play Bhangra and/or Hindi film music when they grow up. Throughout East London, the pattern repeats itself: the musics studied by the majority of the pupils at primary or GCSE level are popular and/or ethnic-classical, rather than the carefully preserved Western classical canon.

'Thatcherism had an impact at the local level on the conceptualisation of cultural policy'

It is particularly unfortunate, then, that music education in these skills at higher levels is unavailable locally. Some colleges provide basic introductory courses in rock music, soul, reggae and the new computer-based technologies. There has been for many years liaison between local government and independent recording studios, and though the budgets for these activities are never less than tight, such investment has continued. The Tower Hamlets Youth Music Workshop, for example, was launched in 1982 as a council-supported educational charity. It employed an administrator and, on a part-time basis, teaching staff who were themselves active in music recording and performance. A small 16-track recording studio was built in a disused public swimming bath. The facilities and expertise of the staff were made available at very low cost to target groups such as the unemployed; women taking access courses in music and music production; adults in further education; and local arts and community organisations. The studio was also available for hire at full professional rates for the making of commercial recordings. The charity has continued to operate, and has sought European funding for its redevelopment. A decade later, Tower Hamlets supported the setting up of ATUM, another training project focused on recording studio skills. By this time there was no question of council funding for startup costs, though from the start it was clear that European Social Fund money would be available for staffing costs. In order to claim these it was necessary to be specific about the types of training offered and the eventual vocational destination of trainees. Liaison with the BBC and with local further and higher education institutions such as Guildhall University, produced a range of specifically tailored pre-vocational courses and access to higher education courses, in music production and music video production.

What is not currently provided in the East London area itself is degree-level work which provides theoretical study as well as practical hands-on experience. Such courses are provided in many parts of London (the nearest being at City University in Clerkenwell and the Guildhall School of Music and Drama at the Barbican). African-American and African-Caribbean forms and their local derivatives are comparatively well provided for in these courses (the Guildhall School's big band was one of the sources for the successful professional big band of the mid-1980s, Loose Tubes). However, Asian musics are not available in the same ways. Provision which will build on the primary education in South Asian music, and provide insight into the interactions between these forms of basic training, and the popular musics which so many of the schoolchildren who take them up wish to perform, is sorely needed.

The changing nature of local government-based arts provision, under increasingly restricted central budget control, underlines the priority for expanding musical provision by the new educational corporations. Local government has long played a pro-active role in local musical cultures, by, *inter alia*, supporting festivals and other subsidised concerts; funding adult education in musical appreciation and performance; providing training opportunities for local people in recording studios (as discussed above); and creating facilities for rehearsal and performance. But central government has constantly attacked such provision indirectly, through stringent budgetary control.

Predictably, Thatcherism also had an impact at the local level on the conceptualisation of cultural policy. Recently, arts policy has been seen as an arm of general economic policy: the arts, in other words, are seen as an industry, employing people and attracting tourists and inward investors. (These issues have been raised recently in East London: the borough of Havering, concerned at the economic impact of the loss of consumers to the Lakeside shopping complex, has invested in brighter shopping facilities, and at the end of 1994 was considering regular outdoor musical events in its town centres, in an attempt to win back the shoppers who had been seduced by the motorway leisure city).

Havering is not, however, merely using music to try to entice shoppers. The borough regularly supports concert series in libraries and parks, including a showcase for local popular music bands on National Music Day. It also subsidises a range of professional and semi-professional musical events in the Queens' Theatre. There is an annual free orchestral concert (sponsored by accountants Kingston Smith) in the grounds of The Langtons,

'Local subsidy of pop has been provided only through the student unions of universities and colleges'

what was once a country house in Hornchurch. Regular cheap coach parties attend shows in central London. The Borough's arts officer liaises with amateur and semi-professional performers – there are twelve choirs, ten troops of majorettes, and seven marching bands, for example – publicising gigs, arranging rehearsals and making personnel contacts when possible. All this is done on a shoestring: the 1993-94 annual budget was £250,000 for *all* the arts (inner London boroughs such as Tower Hamlets are currently funded more generously).

But much more could be done even within this budget if the Borough had a suitable venue for concert music. At present, there is nothing suitable for large orchestras, nothing for the better-known rock performers (there are, of course, plenty of pubs, though few offer gigs). All over East London, in fact, arts officers have told me that there was a need for regular performance venues and for large venues in particular. A site is needed somewhere in outer East London to match the excellent facilities of the Fairfield Halls in Croydon. Havering may be able to develop the empty site of the former Romford Brewery in Hornchurch; the funds necessary could come from the National Lottery's capital spending for the arts. The University of East London should also recognise the need for suitable performing spaces, as well as for rehearsal space and teaching/production facilities. Any development of the proposed Docklands site, for instance, should include a fully equipped medium-sized concert hall and general performance space.

One useful source for the discussion of this problem of provision is John Street's article 'Local Differences? Popular Music and the Local State', which discusses the planning, conversion and first few years' running of a new, medium-sized rock venue in Norwich. 'In Britain, much of the public provision of culture falls to elected local authorities'.[12] Whereas this obligation has usually been taken to include musical entertainments such as brass bands in parks on Sunday afternoons and orchestral concerts in town halls, it has seldom extended to pop.

Local subsidy of pop and its derivatives has been provided only through the student unions of the universities and colleges, as a leisure function of further and higher education, with all the implicit elitism of this distinction.

The Norwich Venue Campaign started in 1985. Local musicians and fans claimed that the only local popular music venue of any size, the University of East Anglia, was too far from the city, and the local arts centre too small. With the endorsement of local resident John Peel, but with the opposition of many other local residents, plans to convert an abandoned warehouse got nowhere before the intervention of the UEA itself, which wished to relocate its own drama centre. So, with University and Council cofunding, a 700 capacity rock venue was set up. Prices were low, and booking policy tended towards indie music. Some local performers were given support, but overall the local consumption of a national and transnational culture was fed through the choice of live performers. It was not a great financial success, went into receivership and eventually the University took over its management completely. The venue is now both an urban students' union and an important space for local and student music and drama. This is a model which should be considered by those planning future developments by East London educational institutions.

The East Thames corridor will, no doubt, continue to echo with new sounds, even if the public and corporate provision for the making of music remains at its present low level. Pop, rock, reggae, rave, jungle and whatever is next can and will be made in garages and bedrooms, in pubs and schoolrooms. But more could and should be done, especially for those South Asian musics currently underprivileged within the hierarchy of educational and broadcasting values, and which lack the Atlantic connections that have proved so fruitful for music-making in all its twentieth-century forms.[13]

12. J. Street, 'Local Differences? Popular Music and the Local State', *Popular Music*, Vol 12 No 1, 1993, p43.
13. For a broader discussion of the issues raised in this paper see A. Blake, 'Re-Placing British Music', in M. Nava and A. O'Shea, eds., *Modern Times: Reflections on a Century of English Modernity*, Routledge, London 1995; and A. Blake, *The Land Without Music*, Manchester University Press, Manchester forthcoming.

RENEWAL

Renewal is published quarterly by the LCC in association with Lawrence & Wishart. The latest issue includes: Power for a purpose/**Tony Blair**, What's new in New Labour?/**Paul Thompson**, The SDP and Owen: Lessons for Blair/ **Alex de Mont**.

Subscription rates are as follows:

Standard annual subscription	£20
Single issues	£6
Two-year subscription	£36 (save £4 over two years)
Standing order subscription	£16 (save £4 each year)
Institutions	£30 (annual subscription)
	£10 (single issues)
Students and unemployed	£12 (annual subscription)
Overseas	
Europe	£30 (payment in sterling only)
Rest of the world	£36 (payment in sterling only)

Your details

Name ⎯⎯⎯⎯⎯⎯⎯⎯⎯⎯⎯⎯⎯⎯⎯⎯⎯⎯⎯⎯⎯⎯⎯⎯⎯⎯

Address ⎯⎯⎯⎯⎯⎯⎯⎯⎯⎯⎯⎯⎯⎯⎯⎯⎯⎯⎯⎯⎯⎯⎯⎯

⎯⎯⎯⎯⎯⎯⎯⎯⎯⎯⎯⎯⎯⎯⎯⎯⎯ Postcode ⎯⎯⎯⎯⎯⎯

Method of payment

❏ I enclose a cheque/postal order, made payable to *Renewal* for £ ⎯⎯⎯⎯
❏ I wish to pay by standing order.

Bank details

Please debit my account for the sum of £16.00 immediately and thereafter annually until further notice.

Bank ⎯⎯⎯⎯⎯⎯⎯⎯⎯⎯⎯⎯⎯⎯⎯⎯⎯⎯⎯⎯⎯⎯⎯⎯⎯

Address ⎯⎯⎯⎯⎯⎯⎯⎯⎯⎯⎯⎯⎯⎯⎯⎯⎯⎯⎯⎯⎯⎯⎯⎯

⎯⎯⎯⎯⎯⎯⎯⎯⎯⎯⎯⎯⎯⎯⎯⎯⎯ Postcode ⎯⎯⎯⎯⎯⎯

My account No ⎯⎯⎯⎯⎯⎯⎯⎯⎯⎯⎯ Sort Code ⎯⎯⎯⎯⎯⎯

Please pay *Renewal* A/C no 87658704, sort code 56-00-05, The National Westminster Bank, 32 Corn Street, Bristol, BS99 7UG.

Signature ⎯⎯⎯⎯⎯⎯⎯⎯⎯⎯⎯⎯ Date ⎯⎯⎯⎯⎯⎯

Send this form to: **Renewal, FREEPOST (SE8456), London SE18 3BR.**

Making spaces
or, geography is political too

Doreen Massey

*In an increasingly 'globalised' world what are our
rights to movement? And what should be the
rights of 'local people'?* Doreen Massey *explores
the politics of space and place, arguing that,
from the local scale to the global, geography and
power are inextricably related – and that we have
a responsibility for the geographies we
construct, and in which we live.*

T here is a story – I don't know if it is true or not – about a Native American
chief in the middle of the last century. He had been asked by members of
his society what had been the biggest mistake of the past generations'
leaders. After thinking for a while, he replied 'we failed to control immigration.'[1]
I ponder this story sometimes when I read reports of today's debates in Europe
about immigration; when I hear Jean-Marie Le Pen railing against migration into
France, or Winston Churchill on the same topic in Britain.

Whatever one's view on international migration, it is difficult to base it on any

---

1. I came across this story in Russell King, 'Migrations, Globalisation and Place', in D.
Massey and P. Jess (eds), *A Place in the World? : Places, Cultures and Globalisation*, The
Open University with Oxford University Press, Oxford 1995, pp5-44

simple notion of inalienable rights. There are no abstract, generalisable answers to questions of space and place. One might clearly feel sympathy with the Native American chief (or with Australian aborigines or even, at a more local level, with working-class residents of Docklands faced with an invasion of yuppies – but then what of their response to an 'invasion' of people from Bangladesh?). On the other hand, I have no hesitation in my opposition to the views of Jean-Marie Le Pen or Winston Churchill. The point is, of course, that the two attitudes are set within very different power relations, very different geographies of power.

The mobility of the European immigrants to what was, to them, 'the New World' was the mobility of the relatively powerful and, in the case of some of the earliest settlers, that of the conquering invader. In the case of today's Europe, those who would like to enter (or, certainly, the ones against whom the barriers are raised) are international migrants seeking asylum or work; they are in a relatively powerless position and have a million bureaucratic and racist barriers to cross. The relation of the two groups to space is also therefore somewhat different: the one venturing out with a degree of control and confidence; the other more accurately described as escaping. In the New World (and in countries like Australia and New Zealand) the culture of the invaders and their deliberate military exploits were to destroy altogether the places of the native way of life. They planted flags and claimed total ownership. (In another story of reversal, in the late 1970s, a group of Australian aborigines sailed to the shores of Britain, planted a flag on Dover Beach, and claimed ownership of England. They were barely noticed; and when they were, they were ridiculed.) Today's potential migrants to Europe would certainly produce effects (there would be cultural and economic influences, and probably social conflict), but they would not completely eradicate the places where they settled. Most crucially of all, we are talking here of two migrations set within very different geographical contexts of uneven development. The early migration to the Americas was outwards from the centres of power and economic development. The pressures for migration today are from the underprivileged parts of the world, as Europe battens down its local hatches to defend its existing advantages against those locked into the wrong side of uneven development.

'The mobility of the European 'New World' immigrants was the mobility of the relatively powerful'

194

My point is not to engage in an immediate debate about the rights and wrongs, and difficulties, of migration policy in different situations. It is to argue that what is at issue in each of these cases is a different set of relations to place and to the power relations which construct social space.

T ake another pair of examples: this time where the issue revolves more around the question of what might be the 'rights of local people'. In the first case, groups of indigenous people in a coastal region of Honduras are protesting against a development plan which would allow the entry into their area of large-scale commercial development of such industries as logging, coffee production and oil extraction. The local groups argue that this kind of economic development will destroy the forests, create pollution and, through monocultural practices, threaten precisely the small-scale variety of the natural resource base on which their own economy depends. In short, it will, they argue, destroy the place as they know it, and their way of life.[2]

In much the same period, on another continent, in a First World metropolis, another group of locals is also defending its patch. Here, middle-class people in an expensive suburb (the kind which is defined as 'exclusive') are resisting the building of a community hostel and cheaper housing for rent. Their area is quiet and leafy, and everyone agrees on how to behave within it. That is why they are here: the place and the kind of life they have so carefully constructed over the years go together. An invasion of this place by new and very different people would, so these locals argue ... destroy their way of life.

What *are* the rights of 'local people'? The surburban residents clearly want to exclude the entry of people they think of as different. But so do the indigenous groups of the Mosquitia in Honduras: one of the resolutions they have approved is to prohibit the colonisation of the region by non-indigenous peoples, and to relocate existing colonists to other areas. Indeed, who *are* the locals? Or, more precisely, what does it mean to be 'local'? The wealthy suburbanites claim their status merely on the basis that they are 'already there'. Clearly, they are unlikely to have been the first inhabitants of this place. Even in the immediate past, their leafy roads have been built over land where farmers and farmworkers once lived. So is 'local' just a matter of current possession?

---

2. This case is explored further in P. Jess and D. Massey 'The Contestation of Place' in Massey and Jess (eds), 1995, *op. cit.*, pp133-174

The situation in Honduras is not uncomplicated either. Clearly, the indigenous groups have not been there for ever: they came across the Bering Strait some 15,000 years ago. They arrived first, but what does 'indigenous' mean? One of the groups – the Garífuna – derives from a complex and international history, hailing originally from Africa and arriving in the area courtesy of British-run slave trade. Even the group which is usually recognised as 'the most indigenous' is not in any sense composed of purely local influences. The Miskito have certainly lived in the area for centuries, but over those centuries they have absorbed contacts with many other 'external' cultures – from English pirates to Spanish colonisers. Such influences have been absorbed in the past, so why prevent more outside influences now? Moreover, in the past the Miskito themselves have apparently been none-too-respectful of the local rights of others: they seem to have persecuted another group, for instance, pushing them (with British help) into new areas.

'The "rights of local people" cannot be elevated into an abstract generalisable principle'

Just as with mobility and migration, the 'rights of local people' (whether indigenous peoples, posh residents, or the Isle of Dogs white working class) cannot be elevated into an abstract, generalisable, principle. We are all, somewhere in the past, migrants, and none of us is simply 'local'. Indeed, geography itself may be an important element in establishing our identity, in the sense of defining outsiders *as* outsiders. What has been called the process of 'the purification of space' – that is, the organisation of space into compartments which are strongly classified in terms of the social groups which occupy them – can play an important part in defining the groups themselves. The designation of the expensive suburb as 'exclusive' really means what it says. The social definition of the place involves an active process of *exclusion*. And in that process the boundaries of the place, and the imagination and building of its 'character', are part and parcel of the definition of who is an insider and who is not; of who is 'a local', and what that term should mean, and who is to be excluded. It is a space of bounded identities; a geography of rejection.[3]

The construction of 'the local' is just as much an act of social power as the

---

3. See, for instance, David Sibley, 'Outsiders in society and space', in K. Anderson and F. Gale (eds), *Inventing Places: Studies in Cultural Geography*, Longman, Cheshire, Melbourne 1992, pp107-22

ability, or inability, to prevent the arrival of new migrants. The social and the spatial are always inextricably entwined.

Space, place and globalisation

Yet it is also true that what we are living through today is a reorganisation of that social spatiality, and on very particular terms. It is often said, and with reason, that we are living in a period of accelerated globalisation. People, communications and products – even environmental pollution – can move around the world more, and at greater speed, than ever before. Places and communities are being increasingly opened up to external influences from the farthest-flung parts of the planet.

Yet it is a very unequal globalisation. Even at the macro level of the world economy this is clear. After seemingly endless negotiations, the Uruguay round of GATT agreements was signed earlier this year. It is an agreement which is designed to foster 'free trade'. In effect, it reinforces the power of capital to roam the world. The potential economic implications of this are still hotly disputed, most particularly concerning what its effects on the poorer countries of the world are likely to be.

But what is equally interesting is the one-sidedness of the agreement: there have been no parallel negotiations opening up the world to the free movement of people, or even of labour. Indeed, the very people who are often found most strongly arguing for free trade on the basis of some – unspecified, unquestioned – right to global movement (the term 'free' immediately implying something good, something to be aimed at) are often also the ones who would erect barriers to the free movement of migrants. (Here, too, there is inequality: global migration is far easier for highly-skilled workers and those with capital than it is for those without training or resources.) Right-wing conservatives who, in one breath, assume that free trade is akin to some moral virtue, in the next breath pour out venom against economic migrants ('economics' is, apparently, not a good enough reason to want to move) and asylum-seekers who are always assumed to be trying to worm their way in without sufficient excuse. Michael Howard recently proposed that headteachers, hospital administrators and social security officials be trained and encouraged to identify illegal immigrants and report them to the Home Office.

Yet one of Mrs Thatcher's first acts of government, back in 1979, was to abolish a whole range of restrictions on the movements of international finance (this, incidentally, being a bigger blow to British 'sovereignty', and 'our ability to govern ourselves from Westminster' than many of the proposals Eurosceptics are currently worrying about). The point is that what we are witnessing today is a re-organisation of global economic space on highly unequal terms. In this age of globalisation, the extraordinary success has just been announced of 'sniffer dogs' in detecting people in the holds of boats.

The North American Free Trade Agreement (NAFTA), for example., brings together the United States, Canada and Mexico as a new economic bloc, a free-trade area. It will allow, with various adjustment periods for different sectors, free trade and movement of capital across the national boundaries between those countries. One thing it does, of course, is enable companies – in particular US companies, since these are stronger – more easily to take advantage of different places for production. They can – and this is the classic case – more easily move to Mexico to take advantage of the conditions of production there: cheaper labour (i.e. lower wages) and laxer implementation of environmental regulations. The treaty does not, however, allow the 'free' movement of Mexicans into the United States (although many will continue to find their way 'across the river' by other means).

'Capital and trade can flow across boundaries, while Mexicans are to be held in place'

This is a clear and simple case of inequality in the terms of globalisation, between the freedom of movement of capital and products on the one hand, and of people on the other. Capital and trade can flow across the boundaries, while Mexicans are to be held in place, to be employed and exploited where they are. 'Globalisation' here, then, is a major restructuring of economic space, but in a way which all-too-accurately reflects existing power relations and inequalities. It is, in this case, the transnational corporations whose freedom of movement is enhanced.

Moreover, the reorganisation of economic and social space which NAFTA represents *reinforces* the power of the already powerful. The right to mobility of multinational corporations is increased: their ability to discipline workforces in the United States with the threat of relocation to Mexico if they won't take a pay-cut or accept new 'flexible' working arrangements, and their ability to avoid cleaning up their environmental act (thus making it harder for any government, for fear of losing investment, to attempt to impose tougher environmental legislation), are both enhanced. This is globalisation by and for the already powerful.

From the global to the local

These global-level reorganisations of the world economy trickle down the system to affect also the spaces and places of daily life even at a very local level. It is often remarked that they threaten local identities.

Not long after the inauguration of NAFTA, the people of California approved a Proposition which would deny access to all public services, except those of serious emergency, to 'undocumented migrants'.[4] This was another kind of battle over space and place: here, the power of the relatively wealthy of California was pitted against potential immigrants from Latin America. The ability of the powerful to defend 'their local place' from invasion by 'outsiders' (California, of course, was part of Mexico until 1848), was pitted against the desire for mobility on the part of those from poorer regions to the south. The relationships between space and power could not be clearer.

These relationships were clear, too, at the other end of Mexico in Chiapas, far from the US border. For here another battle over the perceived integrity of local place was being played out. The Zapatista uprising came to world notice on the very day the NAFTA agreement was inaugurated (1 January 1994). The armed rebellion by mainly indigenous peoples in one of the poorest regions of the country was fuelled by many sources of discontent: a long history of being on the wrong side of uneven development had been compounded by the effects of the neo-liberal economic policies of the then president Carlos Salinas. But one of the immediate reasons was NAFTA itself: in an early communiqué the Zapatistas stated that NAFTA is a death warrant for the indigenous peoples of Mexico, who are regarded as dispensable by the government of Carlos Salinas de Gortari. If the Californians want to defend their local place, so do the Zapatistas want to defend theirs.

Central both to the economy and to the belief systems of the indigenous peoples of Chiapas is corn (maize). It is the source of human existence and the

---

4. Proposition 187 was approved in a popular vote in 1994. Its constitutionality has subsequently been challenged. The resemblance to Michael Howard's recent proposals for the UK are notable.

central symbol around which much of life revolves. Three quarters of the *ejidos* (communal land groups) and the agrarian communities which make up the social sector in Chiapas grow corn as their principal crop.

This local, small-scale production has been badly hit by the attempt to insert Mexico into the global free market. World-Bank-encouraged measures to decrease subsidies and to overvalue the peso have generated severe financial pressures, as has the government's shift towards the encouragement of export agriculture rather than growing food for local consumption. In its eagerness to become part of the free-trading world, the Mexican

'In Mexico as a whole some 2 million producers of corn will be unable to survive' government has gone so far as to change the country's constitution. Article 27 of that Constitution enshrined the central gains of the original Zapatistas, the followers of Emiliano Zapata in the Mexican revolution of 1910-17, by establishing the principle of communal landownership. By 1991 about half the country's land surface was owned communally and about 20 million people (a quarter of the country's population) lived on such land. In 1992 the Mexican government modified Article 27, reducing protection for *ejidos* and encouraging private ownership. As many people have pointed out, whatever the changes in landownership which eventually result from this move, the immediate effect on the peasants of Chiapas (and of other regions of Mexico) was 'at the level of expectations, hopes and fears':[5] the end of land reform in Chiapas cancelled the hope, however vain it might have been, of one day having access to a piece of land. A workshop convened by the Diocese of San Cristóbal (capital of the state of Chiapas) just before the alteration of the Constitution concluded, among other things, that the proposed changes to the status of *ejido* land reflected the objectives of the proposed NAFTA.

But this was just preparation: NAFTA itself was a further blow. Despite vociferous opposition from peasant organisations, corn was included in the treaty. Over a period of 15 years, and in the spirit of free trade, all tariffs and import quotas currently protecting local production will be abolished. It has been estimated that, in Mexico as a whole, some 2 million small producers of corn will

---

5. From Neil Harvey, 'Rebellion in Chiapas: Rural Reforms and Popular Struggle', in *Third World Quarterly*, Vol.16, No.1, 1995, p39-73. The figures above are also taken from this article.

be unable to survive. The economic and symbolic centrality of corn to village life would be undermined. 'Free trade' with a neighbour that boasts one of the world's largest grain surpluses will make it impossible for such systems of production to compete. Estimates of the possible consequent displacement of people from the Mexican countryside range from 700,000 upwards to a figure of many millions. Local places and systems of spatial relations will be disrupted. The people will go to the cities, to Mexico City, to the *maquiladora*-land of the north or, if they can get across the border and California does not throw them out again, to Los Angeles.

What treaties such as NAFTA and GATT represent is a potentially massive reorganisation of the world geography of social relations. While multinational companies are freed even more to roam the globe – their already-existing power forcing down borders and further increasing their power – the local production and trade relations of peasants and small farmers are undermined. More people leave the land and make for the cities. Yet they cannot go to just any city. Free trade does not go so far as that. The US border, and the EU border, still remain closed to such people from outside. And so it is that yet more people arrive in unprepared, polluted, Mexico City.

This is a real, global, spatial reorganisation, but one in which different groups are very differently implicated. Different places (Chiapas, California) and different social groups occupy very different locations in this shifting, global power-geometry. Some barriers are torn down; others are maintained. New spaces are created (of global trade and of new squatter settlements in third world cities); others are destroyed (the spaces of more integrated national economies, and those of small-scale agriculture). Some identities (the hybrid-Mayan cultures of Chiapas) come under threat from such spatial reorganisations; while those who already have more strength within the shifting power-geometry can wall themselves more tightly in. Here 'at home', on the day when the call went out to clamp down more severely on the use of public services by illegal immigrants, another story focused on the proclaimed need to teach people, in school, what it means to be 'British'.

The ordinary business of daily life

We all live, then, in complex geometries of social power, and our relationship to place may be, and can be used as, an important component of defining our identities. Moreover, these social geometries stretch from the local to the global with these 'levels' being deeply implicated in each other.

But the crucial point is that we *create* those places and those geometries of power. We create them via the economics and politics which we vote for or allow to happen; we create them through social and cultural imaginings; we create them in the ordinary business of daily life. We have some responsibility for them.

Let's take somewhere completely different – Milton Keynes. It is early autumn, a few years back, and the light is perfect. There are swans on the river, grey willows with twisted bark stand duty along the banks and a dusty path winds past thick hedgerows. The colours of the trees, as everywhere in Milton Keynes, are breathtaking. It is a bit of English countryside, but beautifully planned into the city. A place to walk slowly, to allow your mind to wander as the sun goes down.

Except that you probably won't. I'm told that rapists sometimes operate on paths like these. A number of women have been assaulted. A friend of mine, who lives here, says she will never walk this way after dark. And *her* friend Jane no longer cycles to work in winter: it's not light enough to be safe.

When Milton Keynes was first imagined, issues of space and place, and how they might be organised, were high on the agenda. It was the late 1960s, and above all this was to be a modern city. Its spatiality was planned so as to prioritise mobility, rationality and zoning. Mobility was promised by the road system: through-routes and local roads are separated, with only roundabouts at intersections to slow you down. I'm told there is only one set of traffic lights in the whole of the new city. But there are cycle paths and pedestrian-ways galore. There was once the idea of having a dense network of public transport, too, with frequent buses and diallable services; but that did not happen. So it was not mobility in some abstract sense which was initially envisaged here: there was at least the aim of some *equality* of access and movement too.

'The crucial point is that we *create* those places'

The city is also a 'modern' space in the way that it organises life. Different activities are assigned their own special places: industry in some areas, residential developments in others. Life is zoned. The paths along the river and across the fields are, supposedly, one of the means of linking the zones, and thus the parts of life, together. They were to be spaces to take a breather between-times, to relax.

The threat of violence along these paths is just one of the ways in which that first imagined spatiality of Milton Keynes has been re-worked. The social life of the city is moulding the meaning and the function of its physical form. In this case, what has happened is quite simple. There is nothing inherently threatening about country paths, nor even canalside walkways. It is the existence of these attackers that makes them so. And this in turn restricts the mobility of others; women, though by no means only women, are **'Inequalities are structured into that universal mobility that was the planners' dream'** wary. Fear, warranted or not, has its effects. People devise rules and manoeuvres in order to cope. They adjust their lives. As a result of different forms of social power – in this case violence – the experience of the geography of the city is changed; for some it is restricted. Even in daytime there are those who feel they cannot wander alone, relax in solitude, without continually having to scan for safety.

Inequalities are thereby structured into that universal mobility which was once the planners' dream. Particular time-spaces (pathways-after-dark) become no-go areas for certain groups of people. (And yet today, even more than in the 1960s, the talk is of mobility as the spirit of the age.) The social geography of the city is shifted, reorganised a little, along lines determined by differential social power.

Only one thing seems to be certain about the identity of the attackers: they are men. But in Milton Keynes many people also suppose – without any actual evidence at all – that they are from a particular estate. They are thus pictured, not just as men, but as men 'from the Lakes'. The different residential areas of Milton Keynes may have been born out of nothing, but they have rapidly acquired reputations. And in the imaginative geography of this city, 'the Lakes' estate figures strongly. It is one of the poorest areas, with male unemployment reaching 40 per cent. Originally put up to house the people who came here from north London to begin building the city, there is even an ethnic (Irish) dimension to its place in the geographical imagination. In a few decades the identity of people and place have been merged in folklore. Being from the Lakes estate carries a particular meaning.

But in this case the meaning (that relation between place and identity) has been constructed by those who do not live there. The conflicts and lines of division within the estate remain unknown to outsiders. Indeed, the estate as a whole remains largely unknown to most people in the city. The way the residential areas of Milton Keynes are designed reinforces this. Each is a world unto itself. That separation of through-traffic from local journeys precisely means that the estates – like many 'estates' in this country – are not on the way to anywhere else. They are designed to be gone *to*, not gone *through*. Unless you already know someone in the area, or have a specific reason for visiting, you are unlikely to find yourself there. Spatial seclusion reinforces the sense of the unknown to those not from the place itself. Social difference and spatial separation combine to construct this 'other world'.

This is absolutely not a critique of Milton Keynes. None of these things are unique to that town. Space and place are never just the physicality of plans and bricks and mortar (or even concrete). They are products of our social interactions and imaginations, and we construct them in a constant negotiation with each other.

A place of their own: geography and the middle class

Power over space and place is, then, a major weapon in the negotiation of today's world. That power may rest on economic muscle, on the loudness of your voice in international fora, on ethnicity or country of origin, on violence, on gender... But whatever it is based on, such power differentiates us. Among other things, in Britain, it is very tied up with social class. Indeed, it is possible to argue – at least for purposes of provoking debate – that spatiality and relation to place (geography) may be significant differentiators between socio-economic groups. It seems, for instance, that in England and Wales if you want to be middle class you may have to move. Certainly, your chances are better if you live in the right place.

Some fascinating recent research shows that, in the 1980s, geographical mobility was an important aspect of gaining access to certain social classes.[6] In particular, this is true of the middle class (managers, professionals and the petty bourgeoisie). The statistics show that entry into middle-class occupations was often accompanied by movement from one region to another. The quite reasonable inference would be that climbing into these groups may be easier if

6. See Tony Fielding, 'Migration and Middle-Class Formation in England and Wales 1981-91', in T. Butler and M. Savage, *Social Change and the MiddleClasses*, UCL Press, London 1995.

you are prepared to move house.

There is, moreover, a big difference between these social groups and others. Entry into blue-collar occupations, for instance, shows very little relation to migration between regions. In other words, some groups seem to reproduce themselves in particular places – on the basis of these statistics one might think of working-class communities – while others quite actively gather together from across the country to establish social strata.

Such a picture, and the sharpness of the contrast, can be overdrawn. These statistics refer only to one, recent, decade. The longer historical view shows that

> 'In England and Wales if you want to be middle class you may have to move'

now seemingly stable working-class communities were themselves constructed from long migrations of people seeking work: the trek to the coalfields of South Wales and the North East in the 18th-century, the migration of Scots to work the Corby iron, of rural families to the mills of Lancashire and Yorkshire. Moreover, the statistics relate to a decade when the blue-collar working class was in decline, while the managers and professionals of the middle class were growing rapidly in numbers.

One must not, then, generalise beyond the time and place of these particular statistics. But they do catch something important about the social geography of our times. Some classes, or occupational groups, appear to be formed *in situ* far more than are others.

What is more, the mobility of the aspirant middle class is a *particular* mobility: overwhelmingly it consists of movement to the south east of England. As 'the middle class' has grown in size so it has continued to concentrate in the south of the country. Certainly, not all middle-class people live there and, even more surely, not everyone in the south and east is middle class. But this region is its heartland. As middle-class jobs have proliferated, so the geographical distance between them and working-class jobs has been maintained and at times reinforced. This is not something which *has* to happen; it is not somehow a technical necessity of economic efficiency. The middle class putting geographical distance between itself and manual labour is a *social* phenomenon, part of the formation of the middle-class groups themselves. Occupational, social and spatial identities have been constructed together. Much middle-class movement, within regions as well as between them, had had *as its aim* the creation of a geography of difference.

There is, of course, more to 'mobility' than moving house. But in these other areas, too, the middle class seems to score more highly. It is overwhelmingly the middle class – or, more accurately, it is middle-class *men* – whose jobs take them travelling, whose work-contacts are conducted through international conference calls and the internet. It is middle-class families, on the whole, whose holidays take them further afield; keeping a little ahead, perhaps, of the frontiers of mass tourism. This, moreover, is a mobility of choice, conducted in relative ease and style: quite different from the mobility of the international refugee or the unemployed migrant from Liverpool coming south to find work. Not just the degree of mobility, but also its social meaning and its character as an experience, indeed the way it becomes part of the process of identity-formation, vary hugely between social groups.

But if, for the middle class in this country, the world is increasingly its oyster, the desire for the other side of the coin, for a settled localism, seems equally strong. The mobilities of life are counterposed to, or perhaps even compensated for by, a desire for a place of their own.

I have recently been studying some high-tech scientists, men whose working lives (through the companies they work in, through travel to conferences, through the networks of contacts and debates in which they daily participate) are thoroughly internationalised. And at the end of such globalised days a quite impressive proportion of them go home (should one say 'retreat'?) to a cottage in an 'Olde Worlde' English village whose symbolic essence (if not reality) is stability and localism.

This is, of course, a phenomenon far wider than a handful of scientists. It would be interesting to analyse in the same terms the home-bases of those who work in the City, the prime UK location of untrammelled globalisation. Perhaps the two sides are related. Just as it is often migrants who get most sentimental about 'home', so those whose lives span the globe seem very strongly to want 'a place of their own'. It seems that at least some significant elements of the British middle class today embody in their own lives that tension between the global and the local, between relatively unfettered geographical mobility on the one hand and a commitment to an exclusive localism on the other. (It is, perhaps, a measure of their cultural hegemony that it is *their* experience that is taken as the sign of the times. And it is, of course, primarily they who write about it.)

What is more, these are the groups which have the most power to ensure that they *do* have a place of their own. What is at issue here is not just the happenstance congregation of different social groups into distinct geographical locations but the active making of places. Such a making of place is part of constructing the identity and coherence of the social group itself. This is true of the exclusive suburb, whose 'exclusivity' is an altogether different phenomenon from that of the Lakes Estate. It is also true of the rural English middle class in which, as has often been remarked, a particular kind of white ethnicity is constructed in relation to the symbolic meaning of the countryside.[7] So often, the power to defend an exclusivist localism is greater for those that are already strong, while the places of others (in Chiapas, in Docklands, or in the lands of that Native American chief) come under threat.

I n a fine exemplification of the easy mobility of the professional middle classes, I have recently been in Mali. Mali is *not* one of the parts of the world with which my scientists are much in contact. Indeed, on most maps of the phenomena of globalisation it simply doesn't appear. Most globalisations are, in fact, remarkably selective in the parts of the world which they reach.

But one globalisation which does reach here is that of music: Mali is big in world music. And so, one night, we filmed a group of musicians playing in the yard of one of their houses, a small building which is home to many people. The floor was of sand, the yard open to the night sky and the air unbelievably hot. Everyone from the road (unpaved, no infrastructure) had crowded in to listen and later to dance. On a TV on a stool to one side Arsenal were playing Zaragosa in the Final of the European Cup Winners' Cup.

The music that evening drew on the world. Local instruments (local in the sense of probably having arrived there centuries ago from Egypt) mixed in with electric guitar. There were cadences from the east, hints of Chuck Berry, traces of slave-songs reimported from Cuba. Quite consciously some of these groups have made use of influences from 'outside', but to build a music which they see as specifically Malian. It is a music which draws on the world and is exported back to it. One of the musicians said to us: 'some countries have oil; we have music.'

---

7. See, for instance, Deborah Phillips and Philip Sarre, 'Black Middle-Class Formation in Contemporary Britain', in T. Butler and M. Savage, *op. cit.*

Most of the people gathered in the yard had not been outside Bamako; some knew the rest of the country and stretches of the Sahel, through migrations and family connections; others (the musicians themselves) had been abroad. Some members of the group are on their way to becoming international stars. They come home to towns and villages in a country not on most people's maps of the world. To make major recordings, they have to go to a studio in France.

Here was yet another view of globalisation; another social space being made and constantly re-made. I wondered how we might be affecting things – being there, filming. On the stool in the corner David Seaman came out of his goal just that little bit too far and Arsenal fans thousands of miles away in north London, occupying at that moment another point in the constantly shifting set of relations we know as 'space', were plunged into despair.

Interpretations of the new world

Fred Halliday

Fred Halliday *identifies surprising continuities in the shape of the international scene which has emerged since the end of the cold war. Communism, like colonialism before it, has turned out to be a diversion from the main line of capitalist world transformation predicted by Karl Marx.*

In the last six years the world has undergone a strategic and intellectual earthquake, comparable in its effects (though not, at least as yet, in human suffering) to World Wars I and II. A hegemonic system, and its attendant distribution of power, has collapsed. The map of states is being redrawn. A degree of uncertainty unparalleled since the 1930s prevails in the international arena.

The world created by this set of changes corresponds to no easy model, and has rightly provoked considerable bewilderment. In broad terms, three kinds of response have predominated. One, generally associated with the centre and liberal right, is an optimistic one, that sees the world as having moved decisively forward and as being in a period when certain desirable goals – peace, democracy, greater prosperity – are now available to all. The second is a pessimism of the left which asserts that we are in a new imperialist epoch – that the north is incapable of assisting in the development of the south, that ecological destruction is oncoming, that the USA will, on its own, or in association with its old allies, use the new opportunities to consolidate its domination of the world. An alternative form of pessimism, a gloomy sobriety of the right, sees the breakdown of the cold war order as in many respects a return to the world before 1914, or between the two world wars, leading to greater inter-state conflict, nuclear proliferation and hyper-nationalism. Samuel Huntingdon's 'clash of civilisations' is perhaps the best known of these forebodings.

These approaches have the merit of aspiring to make sense of the world, but in some obvious respects they are all deficient. The hope that the liberal democratic model will within any realistic time-scale be generalised to the world as a whole is, as will be argued later, illusory, as is the belief that war and military competition as a feature of international relations will decline. For a brief period in 1988 and 1989, when the USA and USSR were working together to reduce points of tension, the term 'new world order' had a real, if limited, meaning. But the collapse of the USSR has deprived it of that meaning, and the proliferation of conflict, not only in the third world, but in the Balkans as well, shows how unfounded this oneiric outlook was. Even in its liberal internationalist form, according to which the great powers will do their best to help sort out the world, such liberal optimism is misleading, since it overstates the willingness of the governments, or populations, of the developed world to assume their global responsibilities in either the economic or security fields. The reluctance of any western countries to become involved in Bosnia, the reservations of Japanese politicians, and the confusion about Clinton's reform policy bear this out.

The contrary position, the pessimism of the left, is strongest on economic issues, notably the growing inequalities in the world market, but much weaker in politics. This position gained much credibility from the Gulf war of 1990-1991, and there were many who sought to draw general lessons about the post-communist world from that event. But it is now possible, over four years after the end of that conflict, leaving aside for the time being the analysis of why the war occurred, to see that the critics of the war have, in most respects, and not least with regard to the longer-run significance of the conflict, been proven wrong. First of all, and for all the destruction visited on Iraq, the cost was far less that its critics suggested at the time: total Iraqi dead were around 20,000 – a tenth of what was claimed. Despite rhetoric about Iraq being bombed back to the stone age, most of the war damage had within a year or so of the war been repaired. Secondly, the US has not been able to use its victory to put pressure on its economic rivals, or on other third world countries; militarist sentiment has shown no permanent increase in the US, as George Bush found out to his disappointment in the 1992 elections. And while critics claim the war achieved nothing, it has had some significant, if as yet incomplete, consequences – there has been movement on a range of Middle Eastern issues, including the Arab-Israeli issue, and some increased freedom of expression, for Kuwaitis themselves, in Kuwait. The Gulf war was an important, but essentially diversionary, chapter in world affairs. And if we look at some of the other major international questions of the day, there is no clear 'left' position at all – the range of opinion on Bosnia runs as wide a gamut among socialists as it does on the right, Michael Foot agreeing with Margaret Thatcher, and the friends of Serbia being an equally diverse bunch.

The third perspective of a return to 1914 appears to draw sustenance from new forms of inter-state conflict and from the rise of nationalism, but it forces the analogy too far: the major powers are not, on present evidence, in the grip of nationalism directed against strategic rivals, and are, for the moment at least, relatively uninterested in preparing for military action against each other. There is a torrent of nationalism around, but it takes a communal, inter-ethnic, as distinct from strategic form. The most powerful states involved on the international scene have themselves changed dramatically since 1914, most notably through the universalisation of democracy (no major states had universal suffrage in 1914) and by the growth of economic prosperity. Germany, for one, is not the state it was in 1914, or 1939: neo-nazi youth is repugnant, but it is not yet dangerous for other states, as was the Kaiser or Adolf Hitler. We are, therefore, in what is in many respects a novel international situation, both with regard to the pattern of the post-1945 period, and more generally. Only when this novelty is grasped can a new set of policies, and moral positions, be suggested.

A novel world situation

A perspective, informed by this notion of novelty together with the pattern of events since 1993, gives us at least some context within which to assess the broader pattern of the post-cold war world. The historical outlines and hence originality of what happened in the late 1980s can be summarised in brief. A bloc of states, dominated by the USSR, which had since the 1940s been engaged in great power competition with the west, and which had, in the form of the USSR itself, been challenging the western world since 1917,

'1989 brought to the end a period of history that began in 1789 with the French revolution'

collapsed. The originality of this system's collapse needs recognition: it occurred without inter-state war, in a very short space of time, without the presence of evident forms of political vanguards or organisations and without significant bloodshed. Moreover, in contrast to other revolutions since 1789 which had to some degree claimed to defy the international norm or propound something 'new', those demanding change in this context wanted not, as had hitherto almost always been the case, the creation of something 'new', an alternative to the prevailing world order, but rather conformity to that order, a recruitment and incorporation, as rapid and painless as possible, into what was deemed to be the prevailing norm, be it 'civilisation', 'democracy', the 'west', or 'modernity'.

Certain qualifications of a major kind are necessary: most of those ruled by communist parties since 1988 (1.7 billions) still are (1.4 billions); there is no certainty about what kinds of government will emerge in the former Soviet Union, or in many of its former allies; the future pattern of Russian foreign policy is obscure. Nonetheless a cataclysm of great propositions had occurred, and one that brings to an end not only the cold war and the challenge of the Bolshevik revolution but also a longer period of international history in which a movement of contestation of the hegemonic capitalist form was identifiable. At the risk of what one could term 'megalo-presentism', it could be suggested that 1989 brought to the end a period of history that began in 1789 with the French revolution. If only in this sense, the argument of Francis Fukuyama, that what is new about the contemporary situation is that there is only one set of answers now acceptable on a world scale, is to a considerable degree, and if only for a limited span of time, valid. It is in this above all that the historic importance of 1989 consists. Historical precedent would, however, suggest that this is not a situation that can last: a world of objective inequality, and one where the majority of the world's population is vividly aware of the existence of this inequality, is sooner or later bound to produce movements and ideas of contestation.

The end of 'Great Power' confrontation?

In this perspective the 'end of the cold war' is a composite phenomenon involving several broad historical trends, each of which will take time to work themselves out.

In the first place, the end of the cold war marks the end of the inter-state conflict that has dominated the world since 1945 and the end of the Soviet-US nuclear confrontation. Two obvious prospective issues are whether this marks an end of great power military rivalry as a whole, at least for a generation or so, and whether a new pattern of inter-state blocs and of hegemony will emerge to replace the old. The argument on the former would seem to have considerable historical force – that while for a century since the Sino-Japanese war of 1894 great powers have been engaged in major military confrontation, or in the threat thereof, the prospect of this now seems definitely to have receded. There are those who foresee new great power conflicts in the future, yet the pattern of the past century would appear to have been broken. As for hegemony, we now see a situation of great fluidity in which no bloc of states seems likely to emerge to match the USA, but where the USA itself appears reluctant to play the unipolar 'Roman' role which the collapse of the USSR has allotted to it. The last thing the ascendant Republican right wants is to pay, or assume responsibility, for a larger international role. Moreover, the argument that war between states is almost precluded when they are liberal democratic states has much to recommend it, and, if true, would focus our attention on whether some of the great powers, Russia or Japan, or depression-ridden US, UK or Germany, may in the longer run diverge from this model.

The end of communism?

The second dimension of the end of the cold war is the end of communism as a political force. As already indicated this is, as yet, a phenomenon confined to Europe: but the trend within China would seem to indicate a move towards capitalism, if not liberalism, and the remaining communist states are unable to provide an international alternative (Cuba, Vietnam, North Korea). Two large questions arise here: first, what the future of an alternative to capitalism now is, indeed if such an alternative has a future at all, and secondly, what the historical import of the whole communist experience was. In regard to the first it seems that no programme of revolutionary political challenge to liberal capitalism from the left now has any serious credit or support: the communist challenge is now exhausted. For the moment what remains are variants of social-democratic adaptation within advanced capitalism, but ones that are more and more restricted – in part by international conditions, in part by changing social and political configurations within individual countries themselves. It is conventional to state that the collapse of social-democracy is in part a result of the failure of communism: the reverse may, however be the case – the dynamic of social-democracy and its equivalents was broken in most advanced countries in the 1970s (Britain, USA, Australia, Germany). As recently as 1993 some social-democratic parties were re-elected – in Spain, and in Australia. But that of France was ousted, and the programme of accommodation, evident for more than two decades, continued. The very lack of a credible middle, or third, road meant that the choices facing communist reformers in the late 1980s were all the starker.

'Communism was, as much as liberalism, a product of modernity'

The question of what was communism, too near to allow of an easy perspective, has occasioned several candidate explanations: a dictatorial tendency whereby revolutionary elites seized control of societies, a flawed movement for the self-emancipation of the working class, an expression of messianism, a product of oriental despotism, a failed developmentalist project. Some explanation involving different elements of the candidates listed above may be most appropriate: we should not forget that this attempt to escape the conventional path of capitalist development was for a time remarkably successful, not least in the ideological and military challenge it posed to the west. But in the end it was forced to capitulate, and to do so almost without a semblance of resistance. If nothing else, the communist collapse deserves careful study from the perspective of those who believe in elite-led or state-dictated social and economic development: this is certainly one 'lesson' of communism. But there is another lesson, of equal importance, that is too easily overlooked in current triumphalist accounts: communism was, as much as liberalism, a product of modernity; and of the intellectual and social changes following on from the industrial revolution. It was a dramatic response to the inequalities and conflicts generated by that modernity: the continuation of these same inequalities and conflicts suggests that further challenges, of an as yet indeterminate nature, will result.

Although its collapse is now seen as inevitable, this was not how the communist experiment appeared for many decades: both amongst those who supported it, and those who feared it, there was a belief in the efficacy of socialist state intervention that subsequent events have belied. Nowhere was this more so than amongst those states opposed to communism: faced with the challenge of the Bolshevik revolution and its successors, the capitalist world was forced to modernise its own political and economic systems. Indeed the greatest achievement of communism may well turn out to have been not the creation of an alternative and more desirable system contrasted to capitalism, but the modernisation of capitalism itself: no account of the spread of the suffrage, the rise of the welfare state, the end of colonialism, or the economic booms of Europe and the Far East after 1945 could omit the central role which the communist challenge played. A defiant revolutionary modernity provoked a transformation of its non-revolutionary counterpart.

The breakup of nation states?

The third element in the end of the cold war is that it has broken a 'regime' that prevailed since the end of the Second World War, in terms of which the existing map of the world, for all its iniquities and arbitrariness, was maintained. For all the talk of secession and unification that marked the post-1945 epoch, it is striking how, until 1989, the map more or less held. States became independent, some lost bits of territory, but the actual division into 170-odd states was more or less frozen. Unification or fusion occurred only by force and at moments of uncertainty arising from decolonisation (Palestine, Western Sahara, Timor and, it can be argued, Tibet). Secession only occurred in the case of Bangladesh in 1971, but that was of an entity that was already geographically separated from the rest of Pakistan. Since 1989 both the fusion and fission have come again onto the order of the day: we may assume that the fusion of the Yemens and the Germanies will be followed, albeit with some delay, by that of the Koreas and probably, in some form or other, of the (three) Chinas. On the other hand, fission has been the fate of four of the multi-ethnic states of the former communist system (USSR, Yugoslavia, Ethiopia, Czechoslovakia), with the result that in the space of two years over twenty new

> 'There is not, and never has been, general acceptance of the principle of self-determination'

sovereign states have come into existence.

The breaking of the post-1945 regime will encourage many others to think that they too can achieve separate statehood. This will affect some areas more than others: but parts of Europe and Africa, as well as India, are likely to be subject to increased strains, now that is has been shown that secession is allowed. Yet while such strains have grown, and will continue to grow (even Latin America is now affected by forms of ethnic politics and secessionism) it may well turn out in the end (say, by the year 2000) that the fragmenting impact of 1989 will not be universal, but will be confined only to those countries where there has been a crisis of communist rule. This is plausible for the reason that in most cases where secession has been successful it has been not only – or even not so much – because of the strength of the secessionist movement, but because of a weakening, in war or through abrupt political change, of the power of the central state. Such a weakening is what has characterised the ex-Soviet communist world; is is not a general phenomenon. Indeed the moral of the post-1989 story, far from being that secession and independence are now the order of the day, is a rather different one. On the one hand, it would seem plausible to argue that the breakup of states, however painful, has been of far less importance than its contrary, the fusion of hitherto separate ones: reunified Germany and China matter more than a string of Georgias and Eritreas. On the other hand, for all the formal, and moral, respect it is shown, there is not, and never has been, general acceptance of the principle of self-determination. The map of the world that we have today corresponds in Europe to where armies stopped fighting, in the rest of the world to where European colonialism drew lines. The addition of twenty or so new states (with one or two more to come, such as Palestine) will still produce a system of under 200 states in a world where there are many hundreds, if not thousands, of other potential candidates: there are, after all, 4000 languages still spoken, and even communities with the same language can form separate states, as speakers of German, French, Arabic, Malay and English can show.

A new era of global democracy?

The collapse of communism and the apparent spread of liberal democratic political forms to a range of countries, post-communist and third world, has led some to suggest that a new era of global democracy is at hand. This is in essence the argument of Fukuyama, although he is careful to state that he distinguishes the claim that there is no other viable model on offer from the claim that its consolidation in all countries is imminent or even plausible. In certain respects, this claim is a valid one, in that the end of communism has, in spite of the survival of the Asian communist bloc, underlined the extent to which the old, alternative revolutionary, path of political development is not viable or attractive. In some parts of the third world – *Sendero Luminoso* in Peru, the Khmer Rouges in Cambodia, the PKK in Turkey – dogmatic parties of

> 'If Islamism is a threat to anyone it is to the peoples of the Muslim world itself'

the traditional left continue; but they offer no solution, except further blood-letting, to the problems their societies face. Much is made of the 'Islamic' challenge, not least by protagonists of the Koran themselves, who make out that with the collapse of communism they represent the true challenge to the west. Yet Islamism is no challenge to the west, upon which Islamic societies depend financially and militarily, and its political vocabulary, presented by proponents and opponents alike as an alternative, non-European, discourse is, on closer inspection, vintage populism in a Koranic disguise: anti-imperialism, nationalism, hostility to the corruption of states and elites, promises of economic emancipation. If Islamism is a threat to anyone it is to the peoples of the Muslim world itself, who face the prospect of decades of rule by incompetent, cruel and benighted regimes that have no answers, other than demagogy, gender repression and the gun, to the socio-economic difficulties these countries face.

There is no global alternative to the dominant consensus at the moment, but, as already indicated, it is highly unlikely that one will not emerge at some point in the future. Moreover the system of liberal democracy is far more precarious and imperfect than its supporters imply. First, the attainment of a democratic system is not a rapid or once-and-for-all process, but takes a long period of transition to attain: Britain and the USA became fully democratic, in the sense of one person, one vote, only in the 1960s, after hundreds of years of development. Many other states are still in the process of attaining this through various forms of 'semi-democratic' evolution – Mexico, Singapore and Egypt being cases in point. Second, no-one can be sure if a democratic system is established for at least a generation: the fate of the Weimar Republic and of a range of third world democracies that appeared reasonably secure in the 1960s and 1970s should make that clear (Lebanon, Liberia, Ceylon). The political strains within most countries newly arrived at pluralism indicate that matters may take a very different turn in the years ahead. The early 1990s gave examples enough of that: growing tensions in one of the most enduring third world democracies, India; military overthrow of a recently elected government in Africa (Rwanda); continued crises of democratic rule in Latin America (Venezuela, Peru, Chile, Brazil). Thirdly, while the left authoritarian model has been discredited, there is far from being unanimity amongst capitalist states that democracy on some kind of American-European model is most desirable. In the Far East in particular there are a range of states where alternative forms of capitalism, not of the most brutal, but authoritarian nonetheless, can be identified and which may provide a more attractive model for former communist states, China and even Russia amongst them. Finally, the long-run stability of liberal capitalist states themselves may be insecure, as a combination of socio-economic strains and falling political participation threatens established, and in themselves far from ideal, norms. There are also a number of longer-run trends within advanced industrial society which make for less, rather than more, democracy, not least the new potentialities for electronic and mediatic manipulation and surveillance, and the collapse of the working-class movements which for the first three quarters of this century ensured a degree of political and social compromise in these societies.

'The precondition for world peace is the consolidation of democracy on a world scale'

Precarious democracy

The implications of this precariousness of democracy for the post-cold war world are two-fold. First, if there is some reasonably binding relationship between liberal democracy and peace, then the travails of democratisation will have a major impact on the future course of inter-state relations. The precondition for world peace is the consolidation of democracy on a world scale. Secondly, the process of democratisation itself, and the degree to which all states in the world are pressured into conforming to it, focuses attention on how international norms, and mechanisms such as foreign aid and trading conditionality, can now operate to enforce a single mode of domestic political and economic practice. In other words, it raises the question, of how far, beyond acceptance of certain international norms, states are also compelled by the system to conform internally, or to pay a higher price for not doing so. That has always been one of the underlying dimensions of international relations, but one which recent events enable us to look at in fresh light. Not only in the communist and post-communist worlds, but also in the more advanced states of the west this issue of competition and convergence is visible, as is evident in anxious reflections on the records of economic competitors in the fields of education and productivity: nowhere more so is this clear than in the recurrent references made by politicians in the USA, a country where everything was once held to be of the best, as to how much better Germany and Japan perform on certain key indicators.

The world created by industrial capitalism remains a singularly unequal and divided one, yet what is striking is how states that wish to compete within it are forced, over time, to conform and converge. One can indeed speak here of the pathos of semi-peripheral escape: the repeated effort by states that are at some medium stage of the development process to accelerate this growth by adopting forms of political and economic strategy that circumvent the established norms: communism on the left, fascism on the right have both represented this, as have, at different points, the clerico-conservative regime of Fianna Fail in Ireland, or, in an earlier epoch, the institutionalisation of slavery in the USA. What is striking is how the very attempt to bypass development leads in turn to an international pressure to conform – by war and occupation, in the case of Germany, Italy and Japan, by gradual attraction (to the EEC) and erosion of political exceptionalism in the 1960s and 1970s, in the case of Spain, Portugal, Greece and Ireland.

An agenda for the new world

An agenda for dealing with this new world involves several different components. In the first place, it requires a balanced assessment of the distribution of power in the contemporary world, and of the possibilities open to those states with the greatest amount of it. Neither benign indulgence nor unreconstructed anti-imperialist rejection will help much in assessing how, for example, the US or the UK can be expected to respond to issues of strategic or economic crisis in the contemporary world. If capitalism has disappointed its supporters, by the idiocy of its speculative uncertainty, and its inability to diffuse its wealth, it has also, on occasion, surprised its critics by getting some things right. Secondly, there needs to be a recognition within the richer and more powerful countries that in the post-cold war world a retreat to a narrow definition of 'national interest' is both impossible and morally reprehensible. The refusal to confront issues of ecology or north-south relations except in the most selfish of terms is one index of a failure to grasp the requirements of the situation. So too is the abject failure to act over Bosnia: the permanent members of the Security Council are enjoined, by virtue of their being signatories of Article 24 of the Charter, to assume 'primary responsibility for the maintenance of international peace and security', something they have signally failed to do in the past few years. Logic alone would suggest that if these states do not want to assume this role, then they should resign their seats on the Security Council and leave the door open for others who may be better able to do so.

'Capitalism has, on occasion, surprised its critics by getting some things right'

The prevalence within international conflicts and many other areas of international debate of the issue of nationalism, and of appeals to relativist justifications, reinforces the need for a third component of contemporary policy, namely a cautious, but firm, insistence on universal standards and rights. We have seen an explosion of nationalisms and particularism in recent years, much of it muddled and pernicious: without comment on the particular rights and wrongs of any one case, it could be suggested that a general reduction of sympathy, a period of benign universalist impatience, is now in order. What is most revolting about many of the new nationalisms that have emerged from the post-communist world is their disregard for established norms of political and social behaviour, be it in regard to ethnic minorities, dissenters or women, and the indulgence which this too often receives, from the consensus in the developed countries. In many post-communist countries, obnoxious practices of discrimination on national grounds are being practised – not just in former Yugoslavia, but in the Baltic states, Georgia, Rumania and elsewhere. Islamic countries in their droves are returning to *shari'a* law, without anyone seeming to care that in several respects, not least the equality of men and women before the law, and the infliction of corporal punishments, this code is quite inconsistent with international conventions to which these countries are all signatories. Post-modern relativism and liberal apologia can be the servants of repression and viciousness.

Keeping the peace

At the political-strategic level, the question is how far a system of peaceful and co-operative relations between states can be maintained in a post-cold war world: the question is whether the developed capitalist countries, and in particular the USA, are willing or able to assist in this process, in a way that will certainly provide some benefits to the powerful, but also in some measure meet the interests of the system as a whole. It is precisely this which a range of radical third world movements – from the ANC, and the PLO, to the Eritrean People's Liberation Front – tried to encourage by engaging, critically but actively, with the foreign policy-making process in the USA: long excluded, they in the end attained recognition and the prospect of power. A world of inter-state and intra-state conflict will benefit no-one, and hurt the weaker states most.

The problem of inequality

Beyond these political issues, there is the question of the evident universalising trends in the world political and economic system, and whether these trends will serve to diffuse prosperity and reduce the gap between richer and poorer states. The most important, and apparently intractable, question of all is that of promoting the diffusion throughout the world of the economic standards and political freedoms enjoyed, in a relatively secure way, by about 10 per cent of the world's population. This is an argument that has been much debated within liberal economic and marxist camps for the past four decades: the least one can say is that the jury is still out – incomes in most states are rising, but the gap between rich

'The irony is that Marx was one person who did believe that capitalism could transform the whole world in its image'

and poor is widening, and new problems – ecological, demographic, inter-ethnic – threaten many states. There appear to be very strong rigidities in the international hierarchy: there has been considerable alteration of position within the group of high income states, but over a century and a half none has left this group, and only one, Japan, has joined.

In broad terms, this was precisely the question that communism, it its seven decades of existence, sought to address – it was a crude, very brutal and costly attempt – although for a time quite successful – at an alternative development project, a creation of semi-peripheral states. Now it has foundered, in the face of some more successful developmental projects, and the communist states have been returned, chastened and re-subjugated, like escaped labourers, to their place in the international capitalist hierarchy. Communism failed to come up with an answer that was either politically acceptable or economically competitive. Whether capitalism can do so, for the majority of the world's population, remains to be seen. The irony is that Karl Marx was one person who did believe that developed capitalism could transform the whole world in its image and that, *grosso modo*, it was doing a successful job in the process. In this respect, at least, the new international environment of development looks very much like the old, not least because it has now been stripped of two diversions, both the artificial cover of colonialism (1870-1960) and the chimera of a revolutionary alternative (1917-1991): this international environment turns out, at least in the fundamental issues it raises – peace, democracy and economic growth – to have varied remarkably little over the past century and a half.

Soundings

Soundings is a journal of politics and culture. It is a forum for ideas which aims to explore the problems of the present and the possibilities for a future politics and society. Its intent is to encourage innovation and dialogue in progressive thought. Half of each future issue will be devoted to debating a particular theme: topics in the pipeline include: Law and Justice, Heroes and Heroines, and the Public Good.

Why not subscribe?
Make sure of your copy

Subscription rates, 1995-96 (3 issues)

INDIVIDUAL SUBSCRIPTIONS
UK   £35.00
Rest of the World   £45.00

INSTITUTIONAL SUBSCRIPTIONS
UK   £70.00
Rest of the World   £80.00

Please send me one year's subscription starting with Issue Number _____

I enclose payment of £ _____

I wish to become a supporting subscriber and enclose a donation of £ _____

I enclose total payment of £ _____

Name _____

Address _____

_____

_____ Postcode _____

Please return this form with cheque or money order payable to *Lawrence & Wishart Account No3* and send to:

Soundings, c/o Lawrence & Wishart, 144a Old South Lambeth Road, London SW8 1XX